WILLIAM
CARLOS
WILLIAMS

A Study of the Short Fiction

Also available in Twayne's Studies in Short Fiction Series

Twayne's Studies in Short Fiction

Gordon Weaver, General Editor
Oklahoma State University

William Carlos Williams.
Photograph courtesy of William Eric Williams.

WILLIAM
CARLOS
WILLIAMS

——————— *A Study of the Short Fiction* ——

Robert F. Gish
University of Northern Iowa

TWAYNE PUBLISHERS • BOSTON
A Division of G. K. Hall & Co.

Twayne's Studies in Short Fiction No. 10

Copyright © 1989 by G. K. Hall & Co.
All rights reserved.
Published by Twayne Publishers
A Division of G. K. Hall & Co.
70 Lincoln Street, Boston, Massachusetts 02111

Copyediting supervised by Barbara Sutton.
Book design by Janet Zietowski-Reynolds.
Book production by Gabrielle B. McDonald.
Typeset in 10/12 Caslon by Compset, Inc., Beverly, Massachusetts 01915

Printed on permanent/durable acid-free paper
and bound in the United States of America.

Library of Congress Cataloging-in-Publication Data

Gish, Robert F.
    William Carlos Williams : a study of the short fiction / Robert F.
Gish.
        p.   cm.—(Twayne's studies in short fiction ; no. 10)
    Bibliography: p.
    Includes index.
    ISBN 0-8057-8307-5
    1. Williams, William Carlos, 1883–1963—Criticism and
interpretation.   2. Short story.   I. Title.   II. Series.
PS3545.I544Z58784   1989
811'.52—dc20   89-32961
                                                                CIP

To David Hiatt who knew his Williams.
To Frederick Manfred who speaks the lingo.
To Doc Hagood who lived the life.

Contents

Contents

Preface

I first heard the name William Carlos Williams when I was nineteen. It was then, too, that I read my first Williams poems—"The Yachts," "A Sort of a Song," and "Poem"—and my first Williams short story, "Jean Beicke." Then, in 1959, Williams was identified in the biographical notes of the freshman *Introduction to Literature* textbook I was using as a writer of many volumes of poetry who had published essays, short stories, and novels as well. He was in addition to all this, we were told, a physician. Of all the "new" writers I was introduced to in those formative four months on the threshold of the 1960s and young adulthood, Williams held a special interest for me. I liked the sound, the circularity and Spanish flair of his name. He was East and I was West; however, New Jersey and New Mexico were, at least in their alphabetical proximity, kindred places. He seemed closer in many ways than Shakespeare and Stratford-upon-Avon.

Although I did not understand the complexities behind his stripped-down, understated style, his radiant "simplicity" appealed to me. The words in both his poems and the story we read stood out, at once calling attention to themselves first as words and then as ideas in larger "forms." "No ideas but in things" was something many of us continued to talk about (his "sort of a song"), and we enjoyed the talking. For "things" to precede ideas and not the other way around seemed nicely rebellious. He was either out of step or ahead of his times or both. There was, of course, no mention of semiotics or deconstruction, just "New" Criticism; and that it all certainly was.

His voice, as a poet, storyteller, and physician, talking in and through his writing, appealed to me, made me want to listen. In Williams's voice I heard something of the same straightforward, matter-of-fact, get-the-job-done presence of my own doctor, who in our appointments over the years had become a friend and an advisor. No doubt I projected something of my doctor's presence into Williams—and in the process I romanticized what today might be called the "tough love" of both of them.

Words, as poem and story, did have their special kind of healing, restorative power, I knew even then, for writers like Williams himself, and for reader-listeners like me. My freshman English instructor, who had a passion for words and for Williams, because of the way he used words, formed a reading group consisting of some enthusiastic students. We met in his home and I heard in his voice something of the same thing I heard in Williams—a "rare presence" I wanted to know more about and maybe appropriate for myself.

All of which is to say, by way of preface and acknowledgment, that Williams influenced, during his lifetime, and continues to influence now, not only the course of American literature but a particular course in freshman English and, in a way, the course of an individual life. He occupies a special place in such large and small histories as a physician-poet/poet-physician, one who knows, birthing and burying, that life and literature, teller and listener, can make a special "contact," to use one of Williams's key words.

I want to offer sincere thank-yous to the following individuals who have assisted me in this attempt to share some of my own interest in Williams's short stories: William E. Williams, M.D., for his friendly and fast responses to my questions; Robert J. Bertholf, curator of the Poetry/Rare Books Collection, the University Libraries, State University of New York at Buffalo, and his assistants Michael Basinski and Sue Michels; also Karen D. Senglaup, head of the Circulation Department, Lockwood Memorial Library; Patricia C. Willis, curator of American literature, the Beinecke Rare Book and Manuscript Library at Yale; Alan K. Lathrop, curator, Manuscripts Division, University Libraries, University of Minnesota, and his assistant Vivian K. Newbold; Anthony Teodoro, New York Public Library; Donald Gray, Stanley Lyle, Eva Bonney, Charlene Weber, Rosemary Meany, Lawrence Keifer, and Edward Wagner—all on the staff of the Donald O. Rod Library, University of Northern Iowa; James Laughlin and Peggy L. Fox, New Directions Publishing Corporation; Frederick Manfred, practitioner of the American idiom and prime father in his own right, who, in an interview one cold January morning, told me about his friendship with Williams, his real-life presence; Kate Donahue; Gail Adams, Kansas Public Telecommunications; Linda Wagner, for her books and her 1973 conference on modern literature in East Lansing; James Martin, John Downey, John Somervill, Robert Ward, Nabil Kardosh, and Patrick Roche for important incentives; and Judy, Annabeth, Tim and Georgeann, and Robin and Stu for tolerating interruptions to the larger routines and smaller pleasures of family life. L. J. G. gave her special sanguine advice. Gordon Weaver I thank for being, well, . . . Gordon Weaver, ever encouraging. Liz Traynor Fowler knew what needed to be said and did so with tough, clear-eyed caring. Barbara Sutton listened patiently and helped weigh alternatives. Edward Amend knows what I mean when I thank him for his special "word" way. James E. B. Breslin came through when I needed him, as did Marlene Shea.

Especially in view of the reader "rush" of Williams's stories, any inadequacies here must be attributed, alas, solely to me, not to the stories, and not to those who have helped me.

Robert F. Gish

University of Northern Iowa

Part 1

THE SHORT FICTION:
A CRITICAL ANALYSIS

Go ahead and dig. Let's see what you can haul up in your
buckets or with your thumb.

—William Carlos Williams

"Why the Short Story?":
Theory and Practice

Twenty-five years after his death the canonization of Williams Carlos Williams continues. He is recognized as a great modern American poet, a follower of the exuberant and free-spirited iconoclasm, the "multitudinousness" of Whitman, a friend and compatriot in innovation of Ezra Pound, H.D., and the imagists, and yet very much his own kind of American original—an objectivist, a minimalist, a founder of the triadic foot, a poet whose poems run the gamut from a few lines to the epic, from "The Red Wheelbarrow" to *Paterson*.

But what about Williams and the American short story? Does, or should the short story as he wrote it figure into his canonization? One cannot read his stories without thinking biographically and culturally about Williams's relationships with other artists, all of whom were influential in determining the nature of modern art and literature. His affinities with and aversions to other writers (Pound, Moore, Eliot, Stevens, Joyce, Ford, Hemingway, West, H.D., and Stein), and his friendships with painters and photographers (Demuth, Hartley, Shahn, Sheeler, and Stieglitz, to name a few) are well documented as is Williams's awareness of their theories.

When the final appraisal of Williams's contribution to American literary history is in, it will have to account for his short stories—and his novels, plays, essays, letters—in and of themselves and in relation to his poetry. This is not to say that critics and biographers, fictionists and poets have not analyzed and acknowledged (and, in large part, praised) Williams's prose as well as his poetry. When one turns, however, to the truly staggering amount of critical and hortatory writing about Williams, one realizes that although much is being said about all the forms that Williams's writing took, more still needs to be said about his short stories.

Soon the canonization will be complete and then, no doubt, it will be endlessly reevaluated.[1] More than likely, Williams will not be judged the greatest short story writer—American or otherwise—nor

3

will he be judged as great a fictionist as a poet. (But that prose-poetry dichotomy is bothersome, and will be treated later in this discussion.) In all likelihood Williams will be fully recognized for his masterful contribution to the evolution of the short story, and notwithstanding the limits imposed by such a historical conception, he will be appreciated for the sheer artistry of what he did with the short story form in what was, for his time, a unique, unorthodox variation on the innovations of Joyce and Eliot, Hemingway, Stein, and Anderson. This process of recognition is already under way, and in this study I merely hope to carry it further along.

Part of the richness of Williams as a poet and as a writer of prose is reflected in the seemingly limitless number of approaches that his short stories invite. One unavoidable approach, given both his essentially poetic sensibility and his stature as a poet, is to assess where the short stories fit in relation to his poetry. And, because so many of his stories take the form of anecdotes, conversations, case studies, sketches, and brief "reports," approaches that place Williams's various kinds of short stories in relation to the larger genre and mode of the traditional short story or the oral tale are also profitable avenues of discovery. These comparative critical approaches are in part aesthetic, incorporating stylistic, rhetorical, and structural concerns. More important, they arc back toward biography, revealing Williams's heavy use of autobiography in his short stories which rely so consistently on the point of view and persona of a physician. Approaches that deal with issues clustering around Williams as doctor/narrator are also particularly inviting.

Williams wrote about common people in and around where he practiced medicine in Rutherford, New Jersey, and along the Passaic River, and his "stories" may be approached as examples of regionalism or "localism," or even as sociological study, proletarian portraiture and biography. In this respect particularly, questions arise about just how much editorializing, how much moralizing and politicizing Williams interjected into his stories. For example, his accounts of prejudice and racism in relation to blacks, Native Americans, and Italian and Slavic immigrants are prominent and invite evaluation not only as a reflection of Williams's values, of the values of his local place and era, or of American culture more generally in the 1920s and 1930s, but they also invite comment on race relations today. Furthermore, insofar as many of Williams's stories seem to manifest his rebellion against "puritanism" or evangelical Protestantism, or advocate implicitly a "live and let live," "do your own thing" relativistic attitude about cultural and moral assumptions regarding such volatile things as sexuality, alcoholism, and drugs, his "liberalism" clearly anticipates the "situation ethics" and "new morality" of the 1960s and thereby becomes of interest to certain readers. Another aspect of his work that is of particular interest to contemporary audiences is Williams's depiction of women: because he was so fascinated, so motivated by women, as a man, a physician, and an artist, and because so many of the characters in his stories are women —mothers, wives, girlfriends, sisters, sisters-in-law—his stories may be approached for what they reflect not only about his images of women, but also for what they reveal about images of women that were common to and uncommon to his time.

Given that Williams's work is susceptible to so many approaches, literary historians, deconstructionists, reader response theorists, feminists, formalists, Marxists, Freudians—just about every kind of critic—could well find in his stories "rich plums" and "full buckets" for their "digging" and "mining." My approach to Williams's short stories does not follow from one school or methodology, and is more eclectic and thematic than narrowly polemic or argumentative. I attempt to demonstrate through my readings of some of his stories that he is indeed a complex, if contradictory, master of the modern American short story—although he is yet to be fully, widely acknowledged as such. To carry out such a demonstration in the midst of so many possible critical approaches to Williams and his short stories I have pursued one main line of thinking: Williams's stories are indeed the product of an American physician/poet and this basic fact carries with it some rather far-reaching associations and implications for the short story as autobiography and for the relations between writing and medical professionalism.

To get a glimmering of the complex relationship between Williams's doctoring and his writing, between his poems and his prose, and in what manner he "practiced" the short story in the process, it is necessary to turn to his own theorizing about the short story. It is important to consider, before any attempt at a thoroughgoing analysis of his stories, some of the things biographers and critics—readers—have said about William's stories and their place in literary history. The comments form a fascinating network of biography, autobiography, and critical conjecture both by and about Williams and about his theory and practice as a "word man/medicine man."

His fifty-plus collected short stories are mostly the product of the 1920s and 1930s, although many of these stories also appeared in edi-

tions of his collected stories some decades later in the 1950s and 1960s
(as well as in miscellaneous short story and "literature" anthologies).
Williams's first short stories were written for and appeared in the "little
magazines" of that period—especially literary magazines such as the
Little Review, Others, Contact, and *Blast,*—as did the works of many
other authors who were to become modern literary giants. Since Williams served as either editor or an advisory editor as well as an author,
his contributions are very much a part of the literary and social history
of these magazines and the times they reflect. And since Williams
turned to writing short stories in the midst of working on other longer
prose pieces—novels, novellas, travelogues, improvisations, and so
on—and since he was constantly experimenting with juxtaposing poetry with prose, mention must also be made of that process of alter-
nation and juxtaposing as it affected his short stories. Developments in
his personal theory and practice of the short story must be viewed in
autobiographical contexts if only because his writings are lodged so
solidly in his dual but reciprocal activities as doctor and author.

Williams lived an incredibly full and cosmopolitan life for a man who
was born in Rutherford, New Jersey, in 1883 and who died there, in
1963, after a series of debilitating strokes that left him in his final
months unable to write or read or talk.
He studied in Europe for two years, in Geneva and Paris, when he
was fourteen and fifteen, and then returned, after medical school at
the University of Pennsylvania, to study pediatrics and obstetrics at
Leipzig in 1909 and travel more broadly in Europe for a year.[2] Williams's relationship with his brother, Ed, and their growing up together; his meeting Ezra Pound and Hilda Doolittle (H.D.) while
enrolled at the University of Pennsylvania (1902–06); his marriage to
Florence Herman (1912); their settling at 9 Ridge Road in Rutherford,
where Williams also established his medical practice as a general physician and pediatrician; the birth of their two sons, William and Paul;
along with his many friendships with such individuals as Charles Demuth, Marsden Hartley, Charles Sheeler, Alfred Kreymborg, Robert
McAlmon, Fred and Betty Miller, Nathanael West, Louis Zukofsky,
James Laughlin, David McDowell and countless other artists, writers,
publishers, and luminaries—all of these people and events set lasting
outlines for the "story" that was to be Williams's life.
William Carlos Williams was born to an English father and a Puerto
Rican mother whose mixed Spanish, French, and Jewish ancestry in-

fluenced not only Williams's temperament but also his affinity with
Hispanic language and culture most especially; he would present her
attitudes through her own autobiographical conversations in *Yes, Mrs.
Williams* (1959). As has been pointed out, Williams's combined European and Caribbean heritage somewhat ironically made him value the
local experience of his immigrant parents and his own first-generation
experiences in New Jersey, Garden State, U.S.A., above the experiences to be had in the literary centers of Europe.[3] Perhaps it was this
alliance that, in part, kept him residing in America in contrast to many
of his expatriate peers in the 1920s and 1930s. This English and Caribbean heritage plus the European removals of the literati of his day,
provided a tension in Williams between the cosmopolitan and the regional, the European and the American, or what has been described as
the "exotic and the familiar"—moods and themes that are time and
again apparent in his short stories as well as in such works as *Pagany*.[4]
Paul Mariani writes in his detailed biography of Williams that it was
especially fitting for a man who had kept cultural contact with the literary and artistic pulse of New York and Europe to devote his life and
develop his art in the local environs of Rutherford, Passaic, and Paterson, New Jersey, for in so doing he lived up to the nineteenth-century
criteria for a truly American poet set by Emerson and Whitman in the
nineteenth-century.[5]

Williams's first poem, employing the techniques of imagism, were
published in 1909 and 1913; then in 1915 Williams, Alfred Kreymborg,
and Wallace Stevens joined efforts in an avant-garde little magazine
called *Others*. It was defunct by the fall of 1916, but had planted some
significant seeds of influence for other little magazines and for modern
poetry.[6] Williams's magazines, *Contact* and *Blast*, served a similarly significant role for the short story. The first phase of *Contact*, organized
with Robert McAlmon, who had suggested the enterprise to Williams,
ran for five issues (December 1920–June 1923) and served as a forum
for many of Williams's editorials, poems, and stories. The demise of
Contact was partly due to McAlmon's marriage and move to Europe,
where he started Contact Editions and published Hemingway, West,
and many other soon-to-be major authors.

Williams revived *Contact* in 1932, this time with the assistance of
Nathanael West, author of *The Dream Life of Balso Snell* (1931), who was
working on *Miss Lonelyhearts* (1933) at that time, two of the four novels

that were to make him famous before his early death in 1940.[7] It was a relationship that had important implications for the theory and practice of both authors.

In addition to writing for and editing the original *Contact* and poetry volumes such as *Al Que Quiere!* (1917; To Him Who Wants It), *Sour Grapes* (1921), and *Spring and All* (1923), Williams was busy with the works that made the 1920s and 1930s stand out as a time when he involved himself in much experimental prose writing: *Kora in Hell: Improvisations* (1920)—which combined myth and poetry and expressionist prose into poetic prose pieces much more prose oriented than the poetry/prose ("prosetry"?) found in *Spring and All; The Great American Novel* (1923), now hailed by postmoderns as an important early antinovel or selfreflexive novel; *In the American Grain* (1925), the historical "essays" rendered in a narrative, "story" mode; *A Voyage to Pagany* (1928), the autobiographical travelogue in novel form based on Williams's 1924 and 1927 European trips and the context for his short story "The Venus"; *A Novelette and Other Prose, 1921–1931* (1932), surrealistic musings, conversations and essays again largely autobiographical. And he offered tributes to Kenneth Burke, the music of George Antheil, and the work of Gertrude Stein, Matisse, Marianne Moore, James Joyce, and the short stories of Kay Boyle. The 1920s and 1930s were a time if immense productivity for Williams, theory mixed with practice, practice with theory, and everything blended with autobiography—life experiences he regarded as "rare presences" in the listening to his patients, sensing their hopes and dreams, their essence, in their language, seeing and hearing their obviousness, their "being" as it made itself known before his "listening."[8]

Two of Williams's short story collections were published during the decade of the 1930s: *"The Knife of the Times" and Other Stories* in 1932, and *Life Along the Passaic River* in 1938. Two other volumes of Williams's stories were subsequently published as "collected" stories: *Make Light of It* (1950), which added twenty-one stories (written for the most part before 1950) under the proletarian sounding subsection, "Beer and Cold Cuts," and *The Farmers' Daughters* (1961) wherein only the title story (begun in the mid-fifties) had not been included in previous collections. It is clear that the fifty-two stories that compose these four volumes of short stories point to the 1920s and 1930s, prolific decades for Williams—twenty years in which short stories occupied a significant part of his attention. And during this period he wrote many more stories that appeared in little magazines but were never collected in any kind of *complete* run—something which is still very much needed, as is an inventory of yet uncollected stories in archives at Yale, SUNY-Buffalo, and other depositories.[9]

The 1940s, 1950s, and the early 1960s were a time when prizes and recognition in various forms found their way to Williams: honorary degrees from Rutgers and Bard College and the Russell Loines Memorial Award from the National Institute of Arts and Letters, all in 1948; the National Book Award in 1950; the Bollingen Award for excellence in verse, in 1953; a fellowship from the Academy of American Poets in 1956; and recognition by the Library of Congress first as a fellow then as a consultant in poetry (a position which he had to decline when conservative, McCarthy-era political pressure, growing out of prejudiced assumptions about his friendship with Pound as well as some of his past "Marxist" leaning writings, was brought against him).

Williams's first installment of the Stecher trilogy, *White Mule*, appeared in 1938; the second installment, *In the Money*, was published in 1940; the third novel in the series, *The Build Up*, came out in 1952. His epic, *Paterson*, occupied much of his last twenty years and appeared in five parts, in 1946, 1948, 1949, 1951, and 1958—and he worked on his longest short story, "The Farmers' Daughters," off and on between 1946 and 1961. Plays appeared in 1948 and 1961, and his last book of poems, *Pictures from Brueghel and Other Poems* appeared in 1962, just before his death. Williams retired from medical practice after his first stroke in 1951. He was awarded the Pulitzer Prize two months after his death on March 4, 1963.

Granting Williams's assertion that writing and the medical profession were complementary, life and art the two sides of one coin, his prolific outpouring of writings in such a wide variety of forms, old and new, is all the more impressive when his forty years of "practice" as a physician are taken into account, adding up to, by his own count, a million and a half patients cared for and two thousand babies delivered. In addition to the fifty-two short stories published in collections, others have tallied Williams's literary score this way: forty-nine books "in every literary form we know and in forms we still have trouble classifying"; 600 poems; five plays; four novels, a book of essays and criticism; an American history; an autobiography; a biography of his mother; a book of letters; a major long poem; a translation of a medieval Spanish novel —all of which add up to "the most consequential one-man body of modern literature in American history."[10] If Williams is seen this way, as the "total American writer," it is easy to realize why many critics

9

argue for the "unity" of not just Williams's poetry or prose but of his life and art. Still others—including Williams's son William E. Williams, modern poets Robert Creeley, Diane Wakoski, Denise Levertov, and Paul Engle—would support the view that Williams was "primarily a poet, and his prose was of secondary importance to him."[11]

Even the inheritance of Williams's theory and practice as poet, however, acknowledge his way with narrative, prose, or "story." Diane Wakoski offers a personal recollection of Williams the poet and Williams the prose writer in describing her finding narrative in Williams's poetry (along with an authentic "American voice" less in the tradition of Longfellow than Whitman) and his making her want also to write poems "which combined both poetry and prose."[12] Creeley tells of his attraction to Williams's "commonness," the shying away from the poetic diction and syntax of his predecessors, and of Williams's ability to take the mundane and make it seem heroic, which most imprinted him as a young poet.[13] Engle heard in Williams's words what he himself as an ordinary midwesterner saw and heard in the American language he knew: "It wasn't English porridge he [Williams] wanted for breakfast, / but Quaker Oats, made in Cedar Rapids, Iowa."[14] Levertov, in her reading of *The Descent of Winter*, in which Williams again tried to formulate his theories of the word, attempts to sort out ideas and things in Williams's writing, and finds that many more ideas than are commonly recognized are presented by means of "Chekhovian character" and "Chekhovian narrative."[15] However one divides his work, Williams was compelled to blend both poetry and prose in the most impressive and imaginative ways.[16]

Williams's own theorizing about the short story cannot really be separated from his theorizing about language and words, about his insistence on the importance of the "American idiom." Whether he talked excitedly about "objectivism" or "free verse" or "localism," or his late discovery of the "triadic foot," Williams, early and late, worked from practice to theory and back again, moving toward a kind of "unaware awareness" of the world of words as things to see and things to hear.

The pathos of his *Paris Review* interview, almost one year to the month from his death, is that Williams, showing the effects of his ill health, labored and anguished over his inability to find the words, just the words he wanted to say to the interviewer. When asked if he wrote short stories as an interlude to the poems, Williams replied, "No, as an alternative. They were written in the form of a conversation which I was partaking in. We were in it together."[17]

By coming home to write stories about events that were for the most part absorbed from his daily medical practice he was continuing "common conversations" with his patients and striving for the same intonations of the "real" base of the conversations. He was clearly "in it," as himself (although there are instances where he is variously distanced from his narrator through an assumed but ultimately still autobiographical persona). Williams did not want, he said, to seem a seeker after words, but to write out of his intense concern for "reality" (not a newspaper reality), just as he spoke with an intense awareness of authenticity: "I couldn't speak like the academy. It had to be modified by the conversation about me. As Marianne Moore used to say, a language dogs and cats could understand. . . . Not the speech of English country people, which would have something artificial about it; not that, but language modified by *our* environment."[18] This American idiom, conversational in tone and form, which drew Creeley, Ginsberg, Levertov, Wakoski, Eberhart, Lowell, Berryman—all the "new" poets— to him, was the essential native voice common to oral tradition and the native American, a subject discussed more fully in the next chapter.

In some of Williams's earliest theorizing about his goals as a "word man," he speaks about much the same subject in much the same way as in his last interviews. His credo, and the credo of *Contact* as announced editorially, confirm Williams's lifelong interest in the language of conversation, in native voices and the American idiom. As Williams recounted the purpose of *Contact* and described the "contact" among American writers, he spoke with characteristic urgency and conviction: "The name typified a direct approach to life which typified many of the writers of the period, and in America, at least, a concern with the local idiom. The American idiom dared at last to challenge Oxford English, until T. S. Eliot deserted to the older rules with his way of writing. He won an overwhelming, if short lived, victory with his verse and threw us back on our heels for another twenty years, maybe nearer forty years."[19]

In 1921 and 1922 in *Contact*, in editorials headed variously "Comment" or "Yours, O Youth," Williams hammered away at the principles that undergird his writing, and especially his short stories. Parallels can be drawn between Williams's stories such as those that appear in *Life Along the Passaic River* and Joyce's *Dubliners* and Anderson's *Winesburg,*

The Short Fiction: A Critical Analysis

Ohio, Garland's *Main Travelled Roads* and other "regional" short stories that address the concerns of realism and local color, albeit from different assumptions. Joyce definitely influenced Williams and in an early issue of *Contact* Williams refers to him as a worthwhile model of what all good writing has in common:

> By his manner of putting down the words it is discovered that he is following some unapparent sequence quite apart from the usual syntactical one. That is of course the power behind all good writing but Joyce has removed so many staid encumbrances that his method comes like [a] stroke of sunlight today. He forces me, before I can follow him, to separate the words from the printed page, to take them up into a world where the imagination is at play and where the words are no more than titles under the illustrations. It is a re-affirmation of the forever sought freedom of truth from usage. It is the modern world emerging among the living ancients by paying attention to the immediacy of its own contact.[20]

This is an interesting instance of Williams as a reader ready to treat words in much the same way he treated them as an author in his stories.

Williams agrees with John Dewey's attitudes on localism and quotes Dewey, who believed "We are discovering that the locality is the only universal"; he also quotes Maurice Vlaminick from *The Dial*: "Intelligence is international, stupidity is national, art is local" (*Contact* no. 2, 1921, 7). In a challenge to young writers to take up arms in the battle, "a battle that must be in the end yours, O Youth, yours!" Williams repeats that "contact with experience is essential to good writing or, let us say, literature" (*Contact* no. 3, 1922, 14). The colors of Williams's banner are decidedly local: ". . . contact always implies a local definition of effort with a consequent taking on of certain colors from the locality by the experience, and these colors or sensual values of whatever sort, are the only realities in writing . . ." (*Contact* no. 3, 1922, 14). The resurgence of localism in the 1920s and 1930s, at least for Williams in his talk about "contact" and "color," was clearly conceptualized as an extension of the much earlier "local color" and "veritism" theories of writers like Garland.

Some of Williams's most extensive theorizing about the short story took the form of notes for an address delivered to students at the University of Washington in Seattle, and other Pacific Northwest schools in 1950. Williams and his wife were in Seattle for almost a full week in October. He spoke in one session on the modern novel and some of what he said in workshops and lectures on the theory of the short story was published as *A Beginning on the Short Story* [*Notes*].[21] Williams had given this loose assembly of notes, written in the winter of 1949 and the spring of 1950, to Oscar Baron and the Alicat Bookshop Press in Yonkers as early as March, before the trip West in the fall in which he was to offer workshops during a three-week period at the universities of Washington and Oregon and at Reed College.[22] As he looked back on that trip, in his *Paris Review* interview and elsewhere, Williams confirmed that he enjoyed the West and the students he met who, allowing for his belief in the "cultural drift" of ideas East to West, were "not . . . corrupted by the dry rot of our pseudo sophistication."[23] It is important to note that *Make Light of It*, Williams's collected stories, was also published at this time in 1950. So short stories were somewhat near the forefront of his attention.

His workshop policy as he recorded it was to relax and let the students "Go ahead and dig." He had no formal program, no preparation (other than the "Notes"), and he simply chose a few short stories to consider, asking the basic questions: "What's in this one? What has it done?" (*ABOSS*, 23). His method was to take several stories and discuss them, seeing how they were written, or could have been written, and letting the students take from them what they could. The stories he lists in an "addenda" as candidates for discussion included his own story, "The Inquest," a fascinating narrative that allows for multiple perspectives, Hemingway's "The Short Happy Life of Francis Mc-Comber," portions of *The Bible* (the story of Ruth) and of Plato's *Republic*, and a few unspecified titles by Gogol and Kafka. In his commentary, fragmented as it is , Williams demonstrates an even wider grasp of the concept of "story" in world literature. He alludes casually but significantly to Joyce, Woolf, Kipling, Dickens, and James; to de Maupassant, Cervantes, and Boccaccio; to Poe, Stein, Faulkner, and Jack London. From classic to modern, Williams demonstrates his familiarity with the short story as practiced by others, with "traditions" and results he theorizes about, compares and contrasts.

In these "Notes" Williams does no analysis of his own story, "The Inquest," and merely indicates part of its interest to him by a parenthetical "3 people" beside the title. The characters are ostensibly a woman, a man, and an observer—though the observer at times merges with the woman. "The Inquest" was not quite Williams's favorite among his own stories, unlike "Jean Beicke" or "The Girl with a Pimply Face," but he had his reasons to list it for discussion. "The Inquest" provides fertile ground for workshop discussion, particularly about point of view, description, and social conscience.[24] The story is an inquiry, or "conversation" given in a dramatic monologue about a solitary woman waiting for a bus on a cold day, in transit between an obscure departure and destination. The significance of her personhood, her gender and womanness is central to the story. The "co-eds" on the trip (as Williams called them) no doubt found much to say about the implicit, male, middle-class attitudes toward women, as do feminist readers (of both genders) today.[25] Williams tries to break down stereotypes of both race and gender in this story.

Williams—or his narrator(s) observer(s), somewhat reminiscent of the observer in his well-known poem, "The Young Housewife"—refuses to sentimentalize the bus stop scene, the woman (or women), or his inquiries about her, who she is, and what she represents of womanhood in her developing person. What she represents, finally, is Williams's own imagination—and the possible plots that he imagines and invents in an attempt to explain just why she is there and why she *could* behave, given certain other circumstances, in ways somehow consistent with being female. Although he does not identify this story in context by specific title, outside his "addenda" listing, odds are that what Williams attempts here is to "Imagine a woman looking at herself three ways. . . . Write of three persons as one, . . . three in one" (*ABOSS*, 13).

Behind the woman, in the background, is the softly lighted window of a flower shop described in the most powerfully feminine way, extending to wider associations—male-female and the gift of flowers, kinds of light, kinds of colors, textures and shapes of flowers, the abstract qualities they represent, the variety of it all, and the variety of women, reminding Williams (or the narrator), eventually, in his musings, of his mother and the name, "white-weed," which she had for daisies (*MLI*, 319). From flowers and womanly qualities, Williams modulates to thoughts about dancers, muscles, feet ("The only thing that unites the old and the new"), the anatomical outlines and implications of a woman at a bus stop, as if inquired about by a painter, a physician, a writer—all implicit perspectives of the narrator and Williams himself.

Williams uses these anatomical observations as a basis on which to construct a conceit, in effect, about art, about the very art, the very "dance" he is practicing in this story—a metaphor about the aesthetic or the theory behind it. Williams says of sex and "dance": "You take a woman's body and make it do what it was never meant to do and it's the dance. It really is. Sexless. Only when you make it sexless can it properly express sex. Because it isn't sex any longer. It's the dance. See" (*MLI*, 320). And the dance for Williams is equated closely, magically with poetry. In the final lines of *Paterson*, book 5, he says, "We know nothing and can know nothing / but / the dance, to dance to a measure / contrapuntally, Satyrically, the tragic foot."[26]

The final portion of the story shifts to a sordid vein when a middle-aged man, grotesquely visaged, walks up to the woman, looks at her, then quickly at the pavement, and then goes to the shelter of the florist's doorway. What follows is an "inquest" into sexual attraction, promiscuity, pregnancy, and abortion, and a conversation—only half imagined—between a young girl (a "double" of the bus stop woman?) and her doctor (the narrator?) about her compulsion to have sex automatically with a certain kind of man.

In terms of the setting, the character(s), and the movements, the story is blocked out clearly enough. Against this simple staging is a very complex "inquest" about myriad female potential and the nature of human sexuality. The keen but somewhat cynical observer/narrator is ready to minister to and question the possible reasons for the way things are—at the same time he is matter of factly ready to accept the results. In "The Inquest," as in most of his short stories, Williams joins the host of voyeuristic narrators that have been utilized from Hawthorne and Melville to Fitzgerald and Bellow, et alii, who, as David Minter documents, offer a decidedly quizzical but patterned "interpreted design" of character and event on the American scene.[27] The theory and practice behind "The Inquest" are utterly compatible, fulfilling Williams's sense of the story as conversational "reality," albeit imagined, projected, objectified, made "actual."

In trying to work out his own definitions of the short story and why he wrote his own stories when he did, in the aftermath of the depression, Williams concludes that he wrote the stories when he did, the way he did, because "the materials and the temporal situation dictated the terms." He was there, in New Jersey, and the people he doctored were there:

> I lived among these people. I knew them and saw the essential qualities (not stereotypes) the courage, the humor (an accident) the de-

15

formity, the basic tragedy of their lives—and the *importance* of it. You can't write about something unimportant to yourself. I, was involved.

That wasn't all. I saw how they were maligned by their institutions of church and state—and "betters." I saw how all that was acceptable to the ear about them maligned them. I saw how stereotypes falsified them.

It was my duty to raise the level of consciousness, not to say discussion, of them to a higher level, . . . Really to tell.

Why the short story? not for a sales article but as I had conceived them. The briefness of their chronicles, its brokenness and heterogeneity—isolation, color. (*ABOSS*, 10–11)

Why the short story? Williams's short stories show just how much flexibility the form has. His short stories are not everybody's short story, and some of his definitions point to how he condensed the form and adapted it to his purposes. Williams's modulations of the short story form are today reflected in the briefest narrative forms—minimalist forms, sleek stories that are at once conversational but hardly garrulous.

What is a short story for Williams? Here are some of his "definitions," advanced in his Pacific Northwest workshops: "The principal feature re. the short story is that it is short—and so must pack in what it has to say. . . ."; "It seems to me to be a good medium for nailing down a single conviction. Emotionally."; "The short story isn't a snippet from the newspaper. It isn't realism. It is, as in all forms of art, taking the materials of every day (or otherwise) and using them to raise the consciousness of our lives to higher levels by the use of the art: to get something said."; "I should say that the short story consists of one single flight of the imagination, complete: up and down" (*ABOSS*, 5, 21).

In the midst of these definitions, which are utterly consistent with Williams's practice in his own short stories, he blasts the kind of agents and "accepted" writers who unthinkingly solicit and write formulaic, meretricious stories for popular magazines like the *Ladies Home Journal* and the *Saturday Evening Post*. To Williams the short story is the best form for presenting the "slice of life" incident. He completely ignores fantasy or fable or horror stories, which do not present "slices of life," but he does mention specific regional forms like the story of the Northwest (that is, the stories of Jack London, which he included in his lectures because of the audience appeal in that region), and nationally defined stories like Russian, Irish, and of course American stories.

He is ultimately inclusive in his definitions, not naming specific forms beyond what one might infer from the stories that he actually lists, but remaining open for the unnamable. His criterion for including stories to identify or discuss is that the best short stories raise one particular character, man or woman, from newspaper mediocrity or anonymity to distinctive (if not quite "heroic") individualism through fiction. To Williams, likewise, the author's act is individual, offered not for the sake of a government or an institution, but for the individual —reader, character, and author. In Williams's view, "The finest short stories are those that raise, in short, one particular man or woman, from that Gehenna, the newspapers, where at last all men are equal, to the distinction of being an individual. To be responsive not to the ordinances of the herd (Russia like) but to the extraordinary responsibility of being a person. . . . The real short story will be written privately, in secret, despairingly—for the individual. For it will be the individual" (*ABOSS*, 7–8).

Williams's attitude, his persuasive ploys at establishing his ethos and credentials throughout these lectures and workshops on the short story, are shrewd but sincere. With ironic understatement, he identifies himself, even though his reputation at the time was ascending nationally, as just a "literary guy," "even a poet of all things," who never wrote a saleable, money-making short story in his life. He jokingly identifies the students with him as fellow learners, by saying that he is not a "practical" person to teach short story writing; he is more "theoretical." But his point is that students there must finally find their own way, their own successes.

In his advice to students on the theory and practice of the short story Williams compares the form to a mere brush stroke in painting that does not require complex structural paraphernalia and that allows attention to the manner—"A single stroke, uncomplicated but complete" (*ABOSS*, 16). One of the earliest advocates of free-form and spontaneous composition, Williams recommends loosening up, flinging words: "And be careful not to imitate yourself—like how many others. Remember: the imagination! The short story has all the elements of a larger work—but in petto. Dash off a story in an evening—any old way, trying to follow the action of some characters you can *imagine*. Sit down blind and start to fling words around like pigments—try to see what nature would do under the same circumstances—let 'em go and (without thinking or caring) see where they'll lead you " (*ABOSS*, 16–17). Williams talked much about such spontaneous writing, and his work influenced many later innovative "creative strategies" and composition theories. He did write in a white heat, in "stolen moments," as both he and his biographers make plain. Although he wrote his stories in an evening, perhaps, he also spent much time—and some consultation, with friends, editors, and his wife—discussing a story after a draft, or after a second draft. Some form of revision, often through many drafts, was always part of the process, as his manuscripts confirm.

Although Williams's theorizing about short stories was well received on his college lecture and workshop tour, he gained most national critical attention as a poet—especially because it was for his poetry that he was awarded the National Book Award in that year. The third book of *Paterson* came out in 1949 and it was clearly considered a poem—with prose pieces, stories, anecdotes interspersed, but a poem nevertheless. "So be it," as he phrased his clipped, confirmed "story/history" of his beloved city/person: "The Paterson Cricket Club, 1896. A woman lobbyist. So / be it. Two local millionaires—moved away. / So be it. Another Indian rock shelter / found—a bone awl. So be it. . . . Shield us from loneliness. So be it. The mind / reels, starts back amazed from the reading / So be it." (*Paterson 3*, 98). The amazement came, too, from reading Williams and his personae in *Paterson* as well as the historical "news" of Paterson, New Jersey in life and in the prose/poetry.

Some momentum, initiated only incidentally by Williams, the "literary guy," was building in the recognition of him as a short story writer. After all, *Make Light of It: Collected Stories* provided a counterpart, a 1950 bookend to his *Collected Later Poems* published in the same year. In many ways 1950 was a key year for him, a high point just before a cerebral hemorrhage hit, requiring him to retire from medical practice the very next year.

In 1950 the first book-length critical study to attempt a full-scale appraisal of Williams's achievement to date also appeared. Vivienne Koch's *William Carlos Williams* considered poems, novels, short stories, and other prose. It was a kind of tribute, written by Koch, and sponsored by James Laughlin and New Directions Books, a comprehensive stocktaking of Williams in all his variousness as physician, autodidact, writer, paragon. Koch's consideration of the short stories was notable as the first of such critical looks to come. Koch attributes much of what Williams was attempting in his early short stories to his reading of Gertrude Stein: "Stein's cadenced, clear, syntactically functional prose is suggested over and over again in the easy colloquial flow of the writing."[28]

Williams did read Stein's work seriously and wrote an essay on her in 1930 lamenting the fact that American scholars had overlooked her greatness.[29] Yet more credence is given to Stein's influence on Williams's short stories by Williams's listing her "Melanctha," from *Three Lives*, as a text for discussion in his notes on the short story for his college workshops. Long fascinated by black people and culture, Williams found "Melanctha" much to his liking, both for its life sketch of a black woman, her race and class, and for its directness and technique. Williams quite simply considered it "one of the best bits of characterization produced in America" (I, 350).

To Williams, Melanctha's character became so individualized as to upstage all typicality of scene. His own theory about the importance of fictive character as "individual" perhaps grew out of his reading of "Melanctha." And his own stories, especially "The Inquest," "The Colored Girls of Passenack—Old and New," and "The Dawn of Another Day" provide thematic and technical correspondences with "Melanctha" that are as forceful as those seen by Koch in "The Knife of the Times," a story that offers individualized characterizations of two middle-class lesbians, not proletarian "earth-mothers." In tracing what Koch stresses as Williams's rebellious reversal of values, of the transvaluation of gender stereotypes, of willfulness, and the politics of sex, generally, comparisons of Williams's stories with those of D. H. Lawrence are inevitable.

One of the next critics to take a long look at Williams as a short story writer, some three years after the appearance of *Make Light of It*, was Mona Van Duyn. A poet whose interest in long, narrative poems reflects Williams's influence, Van Duyn attempted to show just how controlled Williams's artistry is in his short stories. In doing so she attempts to raise the stage lights of criticism on Williams's "almost completely neglected" stories.[30] Van Duyn opposes the main assumption that Williams's stories are not stories, really, just "formless slices of life."[31] Van Duyn rightly insists that Williams is much more sophisticated in his ostensibly simple stories than many readers of more symbolic fiction might first imagine: "In form, his short stories take major risks for major achievements."[32] In its recognition and acceptance of Williams's range with first-person, autobiographical form, Van Duyn's essay remains one of the most perceptive essays written on the stories to date.

Into the 1960s, three major studies also tried to probe the question, "Why the short story?" in relationship to Williams's other work. M. L. Rosenthal, who edited *The William Carlos Williams Reader* (which included eight short stories), argues with quiet enthusiasm that readers should find "more than meets the eye" in Williams and presents the short stories as "vital evocations of ordinary American reality—its toughness, squalor, pathos, intensities."[33] Rosenthal compares Williams's method to the pared-down localism and virility of Anderson and Hemingway and holds that "Jean Beicke" is a quintessential Williams short story."[34]

Two other important works on Williams appeared in 1968. Thomas R. Whitaker included a brief chapter on the short stories in his book on Williams, explaining that they represent an attempt to explore in detail "the ground on which Williams walked daily."[35] In his consideration of Williams and the modern short story, J. E. Slate argued, also in 1968, that Williams deliberately downplayed the "literary" quality of his stories—an attitude that distinguished him from Stein, Anderson, and Hemingway—in that he refused to separate himself from "everyday diction, the rhythms of the spoken language, the mind of the nonliterary and anti-intellectual."[36] Hemingway's stories, Williams thought, made ordinary conversation more expressive and not really succinct enough and he complained to Pound in 1928, "I'm afraid Hem doesn't at all understand since it is rarely as expressive as he makes it and twice as succinct."[37] Slate sees this attitude as arising from Williams's sincere belief in his own theory of the short story, rather than from jealousy of Hemingway's commercial successes. And Slate insists that "Williams's theory and practice both make it necessary to redefine the term *fiction*, at least for [Williams], to include almost all of his prose forms: novels, short stories, improvisations, autobiographical works."[38]

J. Hillis Miller is responsible for three ground-breaking essays on Williams published in the mid- and late 1960s and in 1970. Although none of his analyses focus specifically on Williams's short stories, Miller brought new attention to the relationships between Williams's theory and practice and to the implications for prose-poetry relationships and the developing literary theories of structuralism, semiotics, and deconstruction.[39] In his deconstructivist reading of *Spring and All* Miller illustrates new ways of seeing how Williams used prose to offer a doctrine divided against itself, out of which the poems arise as "the happening which the prose attempts to describe and justify."[40] As this study attempts to show, this consideration can be expanded to accommodate the prose of the short stories as well: by reciprocal implication, the stories, like the poems, arise as "happenings," and the one form "justifies" the other. Just as prose and poetry are intimately linked, so are the characters, the narrator, and the author. As Miller notes, "Williams' characters . . . penetrate one another completely and are known by a narrator who has transcended point of view so that he stands everywhere in the story at once."[41] One may view, on a more metaphorical level, the doctor/narrator/writer as the objectifier of his patients, "rare presences" all, *as* poetry.

It was, despite these important studies, not until the 1970s that critical interest in Williams's theory and practice of the short story brought the works to new levels of attention. James E. B. Breslin delves into Williams's decision, as expressed to Kay Boyle (whose stories Williams knew well and wrote about), to turn to the "jewels" that the "prose" of short stories revealed and that were possible to "clean and group," if for nothing else than as a "laboratory for metrics."[42] For Breslin, Williams's turn to the short story form in the 1920s and 1930s is natural enough insofar as Williams "made the episode the basic unit of his longer fiction."[43] For Breslin, the short story form allowed Williams to employ a language "purged of all stylistic pyrotechnics."[44]

Linda W. Wagner's book-length study of Williams's prose remains the foremost published attempt to explore the relationships between Williams's various prose works.[45] Wagner emphasizes that Williams characteristically called for a "prose construction" in his poetry, achieving characterization through monologue or dialogue.[46] In brief, Wagner insists that Williams's poetic theory is applicable to his prose, and that all of his prose and plays are often "too autobiographical to be read in comfort."[47] Wagner sees Williams's overall literary theory evolving from imagism to objectivism to an organic form, "a shape for each piece of writing consonant with its subject, tone, and intended impact" that avoids the formulaic at all costs.[48] Concerning the influence of Williams's stories, Wagner goes so far as to say that they "may have had as deep an effect on contemporary fiction as his poems have had on modern poetry."[49] Wagner does not name the contemporary authors whom she has in mind. The list would surely run, in various ways, from Raymond Carver to Robert Coover, Donald Barthleme, and John Updike, Andre Dubus, Jay Neugeboren, Jane Smiley and Leigh Ken-

nedy, Lawrence Dorr, Alice Adams, Robley Wilson, Jr., Barry Yourgrau, Gerald Haslam and others—major and minor.

Underscoring many of the same assumptions of Wagner, Sondra A.
Zeidenstein contends that Williams's poetry and prose are indeed unified and that his experiments with the short story form gave him the
right proportion of easy flow and artistic control, allowing him to evolve
the new style that he was seeking for his poetry. Furthermore, Zeidenstein claims that the stories served his sense of cultural mission to use
the American language and "serve the people through his art."[50]

With the the publication of Reed Whittemore's biography of Williams in 1975, followed in 1981 by Paul Mariani's even more extensive
look at Williams's life and work—including his stories—the canonization is well underway. This recognition is reinforced by the founding
of the *William Carlos Williams Newsletter* in 1975 and a baker's dozen of
incidental scholarly journal articles and chapters in collections specifically addressing various aspects of Williams's short stories.[51] Now with
one college literature anthology after another including at least one of
his stories, his name is associated with the short story as well as with
poetry and he is finally receiving wider, more "popular" recognition as
a master of the short story, notwithstanding his secure position as a
major modern American poet. By the time of this writing the total
number of articles and books written about Williams in the quarter
century since his death was in the thousands. And although only a
relatively small proportion of critical commentary on Williams deals ex-
clusively with his short stories, it soon becomes obvious that in all of
his writings, poetry and prose, practice and theory are inextricably
yoked. What he theorized he practiced, so that "no theory but in practice" might be the paraphrase of "no ideas but in things." Out of what
he wrote and how he wrote came his articulation and speculation about
"why the short story." Why not? The writer, the poet, the physician,
the man—all were subsumed in William Carlos Williams, a name in
itself suggestive of integration and "self containment." More and more
(though less completely in England despite the comments by Charles
Tomlinson, Tom Gunn and others praising Williams), in literary histories and more generalized reference books on the short story, in anthologies and even on videocassettes and telecourses, Williams is
reaching out to make "contact" with the common reader, with the
kinds of individuals he treated as a physician and about whom he wrote
his stories—ever rare, ever uncommon presences to Williams, "the literary guy," the "word man," the "medicine man."[52]

Word Man/Medicine Man:
In the American Grain

A "word man/medicine man," Williams gained much of his force as an autobiographical storyteller from the oral origins and impulses of the short story and from his particularly keen ear for (and empathy with) what he referred to as the "American idiom," the fundamentally colloquial and nonliterary speech patterns, intonations, and word usage of ordinary, working class Americans. Particularly if one looks at Williams's rather romanticized partisanship for the American Indian and the American landscape—the sense of "spirit and place" and belief in American "primitivism," which he shared, albeit to different degrees, with D. H. Lawrence—one sees not only Williams's affinity with the "stories" of local color as told by Hamlin Garland and Sherwood Anderson, among others, but also how Williams's physician and proletarian stance informs his work. His compulsion to "care" medically and politically for the sick and less advantaged in the face of what (given his Hispanic heritage) might be called "la tristeza de la vida," or the "tragic foot" as he words it in *Paterson*, places him in the American grain of earliest beliefs in the power of the "story." For the tribe, the people, the folk story-telling serves not just to report events and occurrences but somehow, whether in an incantatory or reportorial way, to bring about healing and restoration, to reinstate health over illness, community over isolation, and the better life over the worse. In this study Williams is viewed as something more of an American "aborigine" and a "proletarian" (words in need of defining to be sure) than critical consensus would have it.

Williams had no difficulty in seeing his self-consciously "American" stories as being at least partially within the European, physician/humanist tradition of the doctor as artist, and thought that perhaps he continued this tradition most directly through his parents "who were both born out of the country and who were European minded.[53] In his autobiography he insists that when people questioned his ability to function as both a doctor and a writer they failed to realize that for him "one occupation complements the other (*A*, 359). For Williams in the practice of medicine it was the everyday work that pleased him and made it worthwhile: ". . . the actual calling on people, at all times and under all conditions, the coming to grips with the intimate conditions of their lives . . . has always absorbed me" (*A*, 356). That absorption involved an intense identification and empathy with people. Williams describes this process in terms that seem more explainable by the methods of story than by the methods of science. Once he saw a patient the details of the case would formulate themselves in a flash, and the diagnosis would make itself known—or it would not. The patient's personality and behavior would take the form of something needing attention. The patient's case would either attract or repel Williams and he would rely on something he refers to as "professional attitude" (an attitude not all that easily inferred in his short stories). That attitude, although ostensibly a physician's, is also a writer's—an attitude that involved, he says, "a man . . . watch[ing] the patient's mind as it watches him, distrusting him, ready to fly off at a tangent at the first opportunity" (*A*, 357). But it is exactly this process of empathy, of adopting the patient's condition that rejuvenated Williams as a physician and as a writer: "That is why as a writer I have never felt that medicine interfered with me but rather that it was my very food and drink, the very thing which made it possible for me to write. Was I not interested in man? There the thing was, right in front of me. I could touch it, smell it. It was myself naked, just as it was, without a lie telling itself to me in its own terms" (*A*, 357).

Part of the spelling out of simple matters, in as profound a way as he could carry out, turned the people he met in his medical practice into characters for his short stories—in one instance resulting in libel litigation because he forgot to change real names into fictitious ones. The restorative aspects of the science-to-story transformations accomplished by means of words perhaps aided him, most directly, as much as other tangible remedies helped his patients. They, no doubt, read few or none of Williams's short stories; but they conversed with him, knew his manner—rehearsed, as it were, what would later be objectified into the other realities of story. The writer worth heeding for Williams, and the one implicit in his short stories, is one who can— empathetically more so than sympathetically—laugh at people in their various "costumes," high and low, and reveal to themselves (and to other readers who see their own reflections), their inner secrets and private motives found out by, told to, and told about by another.

Williams's vocabulary plainly evidences how he saw his patient's lives in relation to the plots, characterizations, and stagings of narrative and drama. By going to the "base of the matter," seeing people for what they are and revealing it to them in ways beyond escape, Williams saw his patients as their own kind of "hero" (*A*, 358). In their ordinary humanity, their commonness, was a very special and rare "presence" through which radiated an awesome nobility. Through his long, forty-year practice, he knew on a day-to-day basis the people he watched, listened to, and talked to in his office, in their homes, in hospitals. Transferring them to the many pages of his poetry and prose, Williams insisted that medicine allowed him to cut through the "chit-chat" that formulaic stories and their publishers might sell or that slick magazine audiences might want to hear, and to get at essences, "the evasive life of things, . . . the secret spring of all our lives" (*A*, 359). To do this—to actualize in a story the rare presences of the lives with which he empathized—he turned to, and, later influenced, the little magazines of the 1920s and 1930s, publishing a number of experimental stories, essays, and poems in the *Little Review, Others, Contact,* and *Blast,* to name a few.

Physicians, more than other readers, have long found special "professional" worth as well as aesthetic pleasure in Williams's short stories. One of Williams's two sons, William Eric Williams, himself a physician, was influenced in his professional calling not just by his father's life work as a doctor, but by his father's spoken and written accounts of his patients' stories, which became "the source of many if not most of his themes."[54] In one particular instance, "The Insane," W. E. Williams himself becomes a character in one of his father's stories. In testimonial to the importance of his father's short stories, W. E. Williams states, "My personal estimation is that the doctor stories in particular give an excellent picture of the state of the art in medicine in the early years of his practice. I suppose they appeal to me particularly because I am myself a physician and can appreciate in a personal and professional way what he has to say."[55]

It is common for Williams's stories to be included in medical ethics courses. Doctors find a unique firsthand account, almost in the fashion of the case study, of patient types and issues that, in all likelihood, will be encountered in practice. The insights offered into Williams's stories

offered by physicians confirms that whether Williams intended it or
not, the physician is not just a narrator or a character in most of his
stories, but an ideal audience as well. Barbara Currier Bell, for instance, thinks that Williams's frequently anthologized story, "The Use
of Force," is as important for young doctors to ponder as is any single
text she can name.[56] One physician reader has used Williams's stories
to help work through emotions directed at certain more difficult, abusive patients.[57] Williams clearly shares with other physician writers, like
Keats, Chekhov, Holmes, Cronin, and Percy not just a muscle and
bone, anatomical intimacy with the human condition, but also an inclination to go through the "somatic part of medicine into the psychic
part," as Williams called it.[58]

More than any other physician-writer, Robert Coles has commented
at some length, and repeatedly, about the special reciprocal relationship between Williams the physician and Williams the writer and his
influence on doctor-readers. Williams steered Coles into medical school
and served as a mentor for Coles in his effort to combine doctoring and
writing—and, indeed, in the pursuit of writing as a kind of doctoring.
Even Williams's medical specialty of obstetrics and pediatrics influenced Coles's interest in children, psychiatry, and medical humanities.[59] Coles admires Williams for many reasons, but he especially
admires his short stories: "These are stories that tell of mistakes, of
errors of judgment; and as well, of one modest breakthrough, then
another—not in research efforts . . . but in that most important of all
situations, the would-be healer face-to-face with the sufferer who half
desires, half dreads the stranger's medical help.[60] Coles is struck by the
human, fallible yet heroic, qualities of not just the patients Williams
transposes into characters, but also the powerful presence of the writer
behind the personae and narrators of the stories, a writer not all that
distanced in his fictions from the ordinary but nevertheless special realities of his practice, as experience by experience it accumulated over
four decades. Echoing Williams's comments on what he was trying for
as a writer, and why he wrote, Coles observes, "It is this *unreflecting
egoism,* as George Eliot called it, which the doctor-narrator of these
stories allows us to see, and so doing, naturally, we are nudged closer
to ourselves."[61] It is Williams's revelation of his own pride, his own
narcissism, "the doctor ailing even as he tries to heal others," which
endears Williams to Coles.

Certainly Williams and his narrators are daringly honest, and con-
vincingly sincere in the stories. But not all readers find him endearing:

readers who have a difficult time demystifying the physician, or whose ideal of the physician does not take to tough-talking revelations (regardless of literary fabrication—confession or report, complaint or act of self-healing); readers who hold tightly to utterly romanticized stereotypes of the physician as more dauntless than doubt-ridden; readers who like tightly plotted stories—no doubt such readers regard the voicings of Williams's stories as cynical, maybe even mean and prejudicial, certainly fragmented.

As Coles suggests, the conflicts evident in Williams's "doctor stories"—caring ministrations contrasted with dulled insensitivity; love and hate between doctor and patient; oscillations between success and failure, disappointment and satisfaction—make for much of their vitality. These stories bespeak their very nature as essentially autobiographical musings, and form an at once invigorated and exhausted doctor's log of the dynamics of healing both patient and would-be healer through another medicinal venue: narrative sketch, short story.

As a writer and as a physician adept in psychoanalytical method, Coles knows keenly the importance of words to teller and listener alike. Readers of Williams's stories soon see that Williams in his visits to patients lay in wait for words that he could use later as "their" words to a physician in his stories. Williams well knew, and said, that cutting through to the psychoanalytical aspect of administering to his patients also involved a "force" of rather deep consequence to his own psychology, and represented something he described as "a descent into myself."[62] As a result, many of Williams's stories are satires of sorts, the workings out of a doctor not all that keen on taking himself or his role totally seriously—"parody turned on the parodist, words used to take the stern (but also compassionate) measure of the doctor who dispensed (among other things), words."[63] Coles simply confirms what Williams himself said he attempted to do with people in life and literature, with words as their own "rare presences"—that is, to reveal much of himself in the revelation of others, to ask the question so integrally important to philosophy and literature generally and autobiography specifically: "How do I live a life?"[64]

In her response to Coles's views on Williams and his short stories Helen Vendler complains that Coles interjects far too much of his own autobiography and his own crusade as a defender of "forgotten folk" in his identification with Williams and his stories; and she insists that Coles confuses art and life, as perhaps (by implication) so did Williams.[65] But Coles is not inventing the belief held by Williams, to which Coles also subscribes, that if life is not ultimately art, art certainly grows out of life. Moreover, a life in the living may become something of an art, an "autobiography" composed of days and months rather than chapters, just as artistry out of words reshapes the realities and metaphors of self.[66] Vendler, although she shortchanges the implications of autobiography and politics in Williams's stories and Coles's commentary, prompts thoughts that are particularly crucial in reading Williams's stories: To what degree are the stories representative of life or art or both? To what degree are they sociological or political case studies and disguised editorializing presented ("doctored up") by a middle-class liberal? To what degree are the stories more protest than art? To what degree are the stories irrelevant to autobiography and non-referential to anything outside their own art?

In order to understand Williams's stories as curatives and the merging of his role as teller and healer, some attention must be paid to the oral tradition and its autobiographical implications. The context for appreciating Williams' modernism, such as it is, is to be found in the linkage between the aboriginal, the "native" voice, and the modern experience described in his short stories. Some of the bases for his alleged "anti-poetic" or even "anti-intellectual" presence (an issue raised by Wallace Stevens and others) are similarly rooted in this connection. Williams was a lifelong advocate of plain English, of the vernacular, of the "American idiom," as he called it—not garrulity, not preciousness, not ultrafelicitous turns of phrase. And that advocacy is related to seeking the aboriginal, upholding the oral tradition. Frederick Manfred observes in this context, ". . . the echo and the feel and even some of the talk of the aborigine is still in our American language. Because it works. Because it reflects our experience. It reflects not an English experience but an American experience."[67]

The oral tradition depends on silences as well as sounds, and Williams's understated style speaks strongly through silences. As N. Scott Momaday makes apparent, in oral tradition silence is as important as sound, and, aside from Williams's ear and poetic sensibility, this in part accounts for the general shortness of his short stories, which often seem prototypic of the four and five-minute "instant" stories written by so many postmodern authors, such as Barry Yourgrau.

N. Scott Momaday—who in his novels and poems demonstrates with his own special modern yet atavistic eloquence just how significant and sacred the word, and storytelling are—reminds us that in humankind's

first prehistoric transposition of mind's image to cave wall or rock, resides the first art, the first story: "For all the stories of all the world
proceed from the moment he [humankind] makes his [its] mark."[68]
Momaday, of course, is speaking about the engendering of all literature
and art, not the short story. His ear for the spoken word and his insights
into the similarities between his own modern narrative and poetic techniques and his own Kiowa heritage have ramifications for Williams's
allegiance to the American idiom, the American grain.

Momaday argues that the native voice in American literature, and in
the American language, must be recognized as a part of the larger impulse of "primal song" in poetry and prose. The great complexity of
the relationships between writing and speaking notwithstanding,
Momaday insists upon the importance of oral tradition and respect for
words, the significance of what they sound like and what they are in
addition to what they "represent." His argument holds a special relevancy for the concept of ideas as things, or words as things. Williams
heard words spoken by his patients and used them in his stories so that
not only he, as author and narrator, but also his readers/listeners might
hear them again. In the oral tradition, Momaday writes, "words are rare
and therefore dear. They are jealously preserved in the ear and in the
mind. Words are spoken with great care, and they are heard. They
matter, and they must not be taken for granted. . . . With respect to
the oral tradition of the American Indian, these attitudes are reflected
in the character of the songs and stories themselves. Perhaps the most
distinctive and important aspect of that tradition is the way in which it
reveals the singer's and the storyteller's respect for and belief in language."[69] Williams is revealed as such a "singer," such a teller in his
stories, for language is always in the forefront, always "rare and dear":
the colloquial, man-in-the-street, on-the-job, ostensibly antiliterary
and unself-conscious "American idiom," is a part of the "rare presence"
Williams listened for and promulgated. This is so much the case in
Williams that in his stories, as in native American oral tradition, expression itself takes precedence over moral statement, social message, political bias, or editorializing.

Several other word ways in the native American oral tradition are
applicable to Williams's short stories. One relevant item is the sacral
nature of words. Words are intrinsically powerful, even magical, as
Momaday stresses: "By means of words can one bring about physical
change in the universe. By means of words can one quiet a raging
weather, bring forth the harvest, ward off evil, rid the body of sickness

and pain, subdue an enemy, capture the heart of a lover, live in the proper way, and venture beyond death."[70] This is not to suggest that Williams, the well-trained medico whom we hear in and behind the short stories, is a superstitious believer of mumbo-jumbo recitations rather than the scientific remedies and methods available to a "modern" doctor. And yet Williams's belief in the power of words, and in the sacredness of art, and his efforts to function "religiously" as a doctor-writer are everywhere apparent in his short stories. You see them in his attitude toward the "girl with the pimply face," Jean Beicke, toward his black women, especially, and in his narrators and personae generally, who, as in "The Use of Force," treat people out of a heightened sense of morality that merges with religion—the religion of work and of words. He knew full well that man, even doctor, ultimately knew little, that life and health, sickness and death are knowable as unknowable by poets just as by physicians: "We know nothing and can know nothing / but / the dance, to dance to a measure / contrapuntally, / Satyrically, the tragic foot," as he says in those reverberating words at the end of *Paterson* (book 5) so full of primal, aboriginal meaning and identification.

In addition to this belief in the sacrality and efficacy of words, Williams shared the second tenet of the oral tradition, and in fact built one aspect of his aesthetic on his similarly cryptic credo in "A Sort of a Song": "no ideas but in things." In the native tradition, Momaday observes, "Often the words are returned upon themselves in a notable and meaningful way. They transcend their merely symbolic value and become one with the idea they express. They are not then intermediate but primary; they are at once the name of things and the things named."[71] Although Momaday is a student of modern poetry, the echoes of Williams in Momaday's phrasing are perhaps as much anachronistic as incipient in and original to the native tradition.

Other qualities of the native voice also apply to Williams: stories are composed of words and the implications on words placed there by the tellers; stories are true to common experience, actual or imagined; the storyteller is preeminently entitled to tell the story; the storyteller creates himself insofar as the mask the teller wears for the telling is of the teller's making.[72] Momaday says nothing about Williams in his listing of such qualifiers, nor need he, in contending that the native voice has always been pervasive in American literature and has been recognized and perpetuated by "some of the major figures of our literary history."[73] When asked just what he meant by the satyrs in *Paterson* and whether they might represent the "element of freedom, of energy within the form," Williams responded, "Yes, the satyrs are understood as action, a dance. I always think of the Indians there."[74] In the expansiveness, energy, and freedom of *Paterson* and *In the American Grain*, as in his stories, Williams was thinking of, indeed, identifying with the Indians in more ways than is usually realized.

The "stories" and "histories" found in Williams's *In the American Grain* evidence and underscore, in probably the purest sense of all of Williams's narratives—fiction and nonfiction—the importance to him of the native voice, the native American presence and the oral tradition. *In the American Grain* might be regarded, then, in this special sense, as yet another instance of Williams's extraordinary versatility with short "stories": fact becomes faction becomes fiction; history becomes story. Strictly speaking, the twenty-one or so narratives that make up *In the American Grain* are not "story" but "history" filtered through Williams's iconoclastic, imaginative reworking of "fact." His subjective substitution of some of the less traditional American heroes for more traditional ones, and his overall partisanship for native Americans results in a transvaluation that gives his title certain ironic overtones: he is writing, in some measure at least, "against" the American grain.

Philip Rahv helps bring into focus Williams's role in perpetuating what Momaday calls the "native voice" in American literature. Rahv describes Williams as "a writer ravaged by this hemisphere's occult aboriginal past"[75]—a comment applied to "The Venus" (originally part of *A Voyage to Pagany* [1928] and first included in *Life Along the Passaic River* [1938] as a short story) that extends to *In the American Grain*. Because "The Venus" is so explicitly concerned with the Indian presence in America, it can be seen as a companion text to *In the American Grain*, for that book reverberates throughout the story. Because this is so, "The Venus" bears discussion here rather than with the stories that appear in *Life Along the Passaic River*.

In "The Venus" an American in Rome, Dev Evans (a fictive counterpart to Williams himself, and the central character in *Pagany*, known as Dr. Evans from New Jersey) tries repeatedly to answer Fräulein von J., her companion, Frau M., and Clara, a late arrival—all headed for Frascati. Words and communication are a theme of the story, which first becomes apparent as Evans struggles to make himself understood in German. (He is also disturbed by the babbling Englishwomen passengers.) Once in Frascati, Evans and Fräulein von J. leave the others and head for the open air and the Italian springtime. Evans, though somewhat preoccupied with thoughts of his absent sister, Bess, is erotically drawn to the young German girl. He admires her coloration, hair, eyes, hands, and her firm, peasantlike ankles. He likens her to Venus. But the question, "What is it like, America?" is ever on the girl's lips; her longing, more obliquely, mystically sexual, is to give herself to something like the idea of a primitive America—once the idea has been comprehended, that is.

The girl persistently wonders whether or not Evans is somehow America personified. He tells her first that America is a place "to . . . hide everything that is secretly valuable" to him so as not to "have it defiled" (*MLI*, 215). He, in fact, has something with him that is spiritually emblematic of that hiding—and the notion becomes all the more ironic and literal when he shows Fräulein J. the Indian arrowhead that he carries around in his pocket, an object that could indeed be "defiled" just as surely as it was "filed" when it was shaped from flint. He tells her that more and more America offers less and less of all that is valuable—except for its seclusion and primitivism: ". . . To me it is a hard, barren life, where I am *alone* and unmolested (work as I do in the thick of it) though in constant danger lest some slip send me to perdition but which, being covetous not at all, I enjoy for the seclusion and primitive air of it" (*MLI*, 216). That hard work, seclusion, and primitivism is augmented for Evans by all that makes up the natural, inanimate "placeness" of his youth: ". . . shapes, foliage, trees to which I am used—and a love of place and the characteristics of place—good or bad, rich or poor" (*MLI*, 216).

For the girl America seems something worthwhile to which she could lose her innocence, her "virginity." Evans responds cynically, though the girl does not really hear him, that America is a paltry society for women, damaged by fears of racism, rape, poverty, and harsh climate. But again, more idealistically, he says of America, as he struggles with the undefinable, struggles to say what he thinks he means, "I think it is useful to us, . . . because it is near savagery" (*MLI*, 218). Evans does not define "savagery," however, Fräulein J. enthusiastically accepts what he says, equating Evans with a man having in America and in himself the "savagery" that she knows Europe and Europeans lack. He is, in effect, on the verge of her psychic seduction.

In convenient, devoted proof of his "point," and her acceptance of it, he retrieves a flint arrowhead from his coat pocket and shows it to her. As if in justification of his right and motive to carry the arrowhead, given his savage sympathies, he says, "I am not the typical American. We have a few natives left but they would not know me—" (*MLI*, 219). She takes the arrowhead and places it in her hand in a scene—so characteristic of Williams—with definite erotic undertones, as if the consciousness of the girl's sexual and psychic ripeness is now physically targeted for penetration: "She was impressed. She held it hard in her hand as if to keep its impression there, felt the point, the edge, tried it, turned it over" (*MLI*, 219). Here the Fräulein is, in effect, "ravaged" just as Evans has been, by America's "occult aboriginal past," as Rahv says Williams has been.

As a result of this moment of penetration, Evans and the girl are united in a special kinship with "savagery" (muted as it is), a special awareness of the special significance, the "rare presence" of native Americans and the frontier in American history, which is lost to Europeans in their distant past and to most Americans in their more recent past. Evans tells the girl the he found the arrowhead in a cornfield in Virginia, and that few Americans understand what he is saying about the savage significance of America. He carries the flint arrowhead as an emblem, a memento of his own special awareness and allegiance to the "hard history" made by the tragic pioneers whose houses, fast to the ground, he has seen in pictures. The awareness of the "hard history" known to Evans is seen as tremendously meaningful to the girl; it is an epiphany of sorts, though not without a shuddering feeling of the "lonesomeness" of the answer to her question, "What then is it like, America?" Evans and the girl have truly communicated, so much so that the girl, figuratively seduced, is now aware of and dedicated to the savagery of America—an initiate, no longer an innocent, "impregnated."

Rahv carries on no detailed analysis of "The Venus"; however, it is understandable why in the story he hears again the aboriginal voicings of *In the American Grain*. That is why, somewhat condescendingly perhaps, but very accurately, Rahv quips that the voice of Dr. Williams in his short stories is really the voice of a more ancient kind of doctor: "In some ways Dr. Williams is really a medicine man."[78] The America Evans defines for Fräulein von J. is, to be sure, defined exotically. It is exotic enough and intuitive enough for Rahv to call it an outgrowth of Williams's American mysticism. Few have ever fully commented on the importance of the native voice as heard in the oral beginnings of American literary history that are expressed in *In the American Grain*, nor have many commented on how that work relates to Williams's short stories and the "native voice" in those stories.[78] As in "The Venus," Williams's native voice is present in many of his short stories and can be related to the idealization of the American Indian and the sense of story in *In the American Grain* as well as to the proletarian spirit evidenced in Evans's (and Williams's) admiration of peasantlike Fräulein von J.

Rahv, curiously, says nothing about Williams in his well-known classification of American authors as either paleface or redskin.[79] In Rahv's scheme the open-air exuberance of Whitman and the drawing-room intrigues of Henry James serve as the two polar types. Granting the extremes of Rahv's account of the dichotomy between experience and consciousness, savagery and sophistication, which he observes in American authors, Williams is a redskin—along with Twain, Hemingway, and others like Frederick Manfred. Williams was indeed allied with things American over things European, with what Rahv's redskins find interesting: "the lowlife world of the frontier and big cities." It is worth noting that redskin and proletarian merge in this accounting.

Another master of the modern short story and a type of vitalist "redskin" D. H. Lawrence read Williams and particularly *In the American Grain* with fond enthusiasm. Similarities between "The Venus" and such stories as Lawrence's "The Woman Who Rode Away" may be drawn to the extent that, without tracing actual influence, Williams and Lawrence have a recognizable kinship. Given Lawrence's assumption about spirit of place as put forward in *Studies in Classic American Literature* it is little wonder. Perhaps Williams owes a debt to that work, as Henry Seidel Canby suggests.[80] What is perceived as a shared psychological pattern with Williams and Lawrence in the narratives of both *In the American Grain* and *A Voyage to Pagany* is discussed at some length by Thomas R. Whitaker, who views *Pagany* and Lawrence's *Twilight in Italy* and *Mornings in Mexico* as dramatizing similar psychological "descents."[81] Although little direct evidence exists to prove Lawrence influenced Williams, there was an affinity, a "contact" witnessed in Lawrence's words about *In the American Grain* and in the exoticism of the stories of the two authors, concerned as many of them are with the transvaluations and relativity of otherness among dark and light-skinned individuals. In 1928 Lawrence saw Williams as presenting history as "a sensuous record of the Americanization of white men in America" rather than history as "a complacent record of the civilization and Europizing . . . of the American continent."[82] For Williams and for Lawrence much of what is America (its "grain," as Williams would have it) is the native American, the "Red Indian," Lawrence says. As Evans realizes in "The Venus," even the most American of Americans, ever bounded by whiteness, by non-Indian blood, is incapable of actually becoming a "Red Indian." The need to strive toward "Indianness" and the aboriginal, however futile for the American non-Indian, (often the intended readers of Williams) is transformed into an effort to realize and acknowledge the native American voice of America; to see it reflected in the kind of Americans Williams presents; to see it represented in literature, in writing about Americans "in the intensest American vernacular."[83]

From his sympathies with the land itself—America personified as the great female principle ("hembrisma")—its ravishing by Columbus —to his delight in Montezuma's demeanor and habits of dress; through his renderings of the conquistadors Cortés, Ponce de León, and de Soto; through Samuel de Champlain, the Jesuit Pere Sebastian Rasles and the French in Quebec; through the coming of Raleigh, the Mayflower, Mather, Thomas Morton, the Puritans; then Washington, Franklin, Boone; the young French-Indian Sachem Jacataqua; Aaron Burr and Edgar Allan Poe and Abraham Lincoln—throughout all these impassioned and poetic "stories" of *In the American Grain*, Williams's advocacy for the native American voice is heard strong and clear.

In his much quoted opening to "The Fountain of Eternal Youth" Williams proclaims the allegiance Americans owe to the Indians in acknowledging our historical origins in "their world." The bases of most of Williams's "histories" and "stories" are traceable to this sense, and presence of "hard history": "History, history! We fools, what do we know or care? History begins for us with murder and enslavement, not with discovery. No, we are not Indians but we are men of their world. The blood means nothing; the spirit, the ghost of the land moves in the blood, moves the blood. It is we who ran to the shore naked, we who cried, *Heavenly Man!* These are the inhabitants of our souls, our murdered souls that lie . . . agh! Listen!"[84]

The anguish expressed over our murdered souls is part of the sense of tragedy, the "hard history," about which Evans speaks in "The Venus," and which informs both Williams's short stories and *In the American Grain* as a story. In his account of Ponce de León's murderous slave hunting in the islands surrounding Williams's ancestral Caribbean islands, Williams weaves a story filled with some of the same outrage as that which he feels for the conditions of the poor and the ill; the "proletarians" he served as an American physician haunted with the sense and sound of the injustices of the American past. In "The Fountain of Eternal Youth," the soul of the "Carib," its natural and human delights broken by Ponce de León's massacres, weighs heavily, sorrowfully on Williams. In Williams's resplendent racial memory, the place in nature becomes a paradise. "A stream of splashing water, the luxuriant foliage. A gorge, a veritable tunnel led upstream between cliff walls covered by thick vines in flower attended by ensanguined hummingbirds which darted about from cup to cup in the green light" (*IAG*, 40). The ruination of this American paradise, emblematic of the horrors at the beginning of America's history, accounts not just for the naturalistic strain in Williams's telling, but also for the shocking and the grotesque, even the macabre and "pseudomacabre" elements that oftentimes provide a subtheme for his stories of suffering and death—and the longed for restoration, absolution, and healing.

In "The Discovery of Kentucky," his retelling of Daniel Boone's "so-called autobiography" as allegedly written down by one John Filson from Boone's dictation, Williams interjects much of his own self and his longing for the American voice, the American idiom. For it is with the frontiersman Boone (not with that part of his myth which identifies him as an Indian killer) that Williams identifies most fully. It is the frontiersman, the primitive Boone—a kind of analogue to Williams as word man/medicine man—whom Williams calls up for inspiration and hope. For Williams Boone's genius was in the way he lived his life; how he found a ground to take England's place, and how he did so with a savage morality; how he understood the American Indian's relationship to place: "Boone saw the truth of the Red Man, not an aberrant type, treacherous and anti-white to be feared and exterminated, but as a natural expression of the place, the Indian himself as *right*, the flower of his world" (*IAG*, 137–38).

In his retelling of the winning of the "frontier," the Puritans, with their high morality, knew nothing of, or refused to know, the native soul of America. Filson's silly phrases and his artificial recasting of Boone's "rude words," (beautiful words, in Williams's view) disturbs Williams and he projects his own voice, the native voice, in his idealization of Boone and his quest for "peace and solitude" and Kentucky: "There was, thank God, a great voluptuary born to the American settlements against the niggardliness of the damning puritanical tradition; one who by the single logic of his passion, which he rested on the savage life about him, destroyed at its spring that spirituality withering plague. For this he has remained buried in a miscolored legend and left for rotten. Far from dead, however, but full of a rich regenerative violence he remains, when his history will be carefully reported, for us who have come to call upon him" (*IAG*, 130).

Williams projected the image of the frontiersman—his lonesomeness and his idiomatic American language—into his dramatizations of himself in this "story" as well as in his Passaic River stories and other stories. In fact, the prototypical physician figure, whether narrator, character, or author's persona, is a kind of incarnation of Boone and his "regenerative violence."

Transposing Boone's kind of American heroism to an American author, Williams elevates Poe, perceiving in his work sympathy with place similar to that of the Indian: Williams writes that Poe was "a genius intimately shaped by his locality and time" (*IAG*, 216). For his "re-awakened genius of place" Poe represents for Williams the sense of the seriousness of literature, a seriousness Williams also aimed for in his own creations of New Jersey locales in his stories. In "Edgar Allan Poe," Williams writes that "what he [Poe] says, being thoroughly local in origin, has some chance of being universal in application" (*IAG*, 222). If it is Whitman who is Williams's closest American kin as a poet, it is Poe whose sense of locality, organic composition and form influenced Williams conception of the short story. For Williams, as author, the native soul and voice was the beginning of his own "hard history," and Poe's stress on the local offered a beginning to a tradition that he himself, in theory and practice, perpetuated. Williams's sense of Poe as a beginning, an originator, is something one senses also in the thingness, the actualization evident in Williams's "story" about Poe: like Poe's works, Williams's narrative is "Made to fit a *place*" and "will have that actual quality of *things* anti-metaphysical—" (*IAG*, 222).

Seldom do the stories in *Knife of the Times, Life Along the Passaic River, Make Light of It,* and *The Farmers' Daughters* reach the poetic lyricism, the song of the prose found in Williams's *In the American Grain.* Although the stories collected in all the above volumes, if taken together as a panorama of the Passaic River, the American Northeast, possess an epic, done-in-mosaic quality about them, the short stories individually do not attain the epic scope and sweep of *In the American Grain.* In the small, "rare presences" of all his short stories the same soul, the same spirit, the same native voice, the same satyr dance, tragically, contrapuntally occur. Williams's excoriating, angry, and sorrowed self is heard in his understated accounts of the lesser American working-class lives, the heroic antiheroes, just as it is in his more archetypal portrayals in the now larger-than-life lives accounted for in *In the American Grain*. Certain of Williams's characters are individuals. He names them and gives them the foregrounding and "fame" of patient and person become "character." They are, ultimately, however, part of the manswarm, the millions of lives unnoticed, anonymous. Williams's stories are ultimately their only history—something quite different from the historical legends he revisits and remythicizes in his *American Grain* histories/stories. For this reason, that is anonymous life become "famous," and legendary name become person, it is important to observe as a kind of first premise for considering his short stories that both in story and history of early and modern America Williams's self and voice prevail with overriding autobiographical influence, the influence of a medicine man of the "word."

Rare Presences: *The Knife of the Times* and *Life Along the Passaic River*

Williams's first two volumes of short stories, *The Knife of the Times* (1932) and *Life Along the Passaic River* (1938), represent the kinds of "rare presences" he found as a doctor in his various encounters with his patients and with people in general; in listening to what they said and how they said it—with the ear not just of a physician formulating a diagnosis or prescription but of a poet tuned in for the music and dance of their words and voicings. Williams's stories are records of those times, those meetings, those places, and of his remembering of them; they are his attempt to turn case history into story and back again through writing. His stories become their own kind of rare presences both as things in and of themselves and in relation to each other. Williams's own rare presence permeates all of the stories—a "new meaning beginning to intervene," the "poetry" under the language that represents the lives of the people who are his characters, his life and his character as author-narrator (*A*, 361).

The Knife of the Times

Outside of two or three of the eleven stories in *The Knife of the Times*—namely "Old Doc Rivers," "The Colored Girls of Passenack—Old and New," and the titular story, "The Knife of the Times"—the eight other stories are relatively neglected by critics, as is the volume as a whole, which has been overlooked in favor of *Life Along the Passaic River* and, most certainly, *In the American Grain*. *Knife*, admittedly, includes only about one quarter of his stories, and early ones at that. But the stories in this first volume are some of Williams's finest, and reveal some of the techniques—style, structure, point of view, and theme —that he carried through and developed in his later stories and that mark the "presence" of a Williams story.

Much of what characterizes his stories must be demonstrated by analyzing individual stories, and by noting comparisons between them. Williams would be the first to admit that different readers find different things to see in a story: "So, let's look at short stories and see what CAN be done with them. How many ways they CAN be written, torturing the material in every way we can think of—from which YOU are to draw what you want" (*ABOSS*, 9). There are, however, a few general traits that bear mention as well as more extensive comment in the discussions below. Williams's stories, it must be reiterated, gain much of their motive and nature from the process of storytelling itself, from the oral tradition and the ancient native voice; he was preoccupied with the native voice, the American idiom, and dedicated himself to finding and experiencing it in daily life. By transferring the voice and the experiences to writing, Williams made a lasting thing out of those experiences for himself and for readers.

Given Williams's interest in storytelling, it is not surprising that his stories thus often take the form of stories within stories, making for multiple narrators and for a succession of linked stories rather than for predictable and formulaic frame narratives. The stories are often recounted in series or layers, much as an event might be related by various individuals, from various perspectives, to one central inquisitor or listener trying to make sense of it all, or trying to find the truth of the matter and then to relate that through the larger telling, which is the frame or "container" identifiable by title as the Williams story.

Significantly, this is the method and form of the case study, written by the scientist or investigator who knows that there are many sides to any story, many versions of character or action or setting that may appear as "truth." This method is also reminiscent of gossip, of hearing and telling about a person and what happened or did not happen to that person, from people who knew, each in their own way, portions of the story, who may have added to the story or even fabricated portions of it. These case stories or reports, or gossipy stories told to an inquisitor-listener who then relates incidents—often in retrospect—give an abiding anecdotal quality to a Williams story. This is not to say that his stories are completely without plot, or without sequenced events. Rather, even in stories that utilize sequenced events and motives, plot takes a decidedly anecdotal and digressive turn. Given an implied listener, Williams's stories seem like a prose variant of the dramatic monologue.

In keeping with their "oral," anecdotal, conversational, reportorial quality, his stories offer some fascinating examples of dialogue that is not really dialogue so much as it is, again, reporting, partially because the reporting is reported as it was reported. Moreover, the narrator does not pronounce judgment on the significance of these conversations. There is, however, more editorializing, more political and moral judgment, more overall value judgment in a Williams story than is commonly pointed out. There are, too, implicit judgments to be drawn, but by and large Williams's stories are not explicitly didactic in the sense that they draw a heavy-handed moral, unless the point is not to draw a moral, certainly not a "puritanical" moral. This is not to say that there is no moral center in his stories, at times even moral indignation. Williams's moral center, his "opinions" are decidedly not bourgeois, at least not overtly. His middle-classness, such as it is—physician, family man, citizen—is subservient to a more radical, left-of-center posturing and self-dramatization.

Because Williams is writing his stories quickly, with a brush stroke here and a fling of paint there (as he describes the process), the spontaneity, as technique, determines some of the form of the story; exposition blends with dialogue, the present of the story proper blends with the present (now the past) of the story related to the principal narrator (for example, the narrator closest in time, place, and psyche to Williams the man, but oftentimes a persona, variously close to or distanced from Williams himself). As a result, there is limited use of quotation and transition, unlike the more traditional short stories of Williams's day.

In terms of personae, point of view, and tone, Williams's stories are, like his other prose fiction, highly autobiographical. A doctor very much like Williams, with a wife like Flossie, with two sons like Williams's, with friends like Williams's, with a philosophy like Williams's, and so on, is quite often the principal narrator. Despite these similarities, the stories are ultimately fiction and not autobiography. At a minimum all characters' names are changed—a need Williams learned with a vengeance when he was sued for not doing so in "The Five Dollar Guy," a story he had tucked away in a drawer and later submitted to the *New Masses* (in 1926) without changing the names as he had intended.[85] The evolution of case history into story, however, goes much beyond mere cosmetic name changes. The vernacular voicings, especially of the narrator, but also of the characters; the finely pared and crafted structures—patterns, rhythms, openings and closures; the usually ironic and oftentimes cynical tonalities; the minimalist "style" and "presence" that is uniquely Williams—all of these ingredients work the marvelous transformations of art.

The case study as source and foundational form notwithstanding, the narrator in these stories, particularly in the early stories, is not always a doctor. Roughly half of the stories in *Knife* are not stories told by a doctor, nor are they, strictly speaking, about a doctor—though the overall attitude of the narrator and/or persona behind the narrator is keenly aware—as a writer and chronicler of humanity and mortality must be aware—of the miseries, "la tristeza," of the human condition as a doctor stereotypically is thought to be. When Williams's stories are about neither physicians nor writers as such, they are nevertheless, invariably (albeit oftentimes obliquely) about the writing process, and most expressly about the storytelling process.

Williams's diction is for the most part decidedly casual and, in keeping with whatever character is speaking, utterly colloquial. The common language of ordinary working class, not particularly well-educated Americans—the "American idiom" – pervades each story. There are also, however, instances in which highly technical language, usually medical language, intervenes. "Profanity" occurs, but there is never "obscene" language as such, for as iconoclastic and "shocking" as he is, Williams makes an attempt to tone down, for the sake of literary presentation or public reception, the blue hues of the people's language and his own language. In his letters and notes to friends and other writers his use of the vernacular illustrates just how fully he toned down his own eloquent use of profanity for the more public, artistically crafted stories—texts especially susceptible to public standards of taste or editorial censorship in the 1920s and 1930s.

Certainly the places Williams writes about and the kind of people he writes about (including himself as dramatized by his narrators and characters) give his stories the stamp of local color. In *Knife* he echoes local colorists of Rahv's "Red Skin" variety, such as Mark Twain and company. Somewhat more refined voicings are also heard—Hardy, T. F. Powys (in his village sketches), and behind these the austere voice of George Crabb. And ever so seldom, in a story like "Hands Across the Sea," even Henry James is heard—he is present in the writing to the extent that he is being rejected and replaced by what Williams considered his better ear for American place and people. In more general terms, perhaps part of Williams's voice is the voicing of the modern, an Arnoldian "plangent threnody" of recognition of the "buried life," the Sophoclean tragic "turbid ebb and flow of human misery," flowing mysteriously from the Aegean to the English Channel to the Passaic River, turning, anxious and forlorn, not so much on the intruding forces of naturalism as on the anguish met firsthand by a physician working with disease, illness, and death in the cutting and killing times of the American depression.

The stories in *Knife* are not all depression stories in any all-encompassing sense, in the sense that all the characters depicted are not suffering as a direct result of poverty or economic reversal caused by the failure of the economy. The "knife" and the "times" in the title may well be seen as metaphors for cuts in and cutbacks to the amenities otherwise available in more solvent, stable times. The "knife," however, as it appears literally and figuratively in these stories, takes on many different meanings. In one sense the knife is the stress, the neurosis, the anxiety caused by modern living—separations caused by city/country, love/hate, health/sickness, and other lesions associated with family and self, husband and wife, parent and child, individual and others, home and homelessness, youth and age, or, more uniformly in these stories, of middle age set against youth and old age. Not only are many of these stories "couples" stories or "love" stories that deal with the battle of the sexes, they also deal with the crises of middle age, and appropriately so, given that Williams himself was facing the personal and artistic crossroads of middle age when he turned to writing stories. In certain instances the "knife" is a cutting tongue of verbal insults and abuses; in other instances it is the looming threat of insanity and nervous breakdown, of losing control of one's life, one's job, one's mental as well as physical health. In some instances it is the "knife" of drug addiction and alcoholism; of homosexual rather than heterosexual yearnings; of racism and rape and violence in real and imagined forms; of apprehension about and recognition of infidelity—the "knife" that cuts the knot of marriage, of human emotional and sexual solidarity, whether of lovers, friends, or fellow human beings. In some instances the knife is one of jealousy, of real and metaphorical back stabs and gut stabs and violent assault. As a backdrop to some of the stories, World War I presents one version of the metaphorical "knife." In rare instances it is a literal scalpel, used to remove surgically a major disease or tumor or to perform something as minor as circumcision, tonsillectomy, or appendectomy. And in a somewhat more farfetched sense the knife is not just the tongue but the pen, the stories themselves that bring to the reader short, close cuts of "realism," slices of life. There are then many ramifications of the title in these early stories, ramifications of theme and character and form, of style and technique, which though capable of being isolated in these stories also carry over to Williams's other stories, to his other prose works, and to his longer poetry.

In *The Knife of the Times*, Williams is in a real sense not just involved in a literary experiment or a literary creation for its own sake; he is working through, in writing as healing, his own doubts and despairs as a man who is compelled—like Coleridge's Mariner or the poet persona of Wordsworth—to give relief through a timely utterance and thereby avoid the despondency and madness that comes from an inability to express something akin to "emotion recollected in tranquility" in the face of the observable. There is a certain dimension of the romantic crisis lyric, as well as the conversation poem, in these stories, which also owe something of their form, as well as their impulse, to the tradition of the biographical sketch or life telling, the autobiographical confessional.

"Hands across the Sea" is particularly revealing of Williams's autobiography; however, in "Mind and Body," "The Colored Girls of Passenack," and "Old Doc Rivers," Williams also makes appearances as narrator/character that place him as close as possible to his actual self. This quartet of stories does not represent his best stories (except, perhaps, "Doc Rivers"), only some of his most characteristically autobiographical. These four stories provide Williams with the means and ways of looking at some of the knives of his own disturbing middle age as his autobiographical presence (who he was able to become as a good, productive male and human, and who he might have been, in the fashion of Conrad's Kurtz in the potential of his own and humanity's darker self) shuttles back and forth, in and out of the stories. If one recognizes Williams's presence in these four stories, his already very much felt presence in companion stories is made yet more easily identifiable if we compare "Hands" (to mention just one of the most directly autobiographical quartet) with "The Knife of the Times" and "The Sailor's Son" (where the psychic and physical unions and splits involve more bizarre sexuality), and with "A Visit to the Fair," "An Old Time Raid," "Pink and Blue," "The Buffalos," and "A Descendant of Kings" (where the unions and separations run the gamut of age, friendship, marriage and parentage).

The one story in *Knife* that stands apart, in terms of locale at least, is "Hands across the Sea," though its autobiographical base and its subthemes of infidelity and muted eroticism link it as well to other stories in the volume. "Hands across the Sea," is in some ways an atypical Williams short story, with its Jamesian "American in Europe" or "comedy of manners" inclinations (as in "The Venus," discussed above) and its Geneva setting. And yet it is ultimately pure Williams, not "psychological" in any belabored sense, and utterly American. The central character is Mrs. Robert Andrews, a doctor's wife and a devoted mother of two sons, who finds herself separated from her husband for a year and living at the Christian Hospice Hotel in Geneva after World War I. Dr. Bob Andrews has returned to his practice in America, leaving Mrs. Andrews to enjoy Switzerland and look after their sons' schooling. (A similar separation faced Williams, his wife and their two sons in the 1920s when he was first turning to the short story form, and is the real-life basis for this story of a husband and wife reaching across the sea to maintain and reconfirm their marriage.) The knife that threatens this union is another physician, a less domesticated, more romantic, free spirit. The Scotchman, Doctor McFarland, although engaged to be married to an appealing widow in England, is not at all certain that he wants to marry his fiancée, Miriam. The grounds for foils, doubles, and antiselves are set in patterns of husband, wife, and friend/lover, which Williams uses in his own special variation on the age-old lovers' triangle or Freudian "family romance."

Mrs. Andrews, much attracted to McFarland, counsels him on what a doctor should expect in a wife and what a wife should expect in a doctor as a husband. In this sense, the story allows Williams to give an airing to some of the adjustments and accommodations he and Flossie had to make in their marriage and in their life roles in the face of Williams's need to be a physician (respectable) and a writer (rebellious). For Williams the central concern is not only fidelity in marriage but also freedom and responsibility, being a husband or being a bachelor, and, not incidentally, being an expatriate or remaining an American in America. For Williams the life of the expatriate bachelor promised freedom at too great a price. He did, however, apparently make compromises between fidelity and freedom as a married American doctor in New Jersey who was incapable of resisting extramarital relationships.

In a sense McFarland can be seen as an extension of Williams's friend, the writer, editor, and free spirit Bob McAlmon. Not to make the story more "psychological" than it really is, it may be read as a story of Doppelgängers, two sets of selves (Drs. Andrews and McFarland, Mrs. Andrews and Miriam), real and desired, selves both accepted and rejected. Andrews's wife, understandably from Williams's and his narrator's perspective, is attracted to both kinds of men—her husband and his European counterpart, McFarland. Mrs. Andrews likes McFarland's ability to listen to what she says, "His conversation seemed made providentially perfect for her ears." Furthermore, he (like McAlmon, Williams, the narrator) can tell a wonderful story, his own life story, in fact.[86] McFarland's life story is an exciting one: he had been a soldier in Mesopotamia during World War I and had developed an expertise in cleaning up all forms of contaminations and infestation; now employed by the League of Nations, he travels about as a troubleshooter, returning from time to time to the Christian Hospice to tell more stories and enthrall the guests. He is the epitome of a doctor-"author" in the exotic vein, a white man who has known faraway cultures, not at all like the provincial American doctor Andrews— though Andrews, like Dr. Evans in "The Venus," has his exotic American aborigines too, his own special longing to be "a single fellow to go, to be his own master" contemplating Europe back in America (*KOT*, 23).

The knife cutting Andrews and McFarland cuts both ways. Andrews has talked frequently to his wife of wanting a life like McFarland's, and now McFarland talks to her of wanting a life, married and settled, like the life Andrews—albeit temporarily separated—has with his wife. Mrs. Andrews recognizes this and has often felt her husband would readily give up "his home, his kids, herself, everything, . . . if he could only get out and away—anywhere" (*KOT*, 24). She is now confronted with a similar romantic possibility in her half-realized longings to carry on an affair with McFarland. Williams throws in the added complication of McFarland's divided longings for Miriam. And Mrs. Andrews's lecturing on women's rights and the way a doctor's marriage should be add to the tensions everyone feels about marriage for doctors. Williams handles the underlying sexuality and eroticism quite discreetly—more so than in some of his more explicitly erotic stories in *Knife*. It is clear, however, that Mrs. Andrews is physically attracted to McFarland, always eagerly awaiting sight of him, even at the final moment when she eats her farewell supper at the hotel.

The upshot of the story, however, is that neither a doctor nor his wife, man nor woman, can be in two places at once, can have it both ways (though Williams and Flossie had what by most standards would be regarded as an "open" marriage). Whereas Williams was tempted to flee to the expatriate writer's life of Pound, Hemingway, and Stein, Andrews and his wife (like Williams and Flossie), chose to hold on to each other and the life they had in America. Mrs. Andrews never really overtly attempts to seduce McFarland. It is probable, however, that in his shifting of sexual attraction to the American doctor's wife in the story, Williams is attempting to expiate some of his own guilt for his own expressed longing to be a free-spirited writer, free of doctoring and marriage. He is, however, in "Hands" clearly understanding of the pressures his longings and wanderlust placed on Flossie, who in this story (as Mrs. Andrews) has her chance at some freedom—if only dreamed—from the fidelities and responsibilities of marriage that often are held up most publicly as the province of the wife. Whether such speculations about Williams's and Flossie's marital tensions are "true," "Hands across the Sea" invites them.

In "Mind and Body" Williams's fictional counterpart is the unnamed doctor and friend who listens to and examines an unnamed woman patient. Only the patient's husband, Yates, and the doctor's wife, Emily, are known by name. The main characters—doctor and patient—are not named, and effectively so, since they know each other well, both as friends and as patient/doctor. The woman patient and Yates are, moreover, family friends. Because of the relative anonymity of the characters Williams achieves a kind of authenticity about the confidentiality obligatory between doctor and patient. Names seem to be changed or not given to protect Williams's actual patients and friends.

The setting for this story, the doctor's home with an office upstairs, is very similar to Williams's own residence at 9 Ridge Road in Rutherford. The place is in the northeast—for all practical purposes, New Jersey—and the ambiance is urban. Much of the story involves the doctor's attempts to diagnose what ails the woman, her attempts to explain her symptoms, and in the process her beliefs and opinions on a number of subjects. The knife that is whittling down this patient is anxiety concerning just what is wrong with her and how it relates to what has been wrong with her in the past: her operation some eighteen years ago, and her nervous breakdown, which placed her in a hospital for a time, a hospital where she met Yates, a man with his own kind of problems.

Their conversation is followed by the doctor's physical examination of the woman. Both the mind and the body of the patient are thus considered and ministered to by a physician who offers advice on sexual matters and marriage in a most matter-of-fact way—especially since the physician goes to the extent of telling the woman that perhaps she needs a woman to love rather than a man. The woman's husband,

Yates, seems much more the friend than the lover; but there is no real evidence in the story that the woman actually would prefer a female lover in place of Yates. Maybe she prefers a more masculine one—like the doctor, for their "appointment," has its erotic overtones. (This same kind of acceptance of lesbianism and homosexuality as either a biological or a psychological fact pervades Williams's other stories that address the subject, including "The Knife of the Times" and "The Sailor's Son.")

"Mind and Body" has a convincing air of reality about it: the physician knows his stuff and demonstrates wide past experience as well as familiarity with the latest research found in professional journals. From the attitudes and methods demonstrated one can infer some of the techniques Williams no doubt approved of and demonstrated in his own methods and bedside, examining room manner as a physician. To a certain extent the physician acts more like a psychoanalyst than a general practitioner.

What is impressive about the story, and unusual by today's impersonal clinical standards, is the extent to which the physician talks to the woman as a friend and even escorts her to the bus stop, insisting that she and her husband return for a visit. The basis for this relationship only partially resides in the fact that the doctor and woman are friends. They discuss religion, education, culture, medicine—many subjects all of which ultimately have a bearing on the woman's condition—and on her relationship to her husband. One infers that in Williams's assumptions of what a doctor does, both "mind and body" are important, and society is both part of the ailment and the cure. As in the prototypical portrait of the physician of an earlier era, this doctor, like a writer, listens and counsels, proving very much a human being and not a sterile, faultless scientist detached from the humanity he serves.

As in "Hands Across the Sea," couples—the woman and Yates, the doctor and Emily—again provide a pattern that Williams uses to great effect to describe the patient–doctor/husband–wife types here. Both marriages are vulnerable to being cut asunder given the numerous pressures of the time, such as the selfishness or narcissism announced in the woman's half-believed assertion, which is the first sentence of the story: "For ourselves are we not each of us the center of the universe?" (*KOT,* 59). Williams both gives evidence of egocentrism as a true and almost instinctive aspect of life and attempts, through the words and actions of the physician and his wife, to disprove this view. Not only mind and body but minds and bodies need contact, need to converse, need to care reciprocally about each other.

Williams fuses the woman's narrations with the doctor's narrations, her past and her present, in such a way—without the use of quotation marks or paragraphing, for example—to underscore visually on the page the story's need for greater fusing and welding of hitherto disparate architectonic parts. The woman, as well as the doctor, is quite opinionated about literature, art, and cultural issues, and yet they are both listening to each other and in key instances conceding points of argument to each other. It is no happenstance that the woman is trained in logic and very intelligent and that the doctor is operating throughout by means of the logical processes taught him.

As intelligent and intellectual and reasonable as the doctor and the patient are, they both hold out for a certain pragmatic primitivism, a superstitious belief in what works over what is explainable in their culture's logic about mind and body. She believes in intuition and "second sight," or animal knowledge. And the doctor does not refute her—he even agrees. Although people view the woman as a "nut" and an eccentric, and conjecture that much of her problem is imagined, she knows, as does the doctor, that natural remedies and nostrums, even superstitious religious ceremonials, can be effective—if there is belief. The doctor/narrator advises that everyone should avoid priests with only one answer, one way to be saved, saying that a ceremonial dance by a medicine man "with beating of tom toms to conduct . . . [him] into the other world" would be more comforting "than the formula of some kindly priest" (*KOT*, 89). Williams himself preferred the "poetry" of the satyrs, as he says in *Paterson*. And his analogue Evans in "The Venus" carries the emblematic arrowhead in his pocket, ready to express its secrets to those who care. But the arrowhead is emblematic of much more than words—as are the satyrs. A similar "no one has all the answers" attitude is also found in "Doc Rivers."

Williams's own individualism as a writer, his iconoclasm in the face of traditions of one kind or another, carry over to his characterizations found here in the woman and in the characters of other stories: the story asserts the implicit value of individualism, even quirky individualism. Intellectually, the woman sets herself above many of her former doctors who, she thinks, do not even understand her charts and the terminology on them to the extent that she does. As she tells the doctor her history, offers him her biography, the doctor is simultaneously drawing conclusions based on what he hears and what he is observing—and these processes, too, are blended with the woman's narrative in such a way as to make the disparate pieces whole, and his thinking process organic to the woman's "storytelling," which is her case, her life. The doctor, in coming finally to what he believes is the right diagnosis—attributes her symptoms not so much to a pathological condition ("mucous colitis" or intestinal spasms) as to an anatomical basis (her "short more inert [capillary] loops which account for [her] more lethargic demeanor")—offers an explanation of first causes: "apparently [it] was laid down in the germ plasm when you were created" (*KOT*, 75). The diagnosis tends to have a calming effect on the woman, because it helps her to accept who she is, how she came to be herself. As simple and all-inclusive as the explanation is, it does give her a better sense of what is wrong with her. It seems as good an explanation as any for her anxiety, reconciling in a way that other doctors had yet to do, her "mind and body."

At the end of the story, what the woman tells Emily—whose place in life is as a housekeeper, looking after her husband—is contrary to what she says as the story opens. Now she asserts that "we must live for others, that we are not alone in the world and we cannot live alone" (*KOT*, 74). In part she knows this before she visits the doctor; but the doctor, in his actions and in his listening to her case history, and in his willingness to talk with her and express his own views, has had a healing effect on the woman. One also knows, and can infer from the telling, that the doctor has benefited from the rather bizarre (yet natural) visit from this woman and her nervous, rare presence as a person.

In "The Colored Girls of Passenack—Old and New" Williams, from his perspective as a doctor, serves up an autobiographical reminiscence about five black women he has known, and offers—again through anecdotes, hearsay, and stories narrated within the larger story—short biographies of their lives, including their health and overall physical condition. In most cases the black women have been family maids or housekeepers, either for Williams's parents or for Williams and his wife, but the story does not have to be read for its autobiographical parallels with the lives of the author and his black employees or patients. "The Colored Girls of Passenack" offers an interesting psychological and social "history" of racial and sexual attitudes during Williams's and his parents' times—from about 1895 to the 1920s. Ironically, the very appeal that black culture and black women hold for the narrator-author makes his liberal and, for the time, enlightened attitude toward blacks seem somewhat embarrassing and paternalistic by today's standard. In the 1980s concerns with "racist" stereotypes linger so that the words of the title, "Colored Girls," and the word "girl," used throughout the narrative, plus the narrator's assumption that black women are always erotic, vital, animalistic and attracted to white males, all detract from what the author-narrator no doubt intended as a positive and complimentary portrait. The story is, in its intent, a testimonial to the beauty of black women, who are in some respects set above white women by Williams. Even putting aside the remnant stereotyping as unintentional, the story and the attitudes and issues that surface concerning race and sex remain volatile.

Williams was a virile, sexual male. He constantly made it known that he loved women. His autobiography, his letters, his interviews, and of course his writing make this apparent. And much has been made by critics, feminist and otherwise, about his attitudes toward women. Marjorie Perloff, for example, contends that "it is the poet's peculiar oscillation between *normalcy* . . . and the pressure of desire, a desire neither acted upon nor fully understood, that gives the short stories . . . their particular poignancy."[87] In this story black women especially are portrayed as among the most erotically stimulating women Williams (and his persona-narrator) has ever seen. One of the knives of the times made explicit in this story is just how tempting it was for Williams as a doctor to become sexually involved with women who were his patients or with mothers of the children he treated. Not only is the story a series of anecdotes and conversations, then, it is a kind of "confessional" on the part of the doctor/narrator—but not presented with any real sense of guilt—about how much black women aroused him as a young boy, and as an adult. "The Colored Girls," like many of Williams's stories, takes the form of secrets revealed and confidences shared in the privileged relationship between patient and doctor. Here, in a somewhat "shocking" (more for its time than now) reversal, the doctor shares some of his inner secrets about women, and especially black women, who have been their own special rare presences in his life.

Medical ethics, the oughts and ought nots of doctoring, is always an underlying theme in Williams's physician stories. And the doctor in "The Colored Girls" follows a stricter code of standard propriety, overtly at least, than does Old Doc Rivers, who is involved with women in ways that he should not be—if one assumes standard norms of professional propriety. In any event, Williams knew first-hand the opportunities and urges of a male doctor confronting a beautiful and alluring (and often willing) female patient. For a "story" drawn from the life of a respected physician, the implicit presumption of the doctor making an advance would no doubt be considered inappropriate by certain readers even if admittedly credible.

The story tells of the narrator's first sight of a nude woman, Georgie Andersen, a black from "down in Carolina" who came to work for his parents when he was ten or twelve. He and his brother loved to be with Georgie in the kitchen after supper, where, with her male admirer, Adolph, and the boy's uncle, Godwin (a counterpart to Williams's own relation), stories would be told and jokes would be played. Georgie is particularly (and stereotypically) vulnerable to ghost stories, and Godwin scares her into running out of the house by making a clock jump off a shelf by means of a black string that Georgie fails to see. Notwithstanding the underlying stereotype of the bug-eyed, teeth-chattering "colored girl" whose superstitious practices include eating dirt, what is important here is the immense pleasure storytelling brings the narrator, including the story of Georgie's wild and promiscuous life.

In what amounts to a more playful version of a story like Faulkner's "That Evening Sun" the story dramatizes Georgie's respect for the narrator's father and her fear of her admirers, including Adolph. Despite her ignorance and relative incompetence as a washerwoman and cook, she is admired by the narrator's parents—or, more probably, by the father—because her sexual attraction is so strong; because of "the sheer vitality and animal attractiveness there was in her" (*KOT*, 80). In one scene etched in the narrator's memory (and an archetypal scene it is, for adolescent boys in multicultural, light-skinned/dark-skinned environments), Georgie bathes as the narrator and two of his friends peep into her room through a hole in the attic wall. The narrator does not present the voyeurism in graphic detail, but he is surely more erotic than comic by announcing that Georgie was aware of the show she was presenting, and his description of what was seen as "a thrilling picture" (*KOT*, 82). That sight of Georgie's nude body stays vividly in the narrator's memory, and stands behind every other black woman he knows later in his life as a man and as a doctor.

The doctor-narrator remembers another black woman, Mable Watts, and tells her story retrospectively, beginning with the first time she came to his office for a "pretended examination," stripped naked, and offered herself to him. The narrator does not dwell on whether he accepted or rejected Mable, but offers this description of how the sight of her body affected him: "She was built in the style of Goya's Maja

Desnuda, but her laughter and gestures were pure Africa" (*KOT*, 82). Mable, in any event, becomes a patient of the doctor's, seeking his advice and assistance and telling him everything about the difficulties of her life, most of which center on, and emphasize, her sexuality. She becomes—in a kind of replay of Georgie's role with the doctor's parents—the doctor's maid, and even his wife admires her ability as a servant. That occupation does not last because, as Williams somewhat euphemistically explains it, avoiding the particulars: ". . . she knew too much—and, well, she just wasn't wanted around too long where men were likely to be" (*KOT*, 82). Mable refuses to go into show business, as the doctor suggests, because she does not want to end up in a ditch "with a knife in my back" (*KOT*, 83). The narrator relates the subsequent events of her life in some detail, including her marital misadventures, the way she dresses and, over a period of eighteen years, some of the stories she shares with the doctor during office visits.

It is Georgie and Mable who, as the "colored girls" from the narrator's past (the "old" ones of the title) provide the basis of comparison with the "colored girls" of the present (the new ones)—and with white women generally. All the black women are "remembered" by either the narrator or by those who tell him more details about them. In a manner both digressive and curiously insistent and excessive, Williams, through his narrator, wades into an impassioned exposition on the exceptional qualities of black women: "The American white girl today is shop worn compared to the negress—at her liveliest. All the simplicity of mind which *virtue* should imply lies with the negress" (*KOT*, 85). The young black girls of the times are simply beautiful beyond comparison, possessing a beauty of feature, "which with the manner of their walk, the muscular quality of their contours, the firmness—makes most white girls clumsy, awkward, cheap beside them. There is nothing much in the depths of most white girls' eyes. Colored girls . . . seem a racial confessional of beauty—lost today anywhere else" (*KOT*, 85). Perhaps the narrator praises black women so highly in bold attempt to counter prejudiced "puritanical" or ignorant white opinion to the contrary (an opinion Williams loathed) by asserting what amounts to "black is beautiful" much before that slogan was in vogue. Even so, one wonders why Williams went quite so far with invidious black/white comparisons. He loved black and exotic women, apparently, in a way similar to his longing for the free expatriate writer's life. His bohemian self worked constantly in tension with his more bourgeois self—one edging and tempering the other.

The narrator tells of another "colored girl," visiting in a nearby sub-
urb, who appeared at the door as a "magnificent bronze figure" whose
"actuality," he blatantly says, "made me want to create a new race on
the spot" (*KOT,* 86). Yet another "magnificent physical specimen," also
employed by the doctor and his wife, is described and her story is
related as it was told to the doctor's wife. It is a story of exotic intrigue,
relating how a "Chinaman" she worked for was somehow involved in
the mysterious disappearance of one of her friends. Then the final
"colored girl's" story is told, this time as related by one of the doctor's
patients whose own black laundress insisted that no "colored girl" over
sixteen was a virgin, and bemoaned the fact that her own husband was
ruined by the promiscuous attentions of all the young "colored girls"
in Passenack.

On this note the story ends, with no final wrap-up by Williams, no
disclaimer, moral or otherwise, by the doctor-narrator—just this list, a
record of five old and new black women and their voluptuousness. The
reader is stunned with the eroticism of the story, its libidinal attrac-
tions, made all the more acceptable and ordinary by the endorsement
of physical magnetism by a sanctioned, professional man of medicine.
The aboriginal has somehow gained a civilizing stamp of approval, an
authorization. If the narrator's or the author's attitudes toward "colored
girls" is "shocking," more so even than the "facts" of the lives listed,
it is so only to the sensibilities and assumptions of certain puritanical
or prejudiced readers. The doctor-narrator and Williams behind him
seem shocked at nothing at all, least of all his own sexual instincts and
appetites as a white man turned breathless by black women and their
rare presences. So be it, say Williams's more empathetic readers. So be
it.

Williams's presence in "Old Doc Rivers" is most directly seen,
again, in the narrator who is also a character in the story (the narrator
is a young doctor who was an assistant to Rivers in a few operations).
There is something of Williams in Rivers himself as well, however—
another double, at least of Rivers's better side. The narrator is, again,
an observer, a historian, a biographer who sets out to understand Rivers
and to discover what made him tick as the doctor and man he was.
Historical records and hospital logs are "researched" by the narrator,
and "interviews" are held with patients and people who knew Rivers.

Rivers is fascinating as a story unto himself, but the narrator's interest in Rivers results not simply from curiosity. The young doctor seems

to need to learn about Rivers in order to learn about himself, his profession, and the code that defines it. The narrator's own professional conduct is defined in relation to where Rivers failed and where he succeeded. This story is thus a testimonial to the power of the oral tradition, to the real curative and informative role that stories and storytelling play in understanding "how to live a life" in and beyond middle-age crises—a role that short stories as process seem to have consistently served for Williams.

Rivers is a doctor involved, like Kafka's "Country Doctor," with horse-and-buggy house calls and personal contact with his patients, who see themselves in him just as he sees himself in them. His life has a hellish, darker side like that of Kafka's doctor (although it is not presented surrealistically); the knife of the times, the stress of his profession and of his confrontation with human mortality and misery cuts at him. Drug addiction, alcoholism, and sexual debaucheries take him to the very depths of personal and professional mistake and failure. (There is nothing in Williams about "sin.") And yet Rivers also lives as a legend, not so much in his own mind as in the mind and times of others who need to mythologize the doctor as savior. In effect, the story is Williams's own thorough attempt to demystify and demythologize the doctor, to humanize the M.D. and depict the personal failings and the hypocrisy behind the external appearances and false assumptions about a physician's life—as viewed by patients, other doctors, and the public.

Throughout the course of what is Williams's second longest short story, Rivers outlives his own time. He is seen first as a physician who depends almost entirely on horses for transportation as the age of automobiles dawns. By story's end he is semiretired in a fine house, with garden, lawns, and a double garage and two good cars "always ready for service," though by this time Rivers, significantly, never sits at the wheel (*KOT*, 164). His wife breeds and raises quaint little dogs. Together they, outwardly at least, represent utter happiness and respectability. And yet his career has run from the heights of ability and respect to the depths of drug addiction and questionable diagnoses and treatments, which for most of the physicians of his day would constitute malpractice. Only his reputation as a venerable type, an institution, prevents patients and fellow physicians from bringing him to an accounting. The narrator, himself nettled by his wife's questions and urgings, struggles not to accuse Rivers and find him guilty of professional misdeeds. The story, at once an indictment and a testimonial, is the narrator's attempt not just to accuse and find Rivers guilty but to weigh and balance his good points with his bad points.

Rivers's manner as a doctor is decisive and rough. But it is the kind of tough, almost abusive manner that patients accept, even find endearing; his manner helps to make him the living legend, the colorful character he is. Rivers bossed and talked down to the narrator more than once. But the narrator and the patients never felt humiliated— roused or angered perhaps—but never really offended and abashed. More than in any of his other stories in *Knife*, Williams demonstrates, through Rivers's dialogue with his patients and with his nurse, Maggie, just what kind of "lingo" the doctor used, how he sounded to his patients and to other doctors with whom he worked, including the narrator.

Williams presents, too, exactly what the doctor saw: the places of his rides and house calls, and the kind of people who made up his changing lists of patients over many years of practice. The narrator never visits the small hospital in the nearby city where Rivers did many of his operations, for he was primarily a surgeon, a man who had a way with the "knife." Rather, the narrator visits St. Michael's Hospital and checks through the registry of cases, in volumes stretching back all the way to 1898. Looking at the records the narrator admits, "I felt a catch at the throat before the summary of so much human misery." The narrator as doctor, like Rivers, also knows about misery, "la tristeza de la vida," in his own way, and this knowledge and sensitivity mitigates the harshness of some of his judgments against Rivers (*KOT*, 126). Here the narrator, through Williams, functions as a historian in much the same way that Williams attempts to chronicle the history of Paterson and life along the Passaic, which reinforces the idea that Williams's stories provided certain ground work for his masterwork, *Paterson*.

The narrator is struck by human misery and mortality, by the mutability of life and the speed of change, for even in the relatively recent past of 1908, patients' occupations seem totally different from those of the narrator's own times some quarter of a century later. Rivers himself was among the first people in the region to have a telephone. Medical practices and the role of doctors had changed too—and yet much remained the same, and Rivers in his glory days typified just how important human understanding and skill, along with luck and the blessings of the gods, were in healing patients—though in the end they all die anyway. The list of ailments and remedies, saves and losses the narrator finds entered next to Rivers's name in the registry is amazing and Williams goes on about them for three-quarters of a page in a litany of woes that seems digressive, not to mention oppressive. Williams's world-weariness and the narrator's soon becomes the reader's.

The narrator knows that it was not money or acquisitiveness that drove Rivers so, but the antithesis of greed for money—"Nervous, he accepted his life at its own terms and never let it best him—to no matter what extremity he was driven" (*KOT,* 128). This seems a tribute to Rivers infused with much of Williams's own perception of himself —as a physician who must write and as a writer who must be a doctor. What made Rivers the good doctor he was was attributed first to his sense for diagnosis, then to his thoroughgoing, conservative surgical instincts that could lead him to conclude that something as simple as a circumcision would cure a little boy whose symptoms had baffled many a lesser physician.

Anecdote follows anecdote, case history follows case history, as the narrator, as best he can, reassembles a kind of case history of Rivers's life and offers a kind of diagnosis after the fact—biography as post-mortem. One patient, Frankel, dies after surgery for ruptured appendix and peritonitis. During the operation Rivers drank great amounts of whiskey, which seemed to steady his nerves and allow him to get on with the operation. The narrator, assisting with the anesthetic during this operation, refused to drink with Rivers during the surgery but refrains from judging him: "I thought carefully over what had occurred but I did not come to any immediate conclusion" (*KOT,* 135). Seldom, even in instances that seem as blatantly blameable as this one, does Williams judge any of his characters as simply wrong. Such absolutism is just not present in his short stories, although in "Old Doc Rivers," as in his tribute to black womanhood in the "Colored Girls of Passenack," Williams does editorialize. As the narrator traces Rivers's descent into drugs and whoring, Williams's narrator acknowledges that the dope he took—morphine, heroin, cocaine—for a time relieved him from his "nerves," which threatened in and of themselves to undo him. As the narrator observes, "He was far and away by natural endowment the ablest individual of our environment, a serious indictment against the evangelism of American life which I most hated—at the same time a man trying to fill his place among those lacking the power to grasp his innate capabilities" (*KOT,* 140). Williams refuses either/or pronouncements and explicit moralizing in "Old Doc Rivers," preferring instead to present acts, whether good or bad, in relation to many variables, many shades of gray.

The Short Fiction: A Critical Analysis

"Old Doc Rivers" presents an ambivalent, but finally more positive than negative portrait of Rivers as a man who, Williams suggests, was who he was and did what he did. The "judgment" of him is something of a moot point. Even those actions that would be judged reprehensible by more absolute systems of law and ethics are not so much excused or justified by Williams as they are simply presented. Many readers no doubt find Williams's personae a bit too accepting of the human condition, or think that the narrator's ethics are capable of being perceived in the best light as "situational," and in the worst light "amoral." This is an ironic misreading, for if anything comes across in Williams's plot and narrative tone it is that he is very much on the side of goodness and truth and beauty (defined according to his best lights) and life. But his pursuit of beauty and truth is usually more implicit than explicit and can be discerned in the loving crafting and shaping he gives his experiences and imaginings turned "fiction."

Another physician who knew Rivers, Dr. Trowbridge, fills in some of the details of Rivers's life—when he began to "take to the woods," visit a Frenchman at his mansion in Crestboro, play cards, drink fine wine, and get back in touch with himself. The lure of the primitive, deer hunting trips in Maine, helped for a while. Williams's idealization of the aboriginal, the atavistic, the primitive is a common subtheme in his stories, and is voiced in this story by Dr. Trowbridge, who explains that Rivers needed the escape because in the jumble of big cities "we have lost touch with ourselves, have become indeed not authentic persons, but fantastic shapes in some gigantic fever dream. He, at least, had the courage to break with it and to go. . . . He wanted to plunge into something bigger than himself. Primitive, physically sapping" (*KOT*, 141). This Daniel Boone-like escape from the modern urban confusion and complexity ends badly for Rivers, however, because he accidentally kills his best friend and guide—a naturalistic twist by Williams.

Another informant tells the narrator an anecdote about his times with Rivers that turns regrettable, revealing a darker side of Williams's Daniel Boonism. As a young kid he boarded with Rivers for a few months and Rivers let him have free reign. One time, while carousing with Rivers, he remembers holding a woman "while he [Rivers] did the job" (*KOT*, 149) and has his way sexually with her. Williams's narrator is silent and lets stand ironically the informant's comment that, as he looks back on those wild times, "That was the romantic period of my life, those four months I lived with him" (*KOT*, 149). This wild-man romanticizing of macho willfulness and rape epitomizes the callousness of the likes of Rivers, who both wields the "knife of the times" and is cut by it himself, a man at one point gone beyond the pale into the extremes of savagery. A patient himself for several sessions at the State Insane Asylum, Rivers did indeed have a darker side to his life, one that, although Williams chooses not to portray it in any kind of Kafkaesque or Conradian way, achieves its own kind of matter-of-fact "horror" in representing the human condition at its best and worst.

The other stories in *Knife* have little to do directly with physicians or with Williams's autobiography, at least his life as a doctor. Williams is not as present—at least some of the more prominent and documented aspects of his life as a physician or husband are not as present —in these relatively lesser-known stories. They do, however, reveal a physician's (and a writer's) caring involvement with the miseries of humanity. Furthermore, most of these stories share with the other stories in the volume a concern with couples, their fidelities and infidelities, their bondings and their separations—all set against the cutting tensions of individual and social hard times: homosexual psychic and physical unions and splits; young and old; longtime friends and cronies; mail-order bride and crazed husband; would-be patriarch and liberated wife; mother and son; sons and lovers.

"The Knife of the Times" and "The Sailor's Son" have received more critical attention than "A Visit to the Fair," "An Old Time Raid," "The Buffalos," "A Descendant of Kings," and "Pink and Blue."[88] But Williams's stylistic presence is so successful in all of these stories that one can only wish he had written fewer stories about the physician's life and more stories like these, which go about their business outside of the more focused world of doctors and medicine. This is not to say that these stories are not autobiographical, for they still deal with the crises of middle age that Williams faced, and they allow him a way to objectify some of these crises, empathetically, through self-as-other portrayals.

"A Visit to the Fair," for example, is a delightful "country" story, much in the tradition of Thomas Hardy or the familiar January/June romance. A wealthy widower, Mr. Tibbet, is so taken with a young neighbor woman, Bess Rand, that after asking her to the nearby fair and extending the day's activities as long as he can, he invites her (as well as her husband and all her family) to live with him in his twenty-eight room house. Although the story does have its humorous, flirtatious moments, it is far from being simply a story about an "old fool" enthralled with a pretty girl; in Williams's treatment of him Tibbet retains a love of life and an appreciation of female beauty that raises him above dirty-old-man stereotyping. Certainly the ironies are every-where at hand, again much reminiscent of Hardy, so that the reader realizes once again how youth is in some senses truly wasted on the young. Moreover, given Williams's pervasive liberalism and icono-clasm, the story points out—without sinking into a narrative precursor of new-age communal living—that social conventions and traditions, including the moral and religious laws by which individuals live their lives, also act as restrictions that oftentimes need severing.

"Pink and Blue" is another enjoyable story about the adventures and misadventures of marriages made by mail. The narrative is structurally more complicated than "A Visit to the Fair," because Williams again uses the story-within-a-story device. An account of George Tompkins's finding a wife named "Belle" by writing to the "Cupid's Club," which is first told by Mrs. Bandler, is now retold by the story's primary nar-rator who has, in turn, heard the story. Mrs. Bandler not only first tells the story, she is very much a participant in it because she employs George at her summer place, the idyllic farm, Ferncrest. Belle turns out to be the mistress of a "quiet, middle-aged man," Favier, and is "what they call a bitch. . . . Just a la-la" (KOT, 117). Her continuing involvement with Favier drives George into lunacy, and Mrs. Bandler has him arrested because of his distraught behavior and his refusal to leave Ferncrest. Mr. Favier tells Mrs. Bandler about Belle's subse-quent death. Belle came into George's life literally "in the pink," and she asks Favier to see that she is buried in blue dress, stockings, and shoes. The colors and the title announce the happy-sad progression of events. In "Pink and Blue" men and women act equally foolish under the spell of love and property. As with Williams's other stories of hu-manity's collective and individual follies and foibles, the ship of fools boards all kinds in their attempted journeys to happiness. The satire, such as it is, is offered in a matter of fact way by one who is not immune from foolhardy mistakes.

In "The Buffalos" Williams works out another ironic account of a skirmish in the continuing battle of male-female wills—this time by means of a conceit founded on his fascination with primitivism. Un-derlying the playfulness of the narrator's tactic to stymie his lover's constant insistence about the equality if not the superiority of women, is a subject at serious issue in all of Williams's stories—how does a man live a life, how does a woman live a life, and how do they live a life together?

The narrator could well be a patient of Williams's telling him the story, or simply a man telling some inferred listener (another dramatic monologue) the story—a war story in the battle of the sexes. There are portions of Williams himself present in the narrator—even if satirically and ironically so. The narrator, after all, like Williams and others of his characters, leaves the age-old, if not stereotypical, impression that women are by turns a boon and a bane, both charming and bothersome in relation to the world of men, a world alternately in need of isolation from women and companionship with them. This paradox provides the basis for the ironies of the story. Williams philosophically believed in equal status for women, and he editorializes on this subject often in his stories, for example, through the figure of the doctor's wife in "Hands Across the Sea," and through the woman patient in "Mind and Body." There is also, however, a streak of the narrator's chauvinistic will to dominate, a hint of the need men have for the world of men, and of the mock self-pity of the bachelor preyed upon or of the male on the lookout not to trapped by the female, which is revealed somewhat in the other stories in *Knife* but most clearly in "The Buffalos." It is an attitude that seems shared at least to some degree by the author behind the rather smug, flip narrator in "The Buffalos." And Williams returns to such tensions in the battle of the sexes and their respective willfulness often in his stories, such as "An Old Time Raid," "A Descendant of Kings," "The Sailor's Son," and "The Dawn of Another Day." In a certain prankish sense, then, the "once upon a time" quality of "The Buffalos," and the fantasy undergirding the metaphor developed in the narrator's "modest proposal" about how men should be treated, reflects some of Williams's own possible impatience as a husband just as the woman in the story, Francie, seems a fictionalized version of some part of Williams's wife, ever the good and faithful housewife, Flossie. Francie is not really the woman's name, for the narrator makes it clear that he is just calling her Francie to mask the name of the "real" woman about whom the story is told. The realism of the original basis of the story is also transposed by the fairy-tale, fundamentally fabulated direction the narrative takes as another story within the story unfolds.

The primary story is told retrospectively by an older narrator about a younger love he once had. It was a wonderful love for a period of time—good times and bad times—spoiled only by Francie's "habit" or "defect" of being "a great talker for woman's rights" (*KOT*, 51). The narrator thinks such talk fine for women "with seamed faces and angry looks" who pontificate on platforms and street corners, but, complains the narrator, "It was nothing for the lovely woman with whom I rushed so eagerly to spend my hardly won minutes" (*KOT*, 52). Bored with her argumentative talk, the narrator decides to stop Francie's "railing" and tell her a story by way of a lesson.

Although the narrator's illustrative story begins realistically enough, with a description of three workers on a ditch gang who live a primitive life in a hut, brave the elements summer and winter, trap muskrats, pick berries—generally live independent bachelor lives of camaraderie—the story soon veers into fantasy, if not farce. The narrator finds such a life a revelation to him, proof that property is the cause of most trouble. So much so that he proposes that men give all their property to women, give them even their rights to vote so that women will possess all the land and all the wealth. The narrator concedes that all of Francie's suffragist arguments are right and that men should, after giving all control to women, "gather in herds about the woods and plains, like the buffalo who used to be seen from the train windows in the middle of the last century" (*KOT*, 57). As he makes clear in his discussion of Daniel Boone in *In the American Grain*, in Dev Evans's clutching an ancient arrowhead, in Doc Rivers's escape to the woods, and in the male carousing of Dago Schultz and company in "An Old Time Raid," and Manuel and the "Kid" in "The Sailor's Son," or Ed and Fred in "The Dawn of Another Day" (stories discussed below), the lure of the primitive and the independence of the original American frontiersman and his latter-day replicas held no small attraction for Williams.

Although the absurd scheme proposed here to silence Francie seems more satirical than serious, Williams does raise the possibility in this story, too, of the necessity and pleasure of male solidarity. Williams ends the story with a question about the real effect of the story on Francie, as perceived in the narrator's mind. It is the end of their romance, given the narrator's mind. It is the end of their romance, given the narrator's comic cruelty in constructing his "allegory," and given the disappointment and deflation it brings to Francie. But as the narrator drives away in his roadster (shades of "The Young Housewife"), he believes he sees the curtain slightly rustle in a second-floor window, but concedes, "perhaps it was only my vanity that made me believe this" (*KOT*, 58).

In "A Descendant of Kings" Williams portrays a slightly different variation of his frontiersman hero in the character of Stewie Worthen, a fine physical specimen "endowed with the frame of a bull," who other than knowing that he loves women and the outdoors, does not know quite what vocation to follow. Long days in the sun and along the shore of Long Island Sound give his life a certain focus of physical pleasure, but at the expense of much school missed, and, by the eighth grade he drops out completely. At seventeen he joins the navy. One major love affair ends when the war does, and Stewie is left with little other than the confidence that "He had a body" (*KOT*, 97).

His life is not exactly carefree, however, and Williams sketches his changing ambitions, which for a time deteriorate into shiftlessness. His mother's knife-edged scoldings keep many of the beach girls away from him for a time, except for Muriel, a model from New York with worldly ways. Her infidelity plunges Stewie into a darkening knife-of-the-times funk—"In woman his world all lay, and woman had cut the world from under him, he was sinking into the night. It was awful" (*KOT*, 100). He winds up playing the ukulele and guitar along the beach, and sexually impotent when the physical aspect of his confidence fails him. In "A Descendant of Kings," Williams offers yet another version of his own longings for the free life, the "king of the road" kind of life so alluring to a respectable doctor tied down by the responsibilities of home, wife, family, and patients. As with Williams's own ambivalent attitude toward such an irresponsible life, the story has sorrowful and even pathetic moments interspersed throughout the lighter and more humorous narrative. Williams turns his ambivalence into irony in the end—for the descendant of kings is not quite the same thing as a king, and the king of the road—or the beach—is oftentimes a bum. Such is the prize and the price.

In "An Old Time Raid," and "The Sailor's Son," the two sets of male friends try to survive the pressures against their mutual personal commitment. In the former story that commitment is rowdy friendship; in the latter story the commitment is rowdy homosexual love. Moreover, in the latter story the male companionship is set against the complications of two women—one a disapproving employer of young Manuel, the other an assenting fiancée who is not bothered in the least by his carousing in the haystack with the wild motorcycler and bad influence from the city: "the Kid."

"An Old Time Raid" is one of Williams's most colloquial stories. Another retrospective accounting of a friend's life, the narrator here relates some of the wild times of his youth with a crazy prankster of a fellow—a good but wild old buddy, Dago Schultz. As such, the story functions as a eulogy of sorts both to the memory of Schultz and to the good old days when a fellow could carouse through the town with a friend. Prank follows prank, mischief follows mischief as the narrator confesses to some meanness carried out with Schultz one day in New York City. They raid restaurants, fruit stands, theaters, businesses and disturb the civic peace and order, hastening a police raid or two.

Williams's expert handling of the opening and the ending of the story makes it clear that Dago's days are surely numbered. In the opening paragraph (which deals with events some three years later) he is presumably clipped by "a freight coming from nowhere in the opposite direction" (*KOT*, 48). But that destiny is not known for sure until the ending, and the ending of the story is nicely reflexive to the opening as the reader learns conclusively from the narrator and crony, "Well, whether he was drunk or not or just didn't see, as he swung out after getting a grip on the rail, a freight coming from nowhere . . . just clipped him—" (*KOT*, 48). It is a fitting outcome for Dago's life, another aspiring roamer, a free-spirited hobo whose freedom and daring lead to death. The consolation, and another ironic, ambivalent one, is that he literally did not know what hit him and thus went out in his own kind of style and gory glory.

Schultz's kindred spirit in "The Sailor's Son" is "the Kid," a free spirit who leads a gang of motorcycle rebels lawlessly through the city streets, and every now and again goes out to the country for a sexual tryst with young Manuel, who is employed by Mrs. Cuthbertson. Once she is aware of what she considers outrageous goings on, Mrs. Cuthbertson orders a stop to it and fires Manuel. Manuel's lovesick and lonesome attitude, his longings for both the Kid's attentions and for letters and visits from his fiancée, Margy, and Mrs. Cuthbertson's overall outrage, are all ironically undercut by Margy's arrival on the scene and her berating of the older woman: "I am engaged to marry him, I don't care what he does. Why should you worry?" (*KOT*, 38). Here again, the narrator takes no puritanical stand on so-called aberrant sexual liaisons. Although Margy seems rather too nonchalant, it is her opinion that rings beyond the story—another commentary on Williams's live and let live physician's acceptance of the human condition in all its forms and manifestations. The Kid provides yet another instance of Williams's alterego, the wild and free rebel ready to live beyond the pale of society's approvals and conventions in an urban counterpart of America's former frontier. Part delinquent, part hero, he is the stuff not just of stereotype but of an American archetype that fascinated Williams—whether as aborigine, frontiersman, mountain man, cowboy, or biker.

In the much-talked-about title story, "The Knife of the Times," the narrator takes a similar live-and-let-live attitude in recounting the long-pent-up lesbian love of Ethel for her old friend, "dark-eyed" Maura. Long married and the mother of six children, Ethel takes to writing passionate, seductive letters to Maura. She finally arranges a reunion in New York where she lures Maura to some pay toilets in Penn Station and makes her desires known in a passionate release of physical fondling and kissing. Maura is awakened to her own repressed love for Ethel and when asked if she would spend at least a week with her, "sleep with her," Maura decides, lucidly, carelessly, "Why not?" One "knife" in the story is the knife of long-repressed sexual desire and a desire to be free (another instance of this common proclivity) of society's expectations and conventions. "Why not?" as Maura announces it, is at once a cry of liberation and a leveling of self-restraint in the face of larger instincts. The actual descriptions of physical contact between the two women seem tame if not quaint by today's no-holds-barred erotic accounts. But in the context of the story, the passion seems anything but silly and allows the reader insights into just how far in the history of the short story the freedom to deal with issues of homosexuality has extended. In this sense Williams needs as much recognition as E. M. Forster and others whose homosexual stories were by and large only published posthumously. Whether his homosexual stories were intended by Williams as a kind of apology for those of homosexual persuasion among his painter and poet friends, or a working out of his own feelings for others of the same sex, as is suggested by Reed Whittemore about Williams and Robert McAlmon, is perhaps beside the point.[89]

The homosexual stories in *Knife* hold forth the possibility—most especially to readers of more conventional (Williams would say puritanical) persuasion and those contemporary with the era in which these stories were written—that male-male friendship or love may be a kind of shield against female barbs and other kinds of knives of the times. Moreover, lesbian or homosexual love, if that is the person's inclination, is presented—more shockingly for Williams's time, and somewhat more ironically in the 1980s given the hysteria over AIDS—as something to be accepted without inhibitions if that is the nature of those involved. All three gender combinations—male-male, female-female, and female-male are accepted throughout Williams's early stories as ways of attempting to get through life, as observed by an author who sees human sexuality and behavior for what it is, diverse as it may be, and vulnerable as it may be, both in fidelity and infidelity, and set against the social and psychological, mental and emotional slicings of the "knife of the times."

Life Along the Passaic River

The nineteen stories in *Life Along the Passaic River* continue some of the same themes and techniques Williams develops in *Knife*.[90] A half dozen of these stories are among Williams's best, and at least two of them, "The Girl with a Pimply Face," and "Jean Beicke," are among Williams's own favorites. In *Passaic* subject and tone turn darker, tending more than in *Knife* to the cynical, the grotesque, and the tragic. Part of the darkness of these stories is attributable to the familiar "knife" of the times: the worries, fears, and miseries of humanity, now focused more on children than on adults of middle age. Although the crises and conflicts in *Passaic* do involve adults peripherally, children's presences are closer to the center of things. Place (setting, locale, ambiance—Williams regarded "place" broadly) also assumes greater importance, reflecting Williams's belief that "In a work of art place is everything." In these stories, the Passaic River itself gives a nodality to Williams's portrayal of character and action.

Williams appears again, quite autobiographically, as the physician-writer, the narrator, the overarching persona who, in watching the Passaic and describing the urban liabilities of lives whose rare presences captivate him, is so moved to empathy that he passes beyond voyeur to participant through the telling and retelling of their lives. Few of these stories involve country interludes, retreats, farms, or the summer cottages on the shore known to the more affluent middle-class protagonists who appeared as the "employers" in *Knife*. Here there is only a provisional escape from the city squalor in which the working-class, proletarian families portrayed in *Passaic* live. Part of the cynicism and part of the hostility expressed here by Williams and his personae is due to the inequalities in class, education, income, intelligence and sensibilities between those who see and those who are seen, those who are told about and those who tell. Here, too, hard times are recorded on more than one level. Williams's own middle-class respectability and security adds to the poignancy of the disparities between class and economic status of the individuals living along the Passaic.

One thing is felt by the author and shared by the reader vividly in story after story: Williams feels the "hard history" of the people, the society, the country. And he takes his job as physician and as chronicler seriously. It is that feeling, again, that turns ordinary presences into rare ones. Williams empathizes with these individuals, with their predicament, with their humanity in a caring, far from condescending way, even though his own status in life could easily distance him from them, and cause him to be disparaging rather than empathetic.

In *Passaic* more than in any other collection of his stories, memorable characters come to the forefront as living people, people with names and desires that at once typify and transcend their kind. For example, the title story, "Life Along the Passaic River," is a wonderfully tough but impassioned overview of the place and the people. Both the river and the local inhabitants of the valley virtually compel Williams and his narrator(s) to pay attention to them, to speak up for them, to say in various ventriloquisms that they matter very much in spite of the larger world's indifference, in spite, to some degree, of their own indifference. The stories could be, and usually are, capable of their own individual meanings, but read together, they gain a special rhythm and structure. As a whole, the volume personalizes the human "swarm," bringing moment and distinction to the larger, generational and historical process that Williams tried to define throughout his career, from "The Wanderer" to *Paterson*, from *In the American Grain* to *Pictures from Brueghel*. He credited James Laughlin with saying that the form of *Passaic*, with its attention to the river as a metaphor for history, might also be well suited to a long poem—a poem that turned out to be *Paterson*.[91] Similar presuppositions about history as process, the flowing of events and persons along time's river also infuse the organic and nature metaphors of *In the American Grain*.

In *"Life Along the Passaic River"* the point of view shifts and blends (now limited, then omniscient); specific scene merges with limited editorializing; vignette dissolves into vignette; showing and telling mix and separate as styles of story; the story proper is reinforced by smaller, internalized stories; the river is knowable first as place and then as idea; the historical past alternates with the present; the language, the vocabulary, the diction, the intonations not only reflect but help define the nature of these lives and their riverscape, or, conversely, the riverscape and its lives. The resultant effect is that of a large canvas done in hasty but impassioned brush strokes. The stories are all essentially Williams—person, physician, narrator, character all combined—teller and technique shaping and being shaped by subject.

As Williams the physician well knew, life is defined ultimately in terms of death and in these stories about life along the Passaic, death is always ready to intrude. This irony of death threatening life is made part of the rhythmic structure of the story in one anecdote after another. The "Polacks" in the city try to cope, like the narrator, with the predicament they are born into, generation after generation. Some, like the young anonymous male hitchhiker in one of the vignettes, possess the saving ambition of wanderlust—the gumption to leave the hometown, like Boone, and travel to "the coast" (*MLI*, 110). The hitchhiker at least has the story of his traveling to tell when he gets in the narrator's car. He has been to one geographical limit, found no work there or anywhere else during his journey "back again through the whole country," and now his glorious westering comes down to a ride to "Westover" just "up here a way."

The small canoe, in the summer-hot, dye-waste, polluted water of the river, which the narrator watches and describes intermittently in the story, is not really going any place very far either. The boy who made the canoe and now floats in it has fashioned hope more than anything else. Others of the youths described are resourceful, if not successful, in their schemes. The intentions of the girls are presented with an air of tragic indulgence and sympathy for their attempts to get their oversized feet into undersized shoes. The narrator's conversation with some listener other than the reader clarifies the attitude: "If your shoes fit you and they're made of good leather, if you know what good leather is, . . . you're getting somewhere. What did you say? The girls' feet look like flat tires in most of the things they don't know enough not to buy and to wear" (*MLI*, 113).

And in another vignette, Williams makes clear that the teenage girl lying on the autopsy slab in the hospital never went very far at all. Neither did her aborted twins. Not just children and youths but young girls especially have Williams's feeling about their hard, rare presences. The pimply-faced girl; Jean Beicke; the young Olson girl in "The Use of Force"; this girl long gone on the slab—all of them face dead-end lives with precious few like the narrator/physician caring to help even if it is only for the sake of helping more than for wondrous "results."

The narrator does not know for sure what the dead girl's story is. She is dead, he sees, a suicide whose death was gruesome, as evidenced by the burn down her throat caused by some concoction she drank. Indignation at the probable motive and the waste of it all, and yet the possible, painful blessing of it, is heard in the narrator's Greek chorus-like judgment: "Good legs. A fine pair of breasts. Well-shaped arms. She's dead all right, and if you get what I mean, that's not such a bad thing either. But good God, what for" (*MLI*, 113)? Trying to deduce the details of her story is not worth it, finally, for the narrator/observer. A woman, a mother, a worker—a waste. But Williams at least makes that point. The reader is convinced that the details would be ghastly whatever they are.

Death in the form of murder along the Passaic cuts short these lives too, as the two bodies fished up out of the river testify—one of them without a head, arms, or feet. And the narrator of this vignette with his "ain'ts" and "gonnas" and "wannas" puts the case plain and hard about those who kill and are killed, "punks," and "suckers" and "gorillas" and "mugs" who as kids grow up to be either cops or criminals. All are still there—". . . they ain't moved away none; that's what I'm saying. They're still here. Still as dumb as ever" (MLI, 114).

In addition to presenting the narrator's flinging of words and throwing of voice, his impersonations of these peoples' voices and views, Williams paints heart-rending and soul-tearing verbal descriptions of the river. Two bridges, one upstream by the new Third Street Bridge between Passaic and Wallington, and the other downstream at the Country Bridge, frame the story's opening and closing. Above the Country Bridge the "Polacks" walk looking for, of all things, gold coins out of some rumored, softer past. And Williams watches them in their looking—for coins, at a diver, at each other; watches one turn up an 1864 copper coin; watches one sit amidst the roots of an upturned tree; watches young, muscular men; watches them want to see "The Babe knock it, just once, out of the lot"—laughs and says, "good luck to you " (*MLI*, 116).

Against such a murallike panorama of persons and presences, such a motley choir of voices in "Life Along the Passaic," Williams modulates back and forth with more individualized prose portraits, as in "The Girl with a Pimply Face." A love growing out of both exasperation and admiration is expressed by the physician-narrator who is faced (literally in the girl's blemished face) with the poverty and ignorance, yet simple humanity of the family whose baby he is called to examine. He does not know their names—tells his flabbergasted wife so once he gets home —but he is smitten with them; with the baby somewhat, and the parents a bit; but with the young sister, "the girl with a pimply face" most especially. She has no life-threatening illness, no bad heart, fever, or diarrhea, just a dirty, pimply face in need of washing. She impresses the doctor as typical, one of hundreds like her, yet very much a magnetic, individual presence, "A tough little nut finding her own way in the world" (*MLI*, 119).

As with numerous encounters, numerous presences described in other Williams stories, there is an erotic element at work too, a sexual attraction felt by the doctor for the young girl. The attraction—a taboo really, given the "correct," "ethical" relations between adult and child, doctor and patient—is more than hinted at, for the doctor takes her on as a patient, not just to heal her or make her healthy, but also to beautify her. He seeks to transform the girl into her own best potential, a change enjoyable to her, of course, but to the doctor too—part of the process of turning back the forces of ugliness as well as those of death. The doctor sees beneath surfaces beneath the skin to the spirit, to essences, ideals—so that even at first meeting he sees, "There was that hard, straight thing about her that in itself gives an impression of excellence" (*MLI*, 117).

While examining the ill infant the doctor is really examining the girl, giving her the once-over—her face, "squeezed up, . . . pimply and coarse"; her breasts, "breasts you knew would be like small stones to the hand"; her muscular legs, her bare feet. He helps the infant, and with a prescription of "lotio alna comp" for her acne, he helps clear the girl's complexion. And, with a curt but caring word or two persuades her to go back to school, to care about herself.

The other physicians portrayed in the story—villainous, jaded, money-grubbers all—despise the girl, her family, and those like them. Williams, through his empathetic narrator, in turn barely tolerates such "colleagues." His greatest sympathies are for the underdogs, the havenots, the pimply ones. And much of the impact of the story results from the ironic juxtaposition of the narrator's attraction to the girl and his alliance with her family—and his own wife's and colleagues' relative disdain. His own feelings go much beyond a certain sexual and temperamental attraction for the girl. Sorrow for the family's squalid circumstances, their small lives inwardly chokes him at one point, forcing him to say for anyone to hear, "Hell! God damn it. The sons of bitches. Why do these things have to be?" It takes Williams many other kinds of words, many other stories to try to work through that very same hard-hit bafflement.

In Williams's most popular story, "The Use of Force," the reader is taken again into the house of another such Passaic River family, where a strange, intimate presence is played out, a battle of wills, of love and hate, cool reason and mindless rage. A relatively simple challenge faces the physician in the story: to examine the girl's throat for infection and signs of possible diphtheria. But out of fear or defiance, the girl, Mathilda Olson, refuses to open her mouth, violently scratches at the doctor's glasses, bites a tongue depressor into splinters, and generally behaves—while in her father's lap—as if the doctor were the embodiment of the disease itself, rather than the means to a cure.[92]

Irony compounds irony and Mathilda's mother and father make matters worse with each word they say to the child. And Williams uses the implications of the semantics in the "argument" at hand to great effectiveness. "He won't *hurt* you," says the mother. "Hurt" is the wrong word to use and irritates the doctor—and the doctor (also the first-person narrator) makes this clear to the reader although he restrains himself in his "professional" dialogue with the parents and girl. "You *bad* girl . . . , The *nice* man . . . , You'll have to go the *hospital*," the mother continues, and Williams, again through the first-person point of view, calls attention to the words and the wrong psychology behind them. Finally he blurts out a remonstrance to the mother with her "bad girl"/"nice man [doctor]" designations: "For heaven's sake, I broke in. Don't call me a nice man to her" (*MLI*, 133).

Since the doctor/narrator (and behind him, Williams) is so keenly tuned to these loaded words in context, it is significant to note that he describes his own persistence toward the end of the struggle with Mathilda as "a final unreasoning *assault*," by which he "overpowers the child's neck and jaw" (*MLI*, 135; my italics).

Williams utilizes his familiar undertones of violent eroticism in "The Use of Force" as well. The doctor's admiration for the girl's beauty (that is, he speaks of her as "an unusually attractive little thing"), which is met by devouring him with her eyes, combined with his hostility to her whimpering mother, become a kind of "rape of the girl's will." The doctor's confessed feeling of "adult shame" notwithstanding, the end justifies the means—the use of force (also exerted by the father) is necessary because Mathilda's tonsils are seriously infected. She cares nothing of such matters, however, and the story ends in her tear-blinded, furious attempt to brutalize the doctor—force returned for force—her own kind of violent attempted "rape of his will." Neither Williams nor his narrator is naive about the sexual implications of the episode. And even if the narrator says, "I had to smile to myself. After all, I had already fallen in love with the savage brat . . ." in an essentially nonliteral way, the adequacy and inadequacy of words in relation to action become a theme of the story.

"Love," "bad," "nice," "savage"—all of the words to which Williams and the narrator call attention, are useless in the face of the infection threatening the girl's very life. The doctor knows the infection is the most powerful force in the equation of forces at work in the small, squalid room. Even the word "diphtheria" with all of its forceful connotations is just a word. The force lies behind the word in the disease and in the will and anger and beauty of the girl's presence, her human essence. But words, inadequate as they are, do have a certain limited, albeit primitive, magical, incantatory persuasive force that will enable the doctor to see, to know the truth of the ailment once he can convince the girl to relinquish her stubbornness. He sees his need to open her mouth, to examine her, as stupidly but admirably thwarted by the girl's resoluteness. Does she hate him? Does he love her? The word "love," as used—perhaps intended figuratively but revealing a more subconscious literalness—and the psychology of the emotion(s) expressed, make for intriguing speculation. Life along the Passaic, like the river itself and the aborigine in Williams's psyche, has its violent, savage aspect.

In "A Face of Stone" Williams pushes the figure of the crotchety, cynical physician to the very limits of reader tolerance. For here the physician seems—at first—not only rude but a misanthrope, the very antithesis of what he should be or perhaps first was as a young doctor. Now he is burned out, not even wanting to treat or tolerate the poor Jewish couple who enters his office and his life, seeking treatment for their child and for themselves. They simply want a family doctor. He is such a doctor and yet his rebuffs seem not just due to overwork; his remarks to the couple, and his thoughts (shared with the reader/listener) make him seem perhaps motivated by anti-Semitism, by cruelty.

The title takes one level of meaning from the poker-faced wife, never smiling, never speaking—until the very end. But on another level, the "face of stone" is the doctor's, an outward evidence, along with his insults and rebuffs, of his apparent heart of stone. But in a wonderfully poignant conclusion the wife loses her cold visage of distrust and the doctor loses his visage of dislike for the couple. The moment of simultaneous recognition and climax brings the story to a release of smiles all around. As is so often the situation in these stories of hard lives and hard histories encountered along the Passaic, the patient seemingly in need of attention is not the real patient at all. In "Face," the doctor is healed as much as anyone—restored in his concern for who he is and why he is helping these poor, illiterate, disadvantaged people.

The wife, only twenty-four, a Polish Jew newly arrived in America who hardly knows the language, is a specific instance of the ignorance that Williams and his narrators allude to in the title story of *Passaic* when they speak of someone who does not know enough to wear the right size or kind of shoe. In "A Face of Stone" the narrator-physician immediately sees that the wife has the wrong shoes and varicose veins (one has ruptured). He prescribes different shoes, an elastic wrapping for her leg, and pills for the leg pain. This prescription, along with her awareness of the doctor's recognition that husband, wife, and child mean everything to each other, causes a smile to spread over the woman's face. The physician's recognition of the humanity he is seeing, their rare presences—manifest most clearly in the love of the husband for the wife, and, in turn, the wife's love for her child—is by implication the pill the doctor must swallow, as he has in the past and must again and again in the future, if he is to remain honest and faithful to his calling.

How Williams works his story so that the first paragraph half-smile of the husband's, which angers the physician immensely, turns by the story's final paragraph to the broad smile of the woman that melts the doctor's heart, is a particularly fine testimonial to Williams's skill with pattern and rhythm. In the story the doctor's basic love of humanity is rekindled, slowly, and his own face of stone softens. What Williams does with the baby's smile is the key: "Fortunately the child grinned and sagged back unresisting in my grasp. I looked at it more carefully then, a smart looking little thing and a perfectly happy fresh mug on him that amused me in spite of myself" (*MLI,* 172).

In effect, and no doubt *for* effect, Williams turns what would strike most readers as an extremely harsh and offensive attitude—an attitude diametrically opposed to the romantic image of the healer/physician—into the excusable behavior of a man worked to a shadow of his younger self. What kind of doctor, after all, thinks to himself, and then says, "He was one of these fresh Jewish types you want to kill at sight, the presuming poor whose looks change the minute cash is mentioned" (*MLI,* 167). Williams, much more knowledgeable than his characters are, knows that his study in prejudice has behind it a much larger social

73

motive in revealing the truths of such sentiments, which in the course of the story he proves utterly unjustified.

Another variation on the theme of the tough-guy, cynical doctor reconfirmed in his work and his love of people with all counts against them along the Passaic, and Williams's most often anthologized and acclaimed story, is "Jean Beicke." Here again the Passaic people take on an individualized identity in a personalized portrait of someone most people would not even bother to think of as more than a statistic or a stereotype. Eleven-month-old Jean is at the center of the story, an ugly and defective infant loved and mourned by the nurses who care for her in the hospital and by the physician who tells her story. Characteristic of a Williams story, it is the narrator that we care about too— Jean's story is also his story, the story of "contact," human reaching out to human.

The whole story is an extended sigh, an elegy for Jean, for her condition (physical and social), and an apology by the physician for his mistaken diagnosis and the fallibility of science, of doctors, of humanity. But it is also a celebration of mankind's need for contact, for the medical profession's (and the writer's) need to know the truth, regardless of the attendant "blame" or "praise," excuse or explanation. Williams underscores all this with a tremendously prominent narrative voice; with a great juxtaposition of technical medical language and friendly, colloquial wordings of conversations; with descriptions that are at once grotesque and beautiful. Speaking of the kind of kids brought to the children's ward, Williams has his analogue physician-narrator say in his tough but compassionate voice: "The ones I mean are those they bring in stinking dirty, and I mean stinking. The poor brats are almost dead sometimes, just living skeletons, almost, wrapped in rags, their heads caked with dirt, their eyes stuck together with pus and their legs all excoriated from the dirty diapers no one has had the interest to take off them regularly. . . . What the hell? We take 'em and try to make something out of them" (*MLI*, 159). Such is Williams's American idiom at its rough, heart-rending best.

The structure of the story is intriguing in that what seems to be the climax of events, Jean's death, comes in the middle of the story, as it is told, rather than at the end. A new climax soon builds, however, to an even more forceful ending as the story blends events before and after her death with the vivid description of Jean's autopsy and the pathologist's opening of her brain while the doctor and the reader look on appalled, puzzled, reverent: "The first evidence of the real trouble

—for there had been no gross evidence of meningitis—was when the pathologist took the brain in his hand and made the long steady cut which opened up the left ventricle. There was just a faint color of pus on the bulb of the chorid plexus there. Then the diagnosis all cleared up quickly" (*MLI*, 165).

Williams's description is not gratuitous medical mumbo jumbo or ghoulish shock effect. The postmortem opening of Jean's brain reveals most directly that spinal taps and x-rays and treatment for meningitis or infantile paralysis or pneumonia were not what was needed. The doctor's suspicion that the left ear was the culprit is confirmed. He and the ear specialist needed to go behind the ear and drain it, not just "incise the drums" of both ears, which they had done. The "clear miss" in diagnosis, confirmed by the ear specialist and the autopsy results, is dramatized by the brief conversation between the narrator and the specialist about the political and social implications of Jean's squalid background and the dirt, poverty, and ignorance contributing to her illness. All the knowledge of medical science applied to saving her was not adequate. When Williams ends the story with the specialist quipping about the wisdom of "[Voting] the straight Communist ticket" to remedy the implied political ignorance and misery of the depression, and their "dumbness" as doctors, he shadows their regret and their ignorance with the ghost image of Jean's sliced and pus-sotted brain held in the pathologist's hands.

In "Four Bottles of Beer" Williams creates the symbol not so much of the toughness of the physician who tries to do the best he can for people, as the tenderness and, indeed, love that bonds doctor, patient, and patient's family. In this story the physician, Dr. Robert Ortiz Watson (an alias for Williams) makes a house call to the home of a Polish boy named Tadke (Theodore) and while observing the sleeping child, converses with the Polish mother of the boy. Her honest and simple life is reflected in her words as much as in the rare presence of the moment, the child resting, still feverish but improved.

Watson and the woman talk of each other's family, their respective Spanish and Polish heritages. Watson defends his black maid to the woman who says she "couldn't eat nigger cooking" and has never eaten outside her own home. They discuss the custom of not cutting the child's hair until spring; of child discipline as advised by her parents and updated by this mother; they listen to the woman's new "1930" $169.00 radio and the song, titled appropriately enough, "If you loved me as I love you"; they look at the woman's wedding picture—and the woman gives him a glass of homemade beer. Then as the doctor starts to leave, the woman's own Polish mother, who cannot speak English, insists that the daughter give him four bottles of the beer—providing that he bring the bottles back.

Watson says little, does not well up with kindness, either when he is drinking the glass of beer or when he is taking the bottles home. But the generosity of the gift—four bottles, four, not one or two—is well registered by the doctor and received all the more lovingly, ironically by the "unemotional" way he accepts such an offering. It is not a replacement of a fee, for the husband will pay that tomorrow. The conversation and the listening to the language "out of the mouths of Polish mothers," has been the real payment, the real poetry of such presence. Williams speaks with great feeling about the human and the aesthetic aspects of such things in his autobiography: "The poem springs from the half-spoken words of such patients as the physician sees from day to day. He observes it in the peculiar, actual confrontations in which its life is hid. Humbly he presents himself before it and by long practice he strives as best he can to interpret the manner of its speech. In that the secret lies. This, in the end, comes perhaps to be the occupation of the physician after a lifetime of careful listening" (A, 362). He heard the American idiom loud and clear in the rare presence of the language of such Polish mothers as those portrayed in "Four Bottles."[93]

Although not all of the stories in *Passaic*, beautiful and significant as they all are, can be discussed here, two other stories do bear mentioning. "Danse Pseudomacabre" and "The Accident" (two of Williams's earliest stories, first published in 1920 and 1921, respectively) raise the general/specific, specific/general rhythm of Williams's narration to further heights of the abstract and the philosophical. For Williams was desperately trying not just to report and describe, but to piece together some meaning to the misery he witnessed, some self-reflexive, word-way of coping with it, of solacing the people, the situation and himself —of reconciling life being born unto death.

In "Danse" a man meditates, in a Kafkaesque way, about life and death, health and illness, time and historical process, self and others —all the metaphysical queries about being and awareness. That process, the living of life, the "doctoring" becomes "la danse" (*MLI*, 208) as Williams suggests. The premise from which the man's ruminations radiate is a paradox: "That which is possible is inevitable," he thinks, the "normality of every distortion to which the flesh is susceptible, every disease, every amputation" (*MLI*, 208). It is the paradox of death in life, of morbidity in health, of the reversals of every kind that physicians see in their training and in their daily practice as it accumulates over the years.

Much of his anxiety is personal as well as professional. He is awakened with an overwhelming sense of death. His wife, sleeping next to him, might die, he thinks. How could he bear such separation, his "boon companion annihilated" (*MLI*, 208)? He hears a taxi leave; hears the "finality" of the clock strike three. Other thoughts come—of death, of a will in need of endorsement, of sickroom talk, a wife's fear of her husband dying, of an unconscious baby with meningitis, presumably, infected at the baptismal font of all places, from "holy" water, a baby, who, if it lives will be an idiot. The moon and street lamps imagistically provide a funereal backdrop to his meditations. The moon's movements, the lighting, are part of the dance and the repetitious visitations of a physician, and the writings and rememberings that grow out of those visits: "And do I repeat the trouble of writing that which I have already written, and so drag another human being from oblivion to serve my music" (*MLI*, 210). Such an imagistic "dance" is confirmation in plotless but still "story" form of the significance, the meaning that writing stories such as this one brought to Williams, "Satyr-like," in counting out the tempos and rhythms heard against his music and giving form to his music, the dance of the river, the place where he happened to find himself, the compulsion to write out an accompaniment to the words, the sounds, "the tragic foot," the dance of life—to death.

In "The Accident" the vignettes that dramatize the event point out that "Death is difficult for the senses to alight on" (*MLI*, 221). For twelve days the speaker struggles to keep a girl alive, but death comes, finally, vividly, grotesquely: "She lies gasping her last: eyes rolled up till only the whites show, lids half open, mouth agape, skin a cold bluish white, pasty, hard to the touch—as the body temperature drops the tissues congeal" (*MLI*, 221).

Which is the accident, Williams seems to say, life or death? The girl's final moments are juxtaposed with another lesser accident, experienced by the narrator/physician, a minor cataclysm on a serendipitous "out-of-doors" trip in spring (a beginning, an "accident") to see four goats "down a red dirt path." The physician now becomes a man who wants to stop to show his son the goats. As in e. e. cummings's "Just Spring," the spring, the boy, the goats, the sexual urges felt by the man toward the woman in the car seat, "hips beside him," or in Williams's "Spring and All," out of all the lustful longing for life and its utter mystery of "death, a sign of life," the child must instinctively touch one of the goats. He does so. Then, walking back along the path, the child stumbles, falls full face into the dirt.

The child's falling is an accident of another kind than the girl's gasping and dying, which opens the account. Death is an accident and spring is an accident. The goats where they are, doing what they are doing as "goats," are an accident. The child's fall is an accident. The story is a kind of accident. Experience is an accident, life, the rarest presence of all, and the rarest absence, in death—all such "accidents" are the stuff of storytelling.

In *Knife* and *Passaic* Williams first tries his hand at doing all of it— the "danse," the "accident(s)," the poetry, the words of it—in short story form. And readers who happen across them, like the six wonderful, sun-drenched women who stop their work and stare, concerned, and finally laugh and wave at the child recovering from his fall, can be thankful Williams cared to tell each and every one of these hard histories, these beautiful stories.

Proletarian Portraits: *Make Light of It* and *The Farmers' Daughters*

Because Williams wrote some of his stories in the 1940s and worked on "The Farmers' Daughters," for example, off and on during the 1950s, it is a mistake to approach Williams's three volumes of short stories as strictly representative of stories written, respectively, early and late during his career—the early to middle portion of his career being the 1920s and 1930s when the majority of his short stories were written and published. Williams is sometimes credited with publishing fifty-one or fifty-two short stories, depending on whether or not one includes "The Farmers' Daughters" (the story from which his second volume of collected stories takes its title). Williams, however, wrote and published stories not included in any of his volumes of collected stories, bringing the total closer to one hundred.[94]

Although each title of Williams's collected short story books is well suited to that particular gathering of stories, there is a wider sense in which the titles could all be interchanged and still preserve the relevancy of the title to the respective collections. *Farmers' Daughters* is, at first glance, incapable of such a switch, for that title pertains in a more limited way to the final story in the volume, which is, despite its countryfied title, essentially an urban, proletarian story. If, however, one considers the more ribald associations of the phrase, as in "Let me tell you the one about the farmer's daughter . . . ," this title is possibly capable of being interchanged with the other volume titles. Williams's short story collection titles characteristically tend, ironically, to understate what is really rather significant and nothing to "make light of." All of which is to say that Williams's collected and uncollected stories, in their variety of theme and technique, are all of a whole, all typically, distinctively Williams.

The mysteries of style as person and person as style are what places his more obscure stories in the same mold as his more well-known stories. What marks Williams's stories is traceable to their origin not for titled volumes of collected stories—though they are wonderfully

The Short Fiction: A Critical Analysis

adaptable to the coherence and unity imposed by "after the fact" arrangements—but to their first publication in, even commissioning for, magazines like *Contact* and *Blast,* two "proletarian" little magazines that represented not just his contributions as a writer, but also his participation as an editor as well. Williams was very much a part of the "story" behind the stories in the little magazines in the 1920s and 1930s, and he backed certain financial schemes associated with them. Some of that story must be told here not just because it is interesting in and of itself, but because it helps in understanding the kind of short story Williams wrote.

To summarize the contents of Williams's various story collections and just what appeared in *Contact* and *Blast,* at the risk of repetition, then (since the positioning of the stories is complicated if not somewhat confusing), it should be noted that *The Farmers' Daughters* is the most recent and most extensive volume of Williams's "collected" stories and is actually a reissue and a retitling of *Make Light of It* with the addition of the title story, "The Farmers' Daughters," which ends the volume. Both *The Farmers' Daughters* and *Make Light of It* include *The Knife of the Times* and *Life Along the Passaic River,* which were published originally as separate volumes, and an additional grouping of workingman and ethnic stories labelled "Beer and Cold Cuts," which is not so much a separate volume of stories as a grouping of twenty-one common or proletarian stories not included in either *Knife* or *Passaic.* *Contact* included stories by Williams and others, as well as poetry, essays, letters, and reviews by Williams, McAlmon, Wallace Stevens, Marsden Hartley, Marianne Moore, and others. One of Williams's stories first published in *Contact* was "The Accident," along with the essay "Youth, O Youth." *Blast* was limited to "proletarian" short stories and ran such fine Williams stories as "Jean Beicke," "The Use of Force," "The Dawn of Another Day," "The Girl with a Pimply Face," (discussed above) and "A Night in June" (discussed below).

The rise of the little magazine in the first decades of the twentieth century included Harriet Monroe's *Poetry: A Magazine of Verse,* founded in 1912; Margaret Anderson's *Little Review* (where *Ulysses* first was serialized), in 1914; Alfred Kreymborg's *Others,* 1915; Max Eastman's *The Masses,* 1913; Herbert Croly's *New Republic,* 1914; and H. L. Mencken and George Jean Nathan's *The Smart Set,* 1914, and later, with Alfred Knopf, *American Mercury,* 1924.[95] These and other magazines such as the leftist, even Stalinist (for a time) *Partisan Review* were both stimulated by a rising tide of cultural nationalism and an attempt, in most cases, to combine interests in art and politics. And with the support of expatriate artists and intellectuals in Paris, magazines such as *Transatlantic Review* (1924), *This Quarter* (1925), and *transition* (1927), Williams, Hemingway, Hart Crane, and others gained a certain avant-garde international credence as well. The revival of the *Dial* in 1920 (edited by Williams's friend Marianne Moore) is credited with mixing "international modernism" with "the native American strain" of writing, and Williams (for his poetry) along with Eliot, Pound, Moore, and others, won the *Dial* award.[96]

The ascendency of literary nationalism and the promise of a new age for writers met head on with the crash of the stock market in 1929 and the Great Depression in its wake. It was during these hard times that Williams turned to the hard histories of his short stories and his first autobiographical short stories in *Little Review* in February-March 1919 at the time Pound was foreign editor.[97]

As Williams's commitments to both *Contact* and to *Blast* indicate— in editorial statements and in his short stories—he was also committed (despite his relatively secure middle-class life as a doctor, and despite accusations by Fred Miller's wife, Betty, among others, that he was at the core merely an aesthete) to the causes of the common man, to the poor and to the disadvantaged. In the first issue of *Contact* he announced, "For native work in verse, fiction, criticism or whatever is written we mean to maintain a place, insisting on that which we have not found insisted upon before, the essential contact between words and the locality that breeds them, in this case America" (*Contact*, no. 1, 1920, 10). As he states in his notes on the short story, "What shall the story be written *about*. That's the final step. Obviously not, if it is serious, the mere sentimental characters. How write about a poor Wop, a Polish gal in her kitchen, a foreign peasant who is barely articulate?" (*ABOSS*, 21). He was their doctor much more than he was a doctor of the monied classes; and he was their spokesperson, trying as much as possible to duplicate their "American idiom" in his stories. Not only did his work seek empathy and contacts with the common people who were his patients, with himself, writing about writing, self-reflexively, but he sought contact with other writers, with readers interested in similar political and aesthetic concerns and the issues between these two powerful, at times contradictory, forces. He was both lionized and condemned in the process.[98]

McAlmon, Miller, and West proved the most important contacts in

Williams's writing of short stories. It should be remembered that Williams and McAlmon edited *Contact* from December 1920 to June 1923; Williams and West revived it in 1923. Miller edited *Blast* and, along with his wife, Betty, critiqued, in a fascinating series of letters, a number of Williams's stories, including "A Face of Stone," "A Night in June," and "The Cold World."[99] Williams's advisory editorship of *Blast* began with the first issue in September–October 1933, under rather guarded, self-protective conditions.

It was McAlmon who suggested to Williams in 1920 that they begin a new magazine to be called *Contact*.[100] It was to be a mimeographed magazine of a half-dozen pages or so fastened together by clips as they came off their own machines—prose and poetry as it came to them. The subscription price was $1.50 for six issues—and only four initial issues had been published in America when McAlmon moved to Paris where he published one more issue and established the Contact Press and Contact Editions. Williams retained the *Contact* name in America. Then Nathanael West, known first to Williams as the brother-in-law of S. J. Perelman, and the author of a manuscript (*Balso Snell*) that Williams read and liked, suggested to Williams, with the encouragement of others, that *Contact* be revived in America. In the summer of 1931 West, with the recommendation from Williams that *Balso Snell* be published by Contact Editions, wrote to Williams praising his *Great American Novel* and invited him to visit in Warrensburg, New York—and maybe plink away at chipmunks and rabbits.[101] Williams did not visit West in Warrensburg; however, by the fall of 1931 West outlined the boundaries of their work—on the east the Atlantic and on the South the Gulf of Mexico—and suggested running issues of about twenty pages, with one feature being a thorough bibliography of little magazines.[102] West was to be associate editor, which made him eternally loyal to Williams.

Jay Martin goes so far as to judge the Williams–West revival of *Contact* as "the culmination of two decades of little-magazine publishing."[103] It was the third number, after successes on topics such as violence and American primitivism, that ran into political trouble. Martin Kamin, one of the magazine's publishers, proposed a Communist issue—an idea both West and Williams rejected. The third issue, including writing by Perelman and Farrell and poetry by Yvor Winters, proved to be the final issue because the differences with Kamin were insurmountable. Williams, in his autobiography, attributes the demise of *Contact* to "scripts that were not distinguished" and West's marriage:

"Then he married an Irish beauty . . . and *Contact* died in that contact" (*A* 302). As for Williams, he had helped found a major little magazine, had been partly responsible for Contact Editions with McAlmon, and had helped "discover" West. At once crusty and celebratory, Williams announced, "Now I understand that all those little reviews ought by necessity to have a short life. . . . When they live too long they begin to dry up. . . . *Contact* has produced N. West. Now it can die."[104] Martin believes that West's imagination helped Williams "sharpen his own sensibility and define the direction he would pursue in literature after this time."[105] Who influenced whom the most is problematic. Williams's short stories, with their themes of the impoverishment of youth in the cities, the same theme Williams praised in West's writing, qualify, along with *The Great American Novel* and *In the American Grain*, as a significant influence on West.[106]

All of this underscores the fact that Williams was not fundamentally a political writer; he was, like West, much on the side of art over propaganda, as illustrated in their unified stand against Kamin. Williams's stories nevertheless have a decidedly proletarian bias to them, a bias made clear in his affiliation with the Millers and *Blast*. That "contact" and Williams's proletarian bias extended only so far. He stated it in agreements with the Millers. They knew it explicitly and sensed it in Williams's life and in his stories.

Williams pinpoints his association with Fred Miller as falling between the publication of *Knife* and that of *Passaic*. Angel Flores's Dragon Press took the stories Williams "had been jotting down for a year or more during the depression"—stories that had never really sold—and brought out *Knife* in 1932. Williams never saw Flores again, and the book did so poorly that by 1935 Williams was able to buy a crate full of copies for fifteen cents each after a friend saw them for sale on the Atlantic City Boardwalk (*A*, 298). And at about that same time Williams was contributing stories to Miller's little magazine, *Blast*, that would later make up part of *Passaic*. Miller was tool designer by profession, and at that time he was unemployed and living over a garage in Brooklyn (*A*, 299).

Correspondence between Williams and the Millers reveals that Fred Miller, along with his wife, had some very definite ideas about the nature of and need for "proletarian" literature. Williams understandably, did not have quite the enthusiasm for the little magazine Miller launched. Even the name Williams thought unnecessarily confused with "Pound's London adventure in Vorticism," the "*Blast*" of Pound and Wyndham Lewis (*A*, 299). In any event, Williams, after suffering difficulties with Kamin and other leftist backers of *Contact*, agreed to a proletarian "contract" of sorts with the Millers. They wanted a story a month from Williams—like those they had read in *Knife*—his name as "advisory editor" alongside Miller and Sam Sorkin as editors, and an editorial every now and then.[107] Williams, too, had his quid pro quo conditions: (1) that he "have no work to do in connection with it"; (2) "that it be and remain a magazine devoted to writing (first and last), though in the service of the proletariat"; and (3) that the magazine adhere to a program that stressed that *Blast* hold that "in order to serve the cause of the proletariat he [the artist] must not under any circumstances debase his art to any purpose. . . . (WCWL&M). Williams insisted that for a writer to help the cause of the proletariat, writing must be good and that most proletariat writing was ineffective precisely because it was bad—because it oftentimes tried to write down to an audience. In short, the writer should "get to the task without first compromising his intelligence" (WCWL&M). The difficulty was, in Williams's view, that the short story writer (artist) who had presumably "perfected a complicated method or methods," had to make contact with readers willing to heed what they understand "but who have no knowledge of the complexities of a difficult technique" (WCWL&M).

The Millers understood both the proletariat messages and themes of Williams's stories, and his complicated techniques. They both attempted much the same thing in their own more limited fiction writing and met with relatively small success. But they responded to the stories Williams submitted in quite fervent, honest, and personal ways. They were, after all, the poor, the proletariat, struggling not only to pay for printing *Blast*, but also to pay for food and lodging, and Betty Miller at one point even gave Williams's Rutherford address and his brother's name (but informed him about it) for a fake reference for the Home Relief Administration.

Although *Blast: A Magazine of Proletarian Short Stories* ran for only fourteen months (September 1933 to November 1934) and published only five issues, they were five landmark issues and featured these Williams stories: "Jean Beicke" as lead story (no. 1, pp.3–6); "The Use of Force" (no. 2, pp. 17–18); "The Dawn of Another Day" as lead story (no. 3, pp. 3–8); "The Girl with a Pimply Face" (no. 4, pp. 15–20); and "A Night in June" (no. 5, pp. 2–4).[108]

From May through September of 1934 the Millers and Williams exchanged letters almost weekly. In that exchange they discussed what they considered to be the strong and weak points of past and current Williams stories: "The Face of Stone," "A Night in June," "Jean Beicke," "Old Doc Rivers," "The Girl with a Pimply Face," "The Impossible Wrestler" (more suited to play form than short story form, Betty Miller insisted), and "A Cold World." Williams and Betty Miller argued in a heated way about the opening of "A Face of Stone," and Fred Miller agreed with his wife that the prejudice and apparent anti-Semitism of the first-person doctor-narrator would be too clearly associated with Williams, much to his detriment. Betty Miller suggested that Williams just omit what turns out to be the fourth paragraph of the story—"People like them belong in clinics. . . . Just dumb oxen. Why the hell do they let them into the country. Half idiots at best."[109] Williams listened graciously and responded by complimenting Betty Miller's critical abilities, and left the passage in.

In their letters the Millers discuss not only the politics of proletarian prose but also the politics of little magazines, the hassles of seeing one through, the rivalries with the likes of Jack Conroy, editor of *Anvil*, who at one time wanted to merge with *Blast* (the Millers saw it as a takeover) and had the audacity, they felt, to assess "Jean Beicke" as a strange mixture of things with no real merit.

Fred Miller's real peeve, however, was *New Masses*, which he saw as broadening the proletarian story too much and relying too heavily on name authors like James T. Farrell and Albert Halper. Similarly, he complained to Williams that *Partisan Review* unjustly favored Farrell over Williams, whose *Blast* stories Miller saw as more proletarian in spirit than *Partisan Review* would acknowledge.[110]

James G. Watson insists that "The best of [Williams's] stories are no more typical of proletarian realism than of any other convention of expression, including conventionally American ones."[111] Williams himself made clear numerous times, including in the pages of the *Partisan Review*, that he was not a Marxist and that he felt Marxism could not be ideologically related to the American tradition.[112] And yet what Miller refers to as Williams's "proletarian spirit" is everywhere in his short stories, from *Knife*, which had so imprinted the proletarian allegiances and aspirations of *Blast*, through the *Passaic* stories, many of which originally appeared in *Blast*, through *Make Light of It* and *The Farmers' Daughters*.

The Short Fiction: A Critical Analysis

In one of her more impassioned letters, Betty Miller tells Williams he cannot really know about the "class struggle," cannot really sympathize with the awakening masses and a leader like Lenin or with the "revolution" because Williams has always been able to solve his personal problems with work and has a devoted wife to comfort him—that he is essentially an "esthete."[113] What Betty Miller curiously fails to acknowledge in her proletarian zeal is that William's work as a physician nourished the very proletarian spirit that is reflected in his stories, and that although personally he was not a member of the proletariat, his empathy for the poor and huddled masses—because it was artistically expressed—was real and more lasting—if not more immediately politically effective—than direct, strident proletarian "propaganda."

Much of Williams's proletarian spirit focuses on children—naturally enough, given his specialty as a pediatrician—as well as on women, blacks, "Polacks," Italians, American Indians, and their oppression as "minorities" in society. The physically deformed, the sick, the mentally ill could also be included in such a classification, and Williams does so. Not all doctors realize the inclusiveness of such a list of "minorities"—and Williams harshly satirizes such doctors in his stories. And those males who dehumanize women, children, and racial/ethnic minorities (even the kind of male who is representative at times of Williams himself) meet with his disapproval, just as males who love and revere children, women and minorities are portrayed approvingly in the stories.

Make Light, with its proletarian subsection "Beer and Cold Cuts," is dedicated to "our Troops in Korea," and *Farmers' Daughters* is dedicated to "our Pets, Grandchildren and Pals." The implied extremes of exile and domesticity point to Williams's deep and abiding faith in family and home and the common people who try to make a go of both of them.

No more proletarian and poignant story (toughly poignant, not sentimental) can be found than "A Night in June," first published in *Blast*. Here the doctor-narrator sallies forth one night in June in a kind of "birth passage" of his own to deliver yet another child of a woman for whom he has, over the years, developed a kind of love. As a young doctor he delivered her first child who died in birth, much to the doctor's sad disappointment.

The narrator describes the woman as a "peasant," an Italian immigrant barely able to speak English—"a woman of great simplicity of character . . . docility, patience, with a fine direct look in her grey eyes. And courageous. Devoted to her instincts and convictions and to me" (*FD*, 136). "Angelina" is the woman's name, ironically but significantly enough, she is angelic in her simplicity. When he gets the call "one beautiful June night," at 3 A.M. on the 10th (he remembers the date vividly), it is the eighth time he has attended her, "delivering Angelina of all her children" (*FD*, 137). In a special way, even a romantic way, the doctor's helping Angelina amounts to a kind of lovemaking. Her husband and sister-in-law are with her, as are some of her children, old and young, and they are much concerned and ready to help. The doctor examines Angelina in candlelight since there is no electricity, takes off his shirt, rests his bare arm on the oil-cloth-covered kitchen table; he gives her an enema as she requests, then returns to his chair and sleeps sitting up, then awakens feeling "deliciously relaxed. . . . The peace of the room was unchanged. Delicious" (*FD*, 141).

He examines Angelina again, decides to give her a shot of pituitrin to intensify the strength of the labor pains, and returns to the kitchen once again to sleep a bit more, resting his head on the kitchen table and an obstetric gown used as a pillow. While he "sleeps" he carries out an argument with himself between "science and humanity" and decides that whereas when he was younger he sides with science, he now is "finding for the older school" of humanity (*FD*, 141). After giving another shot of pituitrin, and as the dawn comes, the doctor decides to help the woman in what amounts to an act of science, humanity, and romantic love of a kind: "With my left hand steering the child's head, I used my ungloved right hand outside on her bare abdomen to press upon the fundus. The woman and I then got to work. Her two hands grabbed me at first timidly about the right wrist and forearm. Go ahead, I said. Pull hard. I welcomed the feel of her hands and the strong pull. It quieted me in the way the whole house had quieted me all night" (*FD*, 142). As a younger, less proletarian-spirited physician, the doctor confesses that Angelina's present condition would have repulsed him. At this time he is refreshed, in a sense reborn to himself and to her circumstance over the years: "The flesh of my arm lay against the flesh of her knee gratefully. It was I who was being comforted and soothed" (*FD*, 142).

Even in her squalid surroundings, the woman is clean, a cleanliness of a biologically ideal birth, and the doctor is tempted to resist science's counsel to put drops in the new baby girl's eyes, "She's as clean as a beast. . . . No chance of gonorrhoea. . . ," but he plays it safe and does treat the baby's eyes. With Angelina counting her children for the doctor and asking about drying up the belly button with boric acid powder, the story ends in an expansive suggestion that the doctor will go on to the next such proletarian presence and be rejuvenated by it: "How many is that? I asked the other woman. Five boys and three girls, she said. I've forgotten how to fix a baby, she went on. What shall I do? Put a little boric acid powder in the belly button to help dry it up?" (*FD*, 143). Amidst such routine the mystery of life continues. There have been past maternity cases and birthings. There will be more such births—and more understated, beautifully commonplace questions for the doctor, he knows—and so does the reader.

Williams's most explicitly proletarian story in an overtly political and sexual sense is "The Dawn of Another Day" (also from *Blast*), which takes the form of two debates one November night. The first is between two down-and-outers of relative means: Ed, a young boat owner, married to a wealthy wife but separated, and an avowed capitalist, and Fred, an older drifter and self-proclaimed Communist, who insists he has read *Das Kapital* so many times he knows it by heart. The second debate is between Ed and his black laundress/mistress, Pauline. As Fred and Ed sit on his yacht and drink whiskey, they talk about Pauline and how sexually attractive she is and whether or not Fred can win her away from Ed. Clearly this issue is more of a joke than a contest. Fred is convinced that the Revolution is here, if for no other reason than he has read Marx's "God damned book three times, in German" (*FD*, 148). Since the capitalists are enslaving the resources of the nation (5 percent of the people owning 95 percent of the money), "We got to have a revolution and take it away from them" (*FD*, 149).

In the drunken, only superficially farcical, dialectic that ensues, Ed counters with a proposal that communism is all right for the Russians but not for America. All Americans need to do is stop inheritances and redistribute everything people have earned when they die. Fred calls for another drink and says such a proposal is preposterous because you would be shot by the army, navy, and the cops.

Ed soon grows tired of the debate and leaves the yacht. On a nearby roadway he meets Pauline returning to the yacht with his laundry. She complains about Fred's presence on the boat and asks Ed to gather another load of dirty clothes since she has to be returning to her husband. Pauline is disgusted by the appearance of Fred, drunk and asleep on the yacht.

Ed and Pauline leave the boat again, but he complains about being low and convinces her to return to the yacht to make love. In a forward stateroom they talk briefly. She undresses erotically and they consummate their passion for each other. Their "debate" now balances the conversation between Fred and Ed in the first third of the story. Pauline wants to make love again, but Ed feels he must tell her—to her bafflement—what their lovemaking has taught him about "class consciousness." But Pauline wants only to hurry home to her husband out of fear of being killed. She is more than willing to continue the liaison with Ed if he will kick out his bum friend, since Fred, ironically, she protests, is not in Ed's class. Despite his passion for Pauline, Ed, loyal to a friend, refuses to turn out Fred.

Williams seems to be closest to Ed in this story—opposed to the politics of Marxist revolution, at least in America, yet aware that a transvaluation in class consciousness as represented by the "change in his head," the recognition that interracial sex between different classes can be a powerfully positive, rejuvenating experience. Ed carries out, in effect, many of Williams's longings that were expressed in "The Colored Girls of Passenack." But the contact and camaraderie with his friends is even more overpowering than political or sexual class revolutions. As usual, the proletarian presence in Williams's stories is not without satirical knots and complications, especially for a middle-class doctor trying to empathize with more disadvantaged individuals and groups.

In "Above the River," one of Williams's many "five-minute" short stories in *Make Light* and *Farmers' Daughters*, the proletariat is represented by a tough supervisor, familiar with the ways of workingmen—metal-lath and bridge construction—who, as tough as they are, also look after their own when ill or injured—even if they are beaten up by their fellow workers. In these sketches Williams again usually follows a conversation/dialectic format. The boss tells a friend, who may be a physician (but of another class), about the kinds of workers he knows. He boasts especially that the American Indian is a rugged worker. These Indians come down into the states from Canada and return to their own country: "Little divisions like Canada and the United States don't mean a thing to them. They're Americans. And do they know it" (*FD*, 252). The physician figure who is listening to all of this is surprised to learn (because he is used to stereotypes) that bridges like the Triboro Bridge in New York City have been constructed by American Indians.

The dialectic focuses on the issue of whether or not American Indians are adaptable in the industrial age. The listener assumes that they were not good industrial workers—and the supervisor-narrator tries to dissuade him: "They go anywhere. Nothin' ever happens to 'em either. You can trust 'em with anything. Fine workers. And they mind their own business . . ." (FD, 252). To illustrate his point the supervisor tells of the time he took the Indians off the bridge construction job to carry metal lath, only to meet with the insults and racial slurs of the metal-lath workers. Although he refers to one of the Indians in his own kind of stereotyping as "Papoose," he takes great pride in the blow by blow account of how the Indian grabbed the metal-lath worker by the flesh of his belly and twisted him to the ground.

In telling his story about the Indians the supervisor reveals more than one racial stereotype of his own, saying such things as "Me Indian" and including a reference to the Indians as "Just like you read about with animals" (FD, 254). But he is far more of an ally than others who refer to the Indians as "God-damned sons of bitches." Williams's intent is clearly a statement against racial prejudice and an illustration of how it can be mitigated—though remnants of such prejudice are bound to remain.

In "The Insane" Williams builds a story around a conversation he once had with his own son, William E. Williams, M.D., concerning his training in medical school in the field of psychiatry. Here the young doctor and his father express their concern for the mentally ill in what amounts to an extension of the proletarian spirit. A doctor, his medical student son, and the boy's mother discuss the "insane" and what can be done about their condition. The father queries the son about any new theories—not about cases with a somatic background, but schizophrenics most especially. The son lists a few possible explanations that place causes in society and family: children being unwanted by parents or rejected in society. Freud is brought up and dismissed as merely one of many theories. What the son does know is that cases of "insanity" seem to be rapidly increasing and he cites statistics from his pediatric rounds in the clinic—only two out of twenty-five free from psychoneurotic symptoms. Much to the father's discomfort the son tells him about a bad case, a compulsive young thief, the product of an alcoholic and physically abusive father and a broken home. The mother is appalled but the son observes that such people are all around them.

The upshot of the conversation is that the individuals who are called "insane" have long and complicated chains of causality behind their conditions. When the medical student son complains to his doctor father that when a medical history like that is presented with an outline of a child's life, it is often dismissed by staff doctors as merely "psychiatric findings." The doctor tells the boy he is right to feel so and he should "Stick to it" (*FD*, 290). Here Williams's allegiance as a doctor and as a father is as much with the humanitarian side of medicine as with the "scientific." Certainly his social consciousness and concern for the insane allows for those knifelike conditions in modern life that drive them "insane."

In a more humorous sketch on a similar theme, "The Pace That Kills," an "old fellow" and a "modern weakling" talk about the changes that take place in one short lifetime, even those changes reflected in as mundane a compendium as the Newark Telephone Directory, originally a listing of only fifty or so names of subscribers. To which the old fellow quips, "Yes, it adds up but it doesn't multiply. No wonder we've all gone nuts, huh?" (*FD*, 301).

In Williams's late, long short story "The Farmers' Daughters" (1956), first called "Relique of the Farm," and a story he worked on for fifteen years, what adds up but does not multiply, and, if fact, amounts to tragedy, murder, and death, is the dissolution of a friendship. It is not only one of Williams's last stories but one of his most diffuse, proving in many ways that his best short stories are indeed his shorter ones. Although a case can be made that the fragmentary quality of the story—anecdote following anecdote, digression following digression—reinforces the division and alienation that face the three major characters in their quest for friendship and belonging, the overall result of this technique is a feeling of incompleteness, which although thematically justified is taken too far architectonically.

The two friends in the story, Margaret and Helen, whose case histories (riddled with neurotic and sexual misadventures) the doctor in the story tries to diagnose, document, and participate in as a physician and as a friend, are from the proletariat. Both Margaret and Helen are farmers' daughters from the South, who, having removed themselves to the North in search of the good life, meet and become friends and, coincidentally, fellow patients in the care of the same physician. Much of the nervous and physical illness that they face comes from trying to better themselves economically and socially. But ambition and upward mobility have their price—part of which adds up to doctor bills—and the anxieties of modern living work toward more unhappiness than happiness, to more nervous and mental strain than peace of mind.

The doctor in the story, who tries to advise and prescribe just what is needed in their lives so that they can make the necessary adjustments to the craziness of the times, represents considerably more economic and emotional stability than the two women—partly because of his wife and home. In a sense the doctor, somewhat akin to Williams, can take a walk on the wild side in his relationships with Margaret and Helen, examine them, joke with them, be entertained by them, try to be their friend and, more erotically, a kind of "lover," because he also has his other, more bourgeois life to keep him tethered and secure. The doctor observes them both and is affected by events only in his emotions, for his condition in life fundamentally does not change.

Much of what happens, especially Margaret's being shot and killed by her husband, is far beyond the control of the doctor. He helps both women as much as he can, but any attempt to travel up and out of one's own class and socially conditioned values and assumptions, and all the genetic and environmental circumstances and causes that determine personality, is proven in this story indeed to be a difficult journey. Helen fares better in most respects than does Margaret.

Through the vantage point of the doctor one first gets an idea about the personalities and "health" of Margaret and Helen. Later, Margaret and Helen reveal some things about themselves through their own interaction—and their roles as part of an unusual "friends/patients triangle" with the doctor.

Margaret grew up being asked to eat chick peas and fatback and wound up not eating it, throwing it under her chair. She is a "skinny-bones," and although Williams does not use the word, she is presumably anorexic—or displays the symptoms. She hates her home and her past in the South; she quit college, married a construction worker in order to leave the place, has one child, and is pregnant again. Similarly Helen hates the South—especially for its violent, savage, red-neck values, which caused her brother to be shot and killed for trespassing and hunting in an old man's woods. Helen is younger, has a prettier body and breasts of a size envied by Margaret, and typically dates "chance guys." Despite Helen's own problem with alcoholism, she sees Margaret as a lonely and neglected woman among strangers, and being a nurse, in effect, tries to nurse Margaret too. The doctor devotes much of his attention to strengthening Margaret's sense of self-worth and pride in her body while he tries to convince Helen that drinking is killing her.

The doctor is more psychoanalyst or psychologist than anything else, and much of his treatment involves talking to his patients a little, but insisting that they keep talking. Each "session" makes a kind of Williams short story—characteristically conversational—in miniature. The attachment the physician has for each patient is not the usual patient–doctor bonding but closer to the kind of strong emotional love bonding associated with psychoanalysis. Both women express their love for the doctor; he, for example, kisses Helen "on the cheek, under the ear" and says he is proud of her, says he admires her when she tells him how she fought off having a drink for a week—day by day, refusal by refusal. At other times Helen tells the doctor she would love him in ways he had never known if he would only stop for tea.

He praises Margaret with all kinds of exaggerated compliments: about her fine complexion and fine eyes, about her pretty face and beautiful black hair (actually getting gray). When she asks if he can give her something to develop her breasts he advises she accept her breasts as the result of having two children, but then jokes about either a special brassiere or a man's hand as alternative ways of "development." What might be regarded as "unprofessional" behavior seems rather to be his version of positive reinforcement in his attempt to get some weight on Margaret and keep Helen sober.

Williams continues to develop his story of these two friends and foils by describing in detail their small houses, their furnishings, their methods of housekeeping, Helen's garden—and the men who enter their lives over a period of several years. Gifts such as a photograph of Helen's garden—"trees blossoming with ice"—are described; Helen recounts her baptism in a creek and talks about what it was like for her to grow up with blacks and like them in a society that whipped and lynched them; Margaret's exquisite post-Thanksgiving, romantic dinners for the doctor are reported as is her mania for housecleaning and her aversion to the church bells across the street from her house. Their bodies are described: Helen's "pink and round" breasts; Margaret's pubic hair—in erotic and exotic detail—"Nothing about her to excite passionate approaches except the savage fistful of black hairs sticking out prominently at the bottom of her belly, heavily matted and, due to her thinness, plainly to be observed under a thin dress—as she well knew" (*FD*, 254).

At certain junctures the story—more in keeping with stereotypically risqué "farmer's daughter" stories—seems to want to turn into a full-throttled erotic telling of a ménage à trois involving the doctor and the two friends who more than once "seem" to display lesbian affection for each other. There is not only an erotic undertone to this story, as is so often the case in Williams's stories; there is also an underlying urge to disregard all bourgeois convention and decorum and turn toward what many would see as pornographic behavior in shocking bad taste. But the story never really takes that kind of "hard-core" direction. Williams makes it clear, however, that the doctor lives outside strict bourgeois moral convention and is fascinated with the range of human sexuality and human behavior. Like Ed with Pauline in "The Dawn of Another Day," the doctor is fascinated by the "earthiness" of these two farmers' daughters, these two women of "peasant" origins. The narrator makes the doctor's attitude toward the two women almost compulsive: "Aside from each other the girls didn't seem to have a friend in the world, anyone they could let their hair down for, except the doctor. He would say: I'm no good for them. But he was fascinated" (*FD*, 353). He says too, by implication, "They're no good for me," but he is fascinated. He is fascinated not only by their class, their proletarian background, by their bodies, by Margaret's tendency toward "indecent exposure" in her sunbathing and in her sheer dresses, but also by their language, especially Margaret's outbursts of profanity, vulgar expressions "that would make a mechanic green with envy" (*FD*, 353).

The fascination that the doctor holds for Margaret and Helen is also attributable to his wondering whether or not the center will hold in their lives, when the breakdown(s) will come. It is inevitable from the beginning that their lives will not be golden, middle-class ideals, although they attain some of the trappings. And the downward spiral occupies the final third of the story, as Margaret gets drunk, disturbs her neighbors and passersby, and then attempts to kill herself and her children. Thwarted in her suicide attempt by her son, she then runs off, withdraws her three hundred dollars in savings, and hits the highways and heads to Miami, lured back to her roots with her new boyfriend, Mac. Helen's life plods along as she follows her friend's flights South, then North, then South again, and follows Margaret's hard history, and the final twists of the screw downward, through scribbled letters and, finally, newspaper clippings. Helen goes to Miami to be Margaret's bridesmaid in her marriage to Mac. Then Margaret returns North when Mac enters the army and is shipped to the Great Lakes region. She works at a Bendix factory doing electroplating but does get a chance to visit the doctor in his office and tell him of the hard work and hard types she sees on and off the job—and asks him to keep her bank book for her. She and Mac divorce after the war and she marries one of the tough-type workers from the plant who had hit her and fractured her eardrum at a party at her house before her divorce.

The doctor and Helen bid a sad good-bye to Margaret as she returns to the South, this time to New Orleans. The doctor tells her that in many ways she is the best of them—"the most direct, the most honest—yes, and in the end, the most virtuous" (*FD*, 369). The next thing he hears is the news that Margaret has been killed by her husband. One version has her shot accidentally by her husband when prowlers broke into her home; another—the one Helen believes—is that her husband shot her deliberately after a quarrel. Either way, the cold reality of the inquest report and the trajectory of the bullet's path certify that she was killed instantly, ending not just her life but the complex network of friendship, loves, and hates participated in, observed, and recounted by the doctor and Helen. Both experience the great loss of her presence. The reader is relieved that such a convoluted narrative has finally found its close.

"The Farmers' Daughters," like all of Williams's other stories, represents, among other things, his continuing fascination with people and their "rare presences." The reason he chose not to focus on middle and upper classes in *The Knife of the Times, Life Along the Passaic River, Make Light of It,* and *The Farmers' Daughters* is not that he did not know about such people, was not himself a respectable middle-class physician with a comfortable life—profession, wife, home, family. He might have likewise chosen to write about the life of the artists—the painters and poets who were his friends and with whom he associated. Few writers or painters are to be found in his short stories. Certainly the writer figure is not the dominating presence that his many oral storytellers— of one stripe or another—are. But the proletarian spirit that Williams felt in his empathy with working-class people, the poor and disadvantaged, and which he characterizes so well in his short stories, depends very much indeed on the power of words, the efficacy of the story, and the rare and special presence of ordinary speech, ordinary American language, and the "native voice" as he heard it spoken by immigrants and first-generation Americans of various ethnic, cultural, and racial backgrounds. In that sense the proletarian presence in his stories—his own and that of his characters—became Williams's own special proficiency as a writer of short stories. In Williams's own words, "I got to love these people; they were all right."

Notes

1. See Peter Schmidt, *William Carlos Williams, the Arts, and Literary Tradition* (Baton Rouge: Louisiana State University Press, 1988).
2. For these and other more complete biographical details see A. Walton Litz, Nathaniel Burt, and Laurence B. Holland, eds., "William Carlos Williams," *The Literary Heritage of New Jersey* (Princeton, N. J.: D. Van Nostrand Co., 1964), 83–130.
3. Litz, Burt, and Holland, *The Literary Heritage of N. J.*, 85.
4. See Litz, Burt, and Holland, *The Literary Heritage of N. J.*, 85; also, for background on the "exotic" short story, see Robert F. Gish, "The Exotic Short Story: Kipling and Others," in *The English Short Story 1800–1945: A Critical History*, ed. Joseph M. Flora (Boston: G. K. Hall & Co., 1985), 1–39.
5. Paul Mariani, *William Carlos Williams: A New World Naked* (New York: McGraw-Hill Book Co., 1981), 770.
6. Mariani, *A New World Naked*, 126.
7. *Contact* was revived yet again in 1959, subtitled a "San Francisco Journal of New Writing, Art, and Ideas," where, in the first issue, Williams told the original *Contact* story and hinted at its implications for the 1960s literary scene as it was developing for the Beats and others wanting to "do their own thing."
8. What Williams referred to as "rare presences" is taken in this study as a significant theme and emblem for his short stories:

"The physician, listening from day to day, catches a hint of it in his preoccupation. By listening to the minutest variations of the speech we begin to detect that today, as always, the essence is also to be found, hidden under the verbiage, seeking to be realized. But one of the characteristics of this rare presence is that it is jealous of exposure and that it is shy and revengeful. . . . It will not use the same appearance for any new materialization. And it is our very life. It is we ourselves, at our rarest moments. . . ."

William Carlos Williams, *Autobiography* (New York: New Directions, 1951), 362. Subsequent references to this work, abbreviated *A*, appear in the text.
9. Stories not in *The Farmers' Daughters* or any other published collection include, "A Black Democrat," about the Irish in East Rutherford; "A Boy in the Family," about a father with four daughters who wants a son—but gets

a tomboy daughter; "The Delicacies," a satire of society types at dinner; "A Difficult Man," about a colorful neighbor, Mr. Hallowel, and his borrowing; "The Fable of the Skunk Mencken," a playful attack on H. L. Mencken; "The Drill Sergeant," a doctor's memory of young Bill Cole not meant for the violent soldiering of World War I; "Effie Deans," about Williams and his wife, Flossie, and a gift painting of the revolutionary heroine, Effie Deans; "A Folded Skyscraper," a look at an aging but spunky grandmother; "The Five Dollar Guy," a patient's story of being propositioned and the source of legal trouble for Williams; "Genesis," a look at five lives as the basis of life in America; "Sister under the Skin," ("The Official Disclaimer"), a woman gives her sister "trench itch"; "Pennsylvania Comes Through," a husband and wife, the woman with a sprained ankle, drive home to Pennsylvania in pain; "The Unfinished Refrain," a singer cannot finish a song line until just before her death; "The Dying Priest," "The Ten Dollar Bill," and various other finished and unfinished stories in the Williams archives at the Lockwood and the Beinecke libraries.

10. Webster Schott, introduction *Imaginations* (New York: New Directions, 1970), ix–x.

11. W. E. Williams, M.D., written interview author, 19 April 1988.

12. Diane Wakoski, "William Carlos Williams: The Poet's Poet," *Sagetrieb* 3, no. 2, (Fall 1984): 45–46; see also Robert Creeley, "A Visit with Dr. Williams," *Sagetrieb* 3, no. 2 (Fall 1984); 29–35; Paul Engle, "William Carlos Williams, M.D.," *Horizon* 1, no. 4 (March 1959); 60–61; Denise Levertov, "The Ideas in Things," in *William Carlos Williams: Man and Poet*, ed. Carroll F. Terrell (Orono: National Poetry Foundation, University of Maine, 1983), 149–151.

13. Creeley, "A Visit with Dr. Williams," 29–30.

14. Engle, "William Carlos Williams, M.D.," 61.

15. Levertov, "The Ideas in Things," 151.

16. Frederick Manfred, who first met Williams in 1945, is another writer, among many, who sees Williams as a kind of influential "prime father," interested in all writing, all writers. See Frederick Manfred, *Prime Fathers* (Salt Lake City: Howe Brothers, 1988), 168. Manfred recalls, "I thought at the time, . . . warm, brown eyes, wispy hair; he had the wonderful way of talking like a warm-hearted doctor, country doctor, not like a hard-nosed guy" (telephone interview with author, 25 January 1988).

17. *Writers at Work: The Paris Review Interviews*, Third Series, ed. George Plimpton (New York: Viking-Penguin, 1977), 8. Those who visited him, talked or corresponded with him during those times—including James Laughlin, as seen in his unpublished short story entitled, "The Visit"—testify to the poignancy of seeing Williams struggle so hard to express himself, make "contact" and communicate.

18. *Paris Review Interviews*, 10.
19. "The *Contact* Story," *Contact: San Francisco Journal of New Writing, Art, and Ideas* 1, no. 1 (1959); 76.
20. *Contact* no. 2, (January 1921): 11.
21. *A Beginning on the Short Story* [*Notes*] (Yonkers, N.Y.: The Alicat Bookshop Press, 1950) Subsequent references to this edition, abbreviated as *ABOSS*, will be made in text.
22. Mariani, *A New World Naked*, 607, 624–25.
23. Mariani, *A New World Naked*, 625.
24. "Inquest," *Make Light of It* (New York: Random House, 1950), 317–21. Subsequent references to this edition, abbreviated *MLI*, will be made in text.
25. See especially Audrey T. Rodgers, *Virgin and Whore: The Image of Women in the Poetry of William Carlos Williams* (Jefferson, N.C.: McFarland & Co., 1987); Marjorie Perloff, "The Man Who Loved Woman: The Medical Fictions of William Carlos Williams," *The Georgia Review* 34, no. 4 (Winter 1980): 840–53.
26. *Paterson* (New York: New Directions, 1963), 239.
27. David Minter, *The Interpreted Design as a Structural Principle in American Prose* (New Haven: Yale University Press, 1969).
28. Vivienne Koch, *William Carlos Williams* (New York: New Directions, 1950), 209.
29. "The Work of Gertrude Stein," in *Imaginations* (New York: New Directions, 1970), 344–51.
30. Mona Van Duyn, "To 'Make Light of It' As Fictional Technique: W. C. Williams' Stories," *Perspective* 6, no. 4 (Autumn–Winter, 1953):230.
31. Ibid.
32. Ibid.
33. *The William Carlos Williams Reader*, ed. M. L. Rosenthal (New York: New Directions, 1966), x.
34. Ibid.
35. Thomas R. Whitaker, *William Carlos Williams* (New York: Twayne Publishers, 1968), 97.
36. J. E. Slate, "William Carlos Williams and the Modern Short Story," *Southern Review* (Summer 1968); 662.
37. Ibid.
38. Ibid., 663.
39. See J. Hillis Miller, "William Carlos Williams," in *Poets of Reality: Six Twentieth-Century Writers* (Cambridge: Harvard University Press, 1965), 285–359; Introduction to *William Carlos Williams: A Collection of Critical Essays* (Englewood Cliffs, N.J.: Prentice-Hall, 1966), 1–14; "Williams' *Spring and All* and the Progress of Poetry," *Daedalus* 99, no. 2 (Spring 1970);405–34.
40. "Williams' *Spring and All*," *Daedalus*, 426.

41. Miller, *Poets of Reality*, 323.
42. James E. Breslin, *William Carlos Williams: An American Artist* (New York: Oxford University Press, 1970), 126.
43. Ibid. 138.
44. Ibid. 139.
45. Linda Welshimer Wagner, *The Prose of William Carlos Williams* (Middletown, Conn.: Wesleyan University Press, 1970); Linda W. Wagner, "William Carlos Williams: The Unity of His Art," in *Poetic Theory/Poetic Practice: Papers of the Midwest Modern Language Association*, ed. Robert Scholes (Iowa City: Midwest Modern Language Association, 1969), 136–44; Linda W. Wagner, "A Bunch of Marigolds," *Kenyon Review* 29, no. 1 (January 1967);86–102; also see Sondra Zeidenstein, "William Carlos Williams' Experiments in Prose," Columbia University, Ph.D. diss., Ann Arbor, Mich.: University Microfilms, 1970, 143–90.
46. Wagner, *The Prose*, 5.
47. Ibid., 12.
48. Ibid., 13.
49. Ibid., 104.
50. Zeidenstein, "Experiments in Prose," 143.
51. See Reed Whittemore, *William Carlos Williams: Poet from Jersey* (Boston: Houghton Mifflin, 1975); Paul Mariani, "Towards the Canonization of William Carlos Williams," *Massachusetts Review* (Autumn 1972):58–70; George Monteiro, "The Doctor's Black Bag: William Carlos Williams' Passaic River Stories," *Modern Language Studies* 13, no. 1 (Winter 1983):77–84; Gilbert Sorrentino, "Polish Mothers and 'The Knife of the Times,'" in Terrell, *Man and Poet*, 391–95.
52. See, for example, James G. Watson, "The American Short Story: 1930–1945," in *The American Short Story, 1900–1945: A Critical History*, ed. Philip Stevick (Boston: Twayne Publishers, 1984), 103–46; Kathryn Zabelle Derounian, "William Carlos Williams," in *Critical Survey of Short Fiction*, vol. 6, ed. Frank N. Magill (Englewood Cliffs, N.J.: Salem Press, 1981), 2441–46; Wendy Steiner, "The Diversity of American Fiction," in *Columbia Literary History of the United States*, ed. Emory Elliott (New York: Columbia University Press, 1988), 845–72; Charles Doyle, ed. "introduction to *William Carlos Williams: The Critical Heritage* (London: Routledge & Kegan Paul, 1980), 1–47; "William Carlos Williams," *Voices and Visions*, Tele-Series, The Annenberg/CPB Project, 1987; also see Williams's stories anthologized in *The Macmillan Concise Anthology of American Literature* gen. ed. George McMichael (New York: Macmillan, 1985), 1663–68; *The Norton Anthology of Short Fiction* ed. R. V. Cassill (New York: W. W. Norton, 1986), 1499–1501; *Textbook: An Introduction to Literary Language* ed. Robert Scholes, Nancy R. Comley, and Gregory L. Ulmer (New York: St. Martins Press, 1988), 15–19.
53. John Gerber and Emily Wallace, "An Interview with William Carlos

Williams," in *Interviews with William Carlos Williams:* "Speaking Straight Ahead," ed. Linda Wagner (New York: New Directions, 1976), 19.

54. William E. Williams, Interview.

55. William E. Williams, Interview.

56. Barbara Currier Bell, "Williams' 'The Use of Force' and First Principles in Medical Ethics," *Literature and Medicine* 3 (1984):143.

57. See Richard E. Peschel, M.D., and Enid Rhodes Peschel, "When a Doctor Hates a Patient: Case History, Literary Histories," *Michigan Quarterly Review* 23, no. 3 (Summer 1984):402–10.

58. Gerber and Wallace, "An Interview," 19.

59. See Robert Coles, introduction to *The Doctor Stories* (New York: New Directions, 1984), viii–ix; also Robert Coles, *Times of Surrender: Selected Essays* (Iowa City: University of Iowa Press, 1988), 45–95.

60. Coles, introduction, xii.

61. Ibid. xii.

62. Ibid., xiii.

63. Ibid.

64. Robert Coles, introduction to *The Knack of Survival in America* (New Brunswick: Rutgers University Press, 1975), x.

65. Helen Vendler, "Art, Life & Doctor Williams," *New York Review of Books* 22, no. 18 (13 November 1975), 17.

66. See James Olney, *Metaphors of Self: The Meaning of Autobiography* (Princeton: Princeton University Press, 1972).

67. Manfred, *Prime Fathers*, 132. See also Wallace Stevens, preface to *William Carlos Williams: Collected Poems* (New York: Objectivist Press, 1934), 2, where Stevens first introduced the "anti-poetic" terminology in describing Williams's art—"His passion for the anti-poetic is a blood passion and not a passion of the inkpot. The anti-poetic is his spirit's cure. He needs it as a naked man needs shelter or as an animal needs salt."

68. N. Scott Momaday, "The Native Voice," in *The Columbia Literary History of the United States*, ed. Emory Elliott (New York: Columbia University Press, 1988), 5.

69. Ibid., 7.

70. Ibid.

71. Ibid., 9.

72. Ibid., 10–11.

73. Ibid., 14.

74. Stanley Koehler, "William Carlos Williams," in *Writers at Work: The Paris Review Interviews*, 3d series, ed. George Plimpton (New York: Viking, 1967 [Penguin, 1977]), 17.

75. Philip Rahv, "Dr. Williams in His Short Stories," in *Literature and the Sixth Sense* (Boston: Houghton Mifflin, 1969), 319.

76. "The Venus," *Make Light of It: Collected Stories of William Carlos Williams* (New York: Random House, 1950), 212.

77. Philip Rahv, *Literature and the Sixth Sense*, 319.

78. Compare Vera M. Kutzinski, *Against the American Grain: Myth and History in William Carlos Williams, Jay Wright, and Nicolas Guillen* (Baltimore: Johns Hopkins University Press, 1987); Paul L. Jay, "American Modernism and the Uses of History: The Case of Williams Carlos Williams," *New Orleans Review* 9, no. 3 (Winter 1982):16–25; Alan Holder, "In the American Grain: William Carlos Williams on the American Past," *American Quarterly* 19, no. 3 (Fall 1967):500–15; Marta Sienicka, "Poetry in the Prose of *In the American Grain* by William Carlos Williams," *Studia Anglica Posnaniensia* 1, no. 1–2 (1968):109–16.

79. Philip Rahv, "Paleface and Redskin," in *Literature and the Sixth Sense*, 1–6.

80. Henry Seidel Canby, "Back to the Indian," *Saturday Review of Literature*, December 1925, reprinted in *William Carlos Williams: The Critical Heritage*, ed. Charles Doyle, (London: Routledge & Kegan Paul, 1980), 84–86.

81. Thomas R. Whitaker, *William Carlos Williams*, 92.

82. D. H. Lawrence, "American Heroes," *Nation*, 14 April 1926; reprinted in *William Carlos Williams: The Critical Heritage*, ed. Charles Doyle, 90.

83. Ibid.

84. *In the American Grain* (New York: New Directions, 1956), 39. Subsequent references to this edition, abbreviated *IAG*, will be made in text.

85. Mariani, *A New World Naked*, 254, 405, 641.

86. *The Knife of the Times* (Ithica, N.Y., The Dragon Press, 1932), 21. Subsequent references to this edition, abbreviated *KOT*, will be made in text.

87. Marjorie Perloff, "The Man Who Loved Women: The Medical Fictions of William Carlos Williams," *Georgia Review* 34, no. 4 (Winter 1980):844. Audrey T. Rogers *Virgin and Whore: The Image of Women in the Poetry of William Carlos Williams* (Jefferson, N.C.: McFarland & Co., 1987), traces the dual images of virgin and whore in Williams's poetry, from "Spring and All" through "Asphodel," and argues that Women as a life force appeared "in endless metamorphoses" in those works.

88. See especially James E. B. [*sic*] Breslin *William Carlos Williams: An American Artist* (Chicago: University of Chicago Press, 1985), 138–46.

89. See Reed Whittemore, *Poet From Jersey*, 165–66, where he states, "The two were instantly close and the closeness was not just spiritual since WCW was taken by McAlmon's physique. . . . The love . . . was not just platonic, it was the real thing and because it was the real thing he [WCW] had to write about it murkily. . . ."

90. *Life Along the Passaic River*, as found in *Make Light of It: Collected Stories* (New York: Random House, 1950), 109–242. Subsequent references to

Life Along the Passaic River, abbreviated as *MLI,* to denote the edition in which they appear, will be made in the text.

91. See Stephen Tapscott, *American Beauty: William Carlos Williams and the Modernist Whitman* (New York: Columbia University Press, 1984), 250.

92. For impressions (and possible impressions) of this story on physicians, see Richard E. Peschel, M.D., and Enid Rhodes Peschel, "When a Doctor Hates a Patient," 402–10; and Barbara Currier Bell, "Williams' *The Use of Force* and First Principles in Medical Ethics," *Literature and Medicine* 3, (1984):143–51.

93. See Gilbert Sorrentino, "Polish Mothers and *The Knife of the Times,*" in Terrell, 391. Sorrentino finds the language of *Knife of the Times* to be the one instance of false language in Williams's stories in that he does not use the language of Polish mothers in it.

94. See note 9; also see Theodora R. Graham, "A New Williams Short Story: 'Long Island Sound' (1961)," *William Carlos Williams Review* 7, no. 2 (Fall 1981):1–3 for a story of about 1,000 words–written during Williams's period of strokes and depression, in a "slump," and concerning Williams's early years and his insistence in the story that "I loved women and should continue to love them to the edge of the grave" (2). Flossie "hated" the story, thought it much inferior to Williams's other work (she was right) and did not want the story published by James Laughlin, who honored her wishes. Also see Donald Gallup, "The William Carlos Williams Collection at Yale," *Yale University Library Gazette* 56, no. 1–2 (October 1981):50–59, and Neil Baldwin and Steven L. Meyers, *The Manuscripts and Letters of William Carlos Williams in the Poetry Collection of the Lockwood Memorial Library, State University of New York at Buffalo: A Descriptive Catalog* (Boston: G. K. Hall & Co., 1978).

95. See Daniel Aaron, "Literary Scenes and Literary Movements," in *The Columbia Literary History of the United States,* ed. Emory Elliott *(New York: Columbia University, 1988), 736–37.*

96. Ibid., 852.

97. Ibid., 930; see also Zeidenstein, "Experiments in Prose," 144.

98. For a more detailed account of Williams's proletarian contacts, see Mike Weaver, *William Carlos Williams: The American Background* (Cambridge: Cambridge University Press, 1971), 89–114; also Dickran Tashjian, *William Carlos Williams and the American Scene, 1920–1940* (New York: Whitney Museum of American Art, 1978), 24–25; Paul L. Mariani, *William Carlos Williams: The Poet and His Critics* (Chicago: American Library Association, 1975), 52, 57.

99. Letters, May–August, 1934, William Carlos Williams Manuscripts and Letters, Poetry Collection, Lockwood Memorial Library, the State University of New York, Buffalo. Subsequent references to material in this collection, abbreviated WCWL&M, will be made in the text.

100. "The *Contact* Story," *Contact: San Francisco Journal of New Writing, Art, and Ideas* 1 (1959):75.

101. West to Williams, July, August [n.y.] but probably 1931, WCWL&M. For a detailed account of the Williams–West friendship and collaboration, see Jay Martin, *Nathanael West: The Art of His Life* (New York: Farrar, Straus & Giroux, 1970), 121–22, 132–35, 143–57.

102. West to Williams, 10 October 1931, WCWL&M.

103. Martin, *Nathanael West,* 144.

104. Ibid., 153.

105. Ibid., 154.

106. See Steven Weisenberger, "Williams, West, and the Art of Regression," *South Atlantic Review* 47, no. 4 (November 1982):1–16, wherein an argument is made for Williams's influence on West.

107. Mariani, *A New World Naked,* 345.

108. Runs of *Contact* and *Blast* are in the Rare Books and Manuscripts holdings of the New York Public Library.

109. *Make Light of It* (New York: Random House, 1950), 167; *The Farmers' Daughters: The Collected Stories of William Carlos Williams* (New York: New Directions, 1961). Subsequent references to these editions, abbreviated *MLI* and *FD*, will be made in text.

110. Miller to Williams, 5 June 1934, WCWL&M: for Williams's difficulties with *New Masses* and *Partisan Review*, see Mariani, *A New World Naked,* 405–06; 812; Also Reed Whittemore, *Poet from Jersey,* 178, 254–65.

111. Watson, "The American Short Story: 1930–1945," in *The American Short Story 1900–1945*, 118.

112. Whittemore, *Poet from Jersey,* 255.

113. Betty Miller to Williams, August 1934, WCWL&M.

Part 2

THE WRITER

Introduction: "Bill iz Bill"

There is nothing quite like hearing Williams speak for himself. His voice is prominent in his work, his presence rare and distinctive in capturing the "American idiom" and "the way it was" for the people in his short stories. As his friend Ezra Pound, the Great "Ez," said to James Laughlin in a jazzy letter, just after having received a copy of *Life along the Passaic* in Rapallo, "SOME BUKK / but as fer Bill bein local / a place wiff some civilization is just as LOCAL as the Passaic Triver / but Bill iz Bill and thaZZATT."[1]

The following selections from interviews and Williams's *Autobiography* show explicitly what Pound meant; "Bill iz Bill," indeed—a man, a physician, a writer fascinated by the people and presences in his life, all part of his grand story. Williams's presence is unforgettable. His handwriting, his notes and poems on his scribbled prescription pads, his letters and manuscripts, and his spirit still dwelling in them, remain etched in memory long after they are seen—and "heard." It is important, too, to hear Williams's wife, Flossie, talk about "Bill." She knew him best, no doubt, in his love—and his loneliness as an artist. For fellow follower of the "American idiom" Frederick Manfred, who knew Williams as someone who spoke deeply and directly to him when he was a beginning novelist, he remains an influence, something of a "prime father."[2]

These selections help show why—for Flossie, for Pound, for Manfred, for all who marvel at the mysteries of literature and life—Williams has our attention and affection, and is so "local" as to be in us all.

Notes

1. James Laughlin, Letter from Pound to Laughlin, 11/15/38, "Letters from Pound & Williams," *Helix* 13–14, 1983:99.

2. Telephone interview, Frederick Manfred with author, 25 January 1988; Frederick Manfred, *Prime Fathers* (Salt Lake City: Howe Brothers, 1988), 168; Williams/Manfred Correspondence, University of Minnesota, Manuscripts Division, University Libraries.

Excerpts from *I Wanted to Write a Poem**

[Edith Heal conducted several interviews with Williams and his wife, Flossie, at their home at 9 Ridge Road, Rutherford, New Jersey, when Williams was seventy-three. These interviews took the form of a note-book by memory of a writer's life. What follow are excerpts from that autobiographical "notebook" and from conversations Heal had with Flossie after Williams's death.]

[Williams:] This [*Life Along the Passaic River,* 1938] is a continuation of the stories in *The Knife of the Times.* I was still obsessed by the plight of the poor. The subject matter is the same as that of the earlier stories but I had matured as a writer. I was much freer. I could say what I had to say. The best stories were written at white heat. I would come home from my practice and sit down and write until the story was finished, ten to twelve pages. I seldom revised at all. Most of the stories were published in a magazine called *Blast.* Fred Miller put it out. He lived with his wife and kids in a poor room on the East Side in New York, had no money. I admired him. What he was doing was for art's sake; he wanted nothing for himself, not to make a name. He was dedicated, wanting only to make the new writing heard. I promised to write some-thing for him every week; that was the start of the stories in the volume *Life Along the Passaic River.*

I have never forgotten the stubborn courage of the man, somehow getting together the $25 a month to pay the printer. He has always reminded me of the line in Villon's *Petit Testament* about ink frozen in the inkwell. . . .

*From *I Wanted to Write a Poem: The Autobiography of the Works of a Poet,* reported and edited by Edith Heal (New York: New Directions, 1958), 63, 105, 106, 109, 115.

108

[Flossie:] He was philosophical about death. Certain patients he became attached to. Jean Beicke for one. He wrote about it; it's in the book of short stories, *Make Light of It*. No, she wasn't pretty. Interesting.

Religion? He accepted it. . . . didn't do much about it.

He wrote by hand for a long time but in later years used the typewriter. He used to bang his feet in time to the rhythm. . . . the boys and I could hear him.

Psychiatry? He used to say, "I'm nuts and everybody knows it," and let it go at that.

We read a lot together.

We liked biography, historical novels, the classics—finding them very satisfying—Dumas, Hardy. And we liked Joyce: *Ulysses, The Dubliners, Portrait of the Artist*—but *Finnegans Wake*—we tried it again and again—no good.

I like what Charles Poore said in his review of *Make Light of It*—something like—"This is poetry—not prose, and in the poetry there is sometimes a line that's prose—the interchanges are there but whatever he wrote was poetry."

His titles were his own, not epigraphs—they are creative titles and he liked punning. *Make Light of It* had two meanings—to take lightly—and to give light on the subject.

Excerpts from *A Beginning on the Short Story* [*Notes*]

*William Carlos Williams**

The principal feature re the short story is that it is short—and so must pack in what it has to say (unless it be snipped off a large piece of writing as a sort of prose for quality of writing which might be justifiable).

It seems to me to be a good medium for nailing down a single conviction. Emotionally.

There's "Melanctha" (and there are the Poe stories), a means of writing, practice sheet for the novel one might *discover*, in it. But a novel is many related things, a short story one.

Plato's discourses: the *Republic*, a walk up from the port of Athens, the stopping with a friend and talking until morning. Socrates as a hero.

You can't "learn" to write a short story—either from De Maupassant or Henry James. All you can learn is what De M. or H. J. did. Or take a reader of the short story like Charles Demuth—and observe what he *did* in the way of painting following the texts.

It isn't a snippet from the newspaper. It isn't realism. It is, as in all forms of art, taking the materials of every day (or otherwise) and using them to raise the consciousness of our lives to higher aesthetic and moral levels by the use of the art.

As in the poem it must be stressed, that the short story uses the same materials as newsprint, the same dregs—the same in fact as Shakespeare and Greek tragedy; the elevation of spirit that occurs when a consciousness of form, art in short, is imposed upon materials debased by dispirited and crassly cynical handling. What the newspaper uses on the lowest (sentimental) level, the short story had best elevate to the level of other interests.

*From *Selected Essays* (New York: New Directions, 1969), 295–98. Copyright 1954 by William Carlos Williams. This essay was excerpted from *A Beginning on the Short Story* [*Notes*] (Yonkers, N.Y.: Alicat Bookshop Press, 1950). Reprinted by permission of New Directions Publishing Corp.

Excerpts from *A Beginning on the Short Story* [*Notes*]

This should make apparent that a mere "thrilling" account of an occurrence from daily life, a transcription of a fact, is not of itself and for that reason a short story. You get the fact, it interests you for whatever reason; of that fact you *make*, using words, a story. A thing. A piece of writing, as in the case of De Maup't, "A Piece of String."

In plainest words, it isn't the mere interest of the event that makes the short story, it is the way it raises the newspaper level to distinction that counts.

This is not easy. At first or perhaps at any time, it won't sell. Hemingway's "Two Fisted" or "Two-hearted River"—was that way. And to *make* a story of any sort, short or long, we use words: writing is made of words—all writing is made of words, *formal things.*

We have Kipling's famous short stories, we have Gogol, we have Dickens' "Christmas Carol."

We also have agents who, seeing some spark of novelty (but a big slab of conventionality) in some recent graduate—will teach her to write *Ladies Home Journal* or *Sat. Eve. Post*—at the rate of $200 to $2000 a throw. And do it every day, more or less. We also have the picture of an "accepted" writer, someone known by her style, that she will not offend or shock us, who long after her final deterioration (repeating the same stock) will go on selling the *Delineator* (note the use of "selling") for $50,000. A THROW. (There's a good story with that, the mag saying the price is too high, dropping the serial or whatever and getting another "good" writer to take on the stint for $25,000. The only trouble was that they, the mag, lost money on the deal, made more money by hiring the first lady at $50,000 to write for it. Except that after that experience her fee went up to $75,000. And they paid it!)

I should think, for myself, that the short story is the best form for the "slice of life" incident. It deals with people and dogs and cats, sometimes horses—those creatures who are the commonest sublimation of man's sexual approaches to woman: Big eyes, magnificently curved haunches and slender ankles, the mane, the dilating nostrils—how exquisitely Shakespeare sketched one in the *Venus and Adonis*—like Dürer at his best. They top monuments and sometimes cathedrals—as at St. Marco in Venice. Kafka and the cockroach.

It is for all that man (as man and woman) from the "Boule de Suif" to the "Murders in the Rue Morgue," a trait of some person raised from the groveling, debasing as it is debased jargon, fixed by rule and precedent, of reportage—to the exquisite distinction of that particular man, woman, horse or child that is depicted. The finest short stories are those that raise, in short, one particular man or woman, from that Gehenna, the newspapers, where at last all men are equal, to the distinction of being an individual. To be responsive not to the ordinances of the herd (Russia-like) but to the extraordinary responsibility of being a person.

Can we not anticipate and look forward with eagerness amounting to despair to the time (past most of our lives) when there will appear those journals, those poems and short stories, being written underground now in Russia as in Ireland of this century by the literary heroes of the future? For it has to be so. And the Russians of all people will be the most persistent, the bravest and the most, I think, brilliant. Any nation that has braved Siberia for eight generations and survived to catch a glimpse of freedom so often dragged, as it has been today, from before their eyes, will be writing the masterpieces of the future.

As we write for the magazines today so they write, officially, for the Politburo. But the real writing, the real short story will be written privately, in secret, despairingly—for the individual. For it will be the individual.

Thus and for that purpose, the great writer will use his materials formally, in his own style, the words, the choice and the mode of his words—like Boccaccio, Stein and Faulkner.

But what right have I who never wrote a successful, that is to say salable, moneymaking short story in my life, to speak to you in this way? I feel like an imposter. I'm just a literary guy, not *practical*—like a one-time atomic physicist. Even a poet, of all things. What a nerve to come to a going institution of learning to teach you how to write?! Even to sell? Why, you might as well have an Einstein. HE at least can play the violin, this is, [sic] fairly well.

There's something to it. And so I object also.

But Hemingway did at first sit at the feet of Gertrude Stein and Ezra Pound. They taught him a lot. And then he went out and capitalized on it—to at least *her* disgust, so they say. And she had written at least one magnificent short story. Pound not even one. But then again Hemingway's not a bad poet and might have been a better one.

So if they did that may we not, conceivably, do this? I'll go the limit, as far as I know any limit. From me perhaps you'll pick up a point or two and make use of it. At the worst we'll fool the trusting faculties who invited me here while you get a laugh. . . .

A Maternity Case
William Carlos Williams*

In February one day I received a call from the office of one of the younger men in town. He used occasionally to take Flossie out to parties when they were kids, but he being a Catholic and she not, that was soon broken up. They were classmates in the public school. It was a call to go to Lyndhurst, the next town, to help a young doctor stuck there on a maternity case. The man whose job it was had sent his young assistant, being himself laid up with the grippe. What could I do but go? I've forgotten what time it was, a holiday, Lincoln's Birthday, that's it. I was pretty sore at being disturbed. Anyhow, I went; a small house in the poorer part of town.

But when I got there, I had a surprise. The door opened as I had my hand out to ring the bell and a burly looking man, in vest and shirt sleeves, said, "Come in."

I entered a dark and narrow corridor, had started to take off my coat when I took my first good look at the guy who had admitted me. He was built like the driver of a beer truck, with his shirt sleeves rolled up. He was beginning to be bald at the temples, and he had more than half a load on, but his pants were what stopped me. Evidently he was a policeman—to be seen, not by the pants alone, but he also wore a belt strung with cartridges and carried a .45.

"Where's the patient?" I said. "Upstairs." And just then I heard screams in a deep woman's voice mingled with enough curses to make your flesh creep.

"Go on up. She needs you, Doc. There's another doctor up there; I don't know how good he is but he's done nothing for her. Why didn't Doctor W. come himself?"

"You got me," I said, and taking my satchel, I walked upstairs. The young physician came to the bedroom door hollow-eyed.

"Am I glad to see *you*!"

*From *The Autobiography of William Carlos Williams* (New York: New Directions, 1951), 247–50. Copyright 1951 by William Carlos Williams. Reprinted by permission of New Directions Publishing Corp.

The Writer

Before I could answer him my eyes were filled with the sight before me. In the poor room was a double bed on which lay the woman— filling it, both from side to side and from the bottom up. The springs rested on the floor. She was a mountain, the rings of fat around her small head only paralleling the size of her belly.

The minute she saw me she let out a string of curses at the young man before her, at Doctor W. and everyone in general who had got her into this state and from which we seemed to have no way of getting her out, at which she dozed off and snored like a hog.

The young doctor had been there since the day before—up all night unable to sleep or eat or so much as leave the place for a moment, because of the man below who, tapping the gun on his hip, told him he'd not leave the place until the baby was born, and that if it was killed or the woman herself was hurt in the process due to his clumsiness and incompetence, by God, he'd go along with them.

"You take over," he said to me. "I'm exhausted."

"Not on your life," I said, "wouldn't that be an acknowledgement of a fault on your part? Stick it out. I'll give her some dope at her next pain and see how it's going."

Then it began. First she would grow restless, then, "Here it comes again!" she yelled, sweating and straining like an ox trying to pull a cart out of the mud where it had been stuck to the hubs. She screamed and cursed and labored.

"It's been going on like this since yesterday," he said. "It's awful."

"Let me examine her," I said.

"It's about time somebody knows what he's doing," she howled at me. "Go on, find out what the trouble is, if you're any better than the other," and she parted her heavy thighs like—there's nothing like it unless you've seen it.

I went in and found the cervix fully dilated, the membranes ruptured and a head presenting. It was fully engaged and nothing as far as I could see wrong. Probably a posterior position, but I didn't stop to find out, no need under the meager circumstances, the low bed, the lack of assistance.

"Have you given any Pit?" I said. Pituitary extract in such cases was very new then and the young man hadn't any with him.

"Have you got any?" he said.

"Yes."

"Won't you take over?"

114

"No. But I'll give her a shot. She's not sick otherwise, is she? How much does she weigh?"

"Three hundred pounds, they say."

So I gave her a c.c. of Pit and went back to the chloroform at the head of the bed. With the first pain after my shot, a terrific contracting occurred and before we could do anything, a male infant, all tangled in the cord and screaming as if we'd stuck *him*, lay in the muck hole in front of the mother's buttocks—there's no other way to say it.

The young doc almost fainted from relief, while the woman, raising up her head, yelled to her husband downstairs, "It's a boy."

"What does it weigh?"

"From the look of it," I said, "not an ounce less than eight pounds."

"Is it injured?"

"What would injure it? No," I said, "he's a regular cop, by the shoulders on him."

"Glory be to God. It's over."

I pulled back the covers enough to get at the woman's belly to get hold of the fundus, to express the placenta. "Wait a minute," I said, and paused. Everyone concerned looked at me.

"Is there anything wrong, Doc?" said my young assistant.

"There's another here!"

"What did you say?" yelled the woman.

"Twins, at least twins," I said. The young doctor damn near passed out.

"Get that first one out of the way over there on the other bed. Here it comes!" And there was the other, bigger than the first, a vertex also, screaming and squirming—cursing if you'd want to believe it.

"Is that all?"

"Yes, that's all," I said. "What do you want?"

"Let me go to sleep," she said.

"Well, give us another minute for the afterbirth," I said, "and you can sleep, forever, for all I care."

When the husband came to the door and I told him he had twin sons, all he said was, "Thank God. How is she?"

"Perfect."

"That's fine. You sure came in the nick of time," said he.

"No, he was doing all right. I was just lucky after the work he'd done to carry her through. And it's, by God, Lincoln's Birthday, at that."

The Writer

"We'll call one of them Abraham and the other Lincoln," he said.

"And what's the last name?" I hadn't had time to find out yet.

"O'Toole," he said.

"Abraham and Lincoln O'Toole," I said, but I didn't laugh. "What's wrong with that?" he said. "Not a thing, unique to say the least. It'll bring them luck, unless I'm far wrong."

"How much do I owe you, Doc?" he said to me, reaching for the wad in his back pocket.

"I'll take it up with Dr. W. I don't know what he wants me to charge you."

"Let him try and get it out of me, after these goings on," said the man.

"He'll sue you," said I laughing.

"Sue me," said the woman waking up. "Let him sue me for the dirty drawers I got on." And that's the way we left it.

The Practice

*William Carlos Williams**

It's the humdrum, day-in, day-out, everyday work that is the real satisfaction of the practice of medicine; the million and a half patients a
man has seen on his daily visits over a forty-year period of weekdays
and Sundays that make up his life. I have never had a money practice;
it would have been impossible for me. But the actual calling on people,
at all times and under all conditions, the coming to grips with the intimate conditions of their lives, when they were being born, when they
were dying, watching them die, watching them get well when they
were ill, has always absorbed me.

I lost myself in the very properties of their minds: for the moment
at least I actually became *them*, whoever they should be, so that when
I detached myself from them at the end of a half-hour of intense con-
centration over some illness which was affecting them, it was as though
I were reawakening from a sleep. For the moment I myself did not
exist, nothing of myself affected me. As a consequence I came back to
myself, as from any other sleep, rested.

Time after time I have gone out into my office in the evening feeling
as if I couldn't keep my eyes open a moment longer. I would start out
on my morning calls after only a few hours' sleep, sit in front of some
house waiting to get the courage to climb the steps and push the front-
door bell. But once I saw the patient all that would disappear. In a
flash the details of the case would begin to formulate themselves into
a recognizable outline, the diagnosis would unravel itself, or would
refuse to make itself plain, and the hunt was on. Along with that the
patient himself would shape up into something that called for attention, his peculiarities, her reticences or candors. And though I might
be attracted or repelled, the professional attitude which every physician must call on would steady me, dictate the terms on which I was
to proceed. Many a time a man must watch the patient's mind as it
watches him, distrusting him, ready to fly off at a tangent at the first

*From *The Autobiography of William Carlos Williams* (New York: New Directions,
1951), 356–62. Copyright 1951 by William Carlos Williams. Reprinted by permission
of New Directions Publishing Corp.

opportunity; sees himself distrusted, sees the patient turn to someone else, rejecting him.

More than once we have all seen ourselves rejected, seen some hard-pressed mother or husband go to some other adviser when we know that the advice we have given him has been correct. That too is part of the game. But in general it is the rest, the peace of mind that comes from adopting the patient's condition as one's own to be struggled with toward a solution during those few minutes or that hour or those trying days when we are searching for causes, trying to relate this to that to build a reasonable basis for action which really gives us our peace. As I say, often after I have gone into my office harassed by personal perplexities of whatever sort, fatigued physically and mentally, after two hours of intense application to the work, I came out at the finish completely rested (and I mean rested) ready to smile and to laugh as if the day were just starting.

That is why as a writer I have never felt that medicine interfered with me but rather that it was my very food and drink, the very thing which made it possible for me to write. Was I not interested in man? There the thing was, right in front of me. I could touch it, smell it. It was myself, naked, just as it was, without a lie telling itself to me in its own terms. Oh, I knew it wasn't for the most part giving me anything very profound, but it was giving me terms, basic terms with which I could spell out matters as profound as I cared to think of.

I knew it was an elementary world that I was facing, but I have always been amazed at the authenticity with which the simple-minded often face that world when compared with the tawdriness of the public viewpoint exhibited in reports from the world at large. The public view which affects the behavior of so many is a very shabby thing when compared with what I see every day in my practice of medicine. I can almost say it is the interference of the public view of their lives with what I see which makes the difficulty, in most instances, between sham and a satisfactory basis of thought.

I don't care much about that, however. I don't care a rap what people are or believe. They come to me. I care for them and either they become my friends or they don't. That is their business. My business, aside from the mere physical diagnosis, is to make a different sort of diagnosis concerning them as individuals, quite apart from anything for which they seek my advice. That fascinates me. From the very beginning that fascinated me even more than I myself knew. For no matter where I might find myself, every sort of individual that it is possible to imagine in some phase of his development, from the highest to the lowest, at some time exhibited himself to me. I am sure I have seen them all. And all have contributed to my pie. Let the successful carry off their blue ribbons; I have known the unsuccessful, far better persons than their more lucky brothers. One can laugh at them both, whatever the costumes they adopt. And when one is able to reveal them to themselves, high or low, they are always grateful as they are surprised that one can so have revealed the inner secrets of another's private motives. To do this is what makes a writer worth heeding: that somehow or other, whatever the source may be, he has gone to the base of the matter to lay it bare before us in terms which, try as we may, we cannot in the end escape. There is no choice than but to accept him and make him a hero. . .

We catch a glimpse of something, from time to time, which shows us that a presence has just brushed past us, some rare thing—just when the smiling little Italian woman has left us. For a moment we are dazzled. What was that? We can't name it; we know it never gets into any recognizable avenue of expression; men will be long dead before they can have so much as ever approached it. Whole lives are spent in the tremendous affairs of daily events without even approaching the great sights that I see every day. My patients do not know what is about them among their very husbands and children, their wives and acquaintances. But there is no need for us to be such strangers to each other, saving alone laziness, indifference and age-old besotted ignorance. . . . .

The poem that each is trying actually to communicate to us lies in the words. It is at least the words that make it articulate. It has always been so. Occasionally that named person is born who catches a rumor of it, a Homer, a Villon, and his race and the world perpetuates his memory. Is it not plain why? The physician, listening from day to day, catches a hint of it in his preoccupation. By listening to the minutest variations of the speech we begin to detect that today, as always, the essence is also to be found, hidden under the verbiage, seeking to be realized.

But one of the characteristics of this rare presence is that it is jealous of exposure and that it is shy and revengeful. It is not a name that is bandied about in the market place, no more than it is something that can be captured and exploited by the academy. Its face is a particular face, it is likely to appear under the most unlikely disguises. You cannot recognize it from past appearances—in fact it is always a new face.

The Writer

It knows all that we are in the habit of describing. It will not use the same appearance for any new materialization. And it is our very life. It is we ourselves, at our rarest moments, but inarticulate for the most part except when in the poem one man, every five or six hundred years, escapes to formulate a few gifted sentences. . . .

Williams's Letters*
To Nathanael West

Aug. 2 (late at night) [1932]

Dear Pep:

May I take lunch with you this Friday at about 1 P.M. or a little earlier? That's a funny way to put it, but convenience is the objective. I want to get away again before three. This new *Contact* (if there is to be one) must be gotten under way. And it must not be dull, at all costs, if we can make it otherwise.

This is what I've been thinking: everything must be put aside for the sake of interest to the reader. Ruthlessly we've got to turn down anything that doesn't fit that purpose even though we make virtual blackguards of ourselves. And the first objective must be not to make this issue just another series of short stories. There's no trick in that. In a way, though it was bad otherwise, our first issue was much better in point of diversified interest than the second. This issue must be different from both those.

The reproduction is worthwhile. Follow it by the—not Brown but perhaps Jonathan Edwards. Then Brown. Then maybe Villa. Then Oppen's fragmentary poems. Topping. The Long poem—(maybe).— The essay by Parkes. And maybe after all I will do a Commentary. Maybe the Ben Franklin—*Miss Lonelyhearts*

Let me know if Friday will be convenient for you. I have a long thing by Sherry Mangan which we may run in two issues. It's censorable tho, I'm afraid. A terrific story of death and perversion.

Yours,
Bill

*From *The Selected Letters of William Carlos Williams*, ed. John C. Thrilwall (New York: New Directions, 1957), 128–31, 265–66. ©1957 by William Carlos Williams. Reprinted by permission of New Directions Publishing Corp.

The Writer

To Kay Boyle

[Kay Boyle, an inveterate contributor to the little magazine, came to know Williams first through her poems published in *Contact I*. The editorship of *Contact II* revived the relationship, and Williams attempted a complete assessment of literature and writers in a letter to her designed for *Contact*.]

[1932]

Dear Kay Boyle:

You say: "Some kind of poetic form has to be found or I'll go crazy. I can't go on taking what you (and others) make possible and beautiful. I think I've got lots to say in poetry and no, no, no form. Lousy—loose—*no punch*—no shape—no agony of line like the back-side or a lovely thigh or whatnot."

Precisely—and a timely reaction of the first importance; it means the present moment for what it is, a formless interim—but those are periods calling more for invention which mask or should mask a feverish activity still out of sight to the generality of observers. There is no workable poetic form extant among us today.

Joyce and Stein have been paramount in knocking the props from under a new technique in the past ten years and enforcing it. They have specifically gone out of their way to draw down the attention on words, so that the line has become pulverous instead of metallic—or at least ductile. Your comment marks clearly for me the definite departure from that sort of thing toward a metrical coherence of some sort—not a *return* to anything, for God's sake let us be clear on that at the beginning. Let us once and for all understand that Eliot is finally and definitely dead—and his troop along with him.

But what remains? For myself, I have written little poetry recently. Form, the form has been lacking. Instead I have been watching speech in my own environment from which I continually expect to discover whatever of new is being reflected about the world. I have no interest, as far as observation goes, in the cosmic. I have been actively at work (if such sketchy trials as I employ can be called such) in the flesh, watching how words match the act, especially how they come together. The result has been a few patches of metrical coherence which I don't as yet see how to use—but they seem to run to groups of lines. Occasionally they give me the feel of authenticity.

You know, I think, enough of me to understand that I have no belief in the continuity of history. To me the classic lives now just as it did then—or not at all. The "Greek" is just as much in Preakness as it was in Athens. Everything we know is a local virtue—if we know it at all—the only difference between the force of a great work and a lesser one being lack of brain and fire in the second. In other words, art can be made of anything—provided it be seen, smelt, touched, apprehended and understood to be what it is—the flesh of a constantly repeated permanence. This must be a lot of bosh to anyone who isn't intimate with the materials. But to one who is working with the stuff it may mean something. If not—

But it doesn't mean enough to create form. It means this however—that whatever form we create during the next ten years will be, in excellence, like all the classic inventions, a new thing, a thing intrinsic in the times. It will probably foretell the decade that is to follow it. It will take its shape from the character of its age, not the "social" character, if so positively, not satirically. It will not be the symptom of a chronic bellyache or—something else. It will be like no classic which has preceded it. Why do we not read more of Juan Gris? He knew these things in painting and wrote well of them.

I have been working with prose, since I didn't know what to do with poetry. Perhaps I have been in error. Maybe I should be slaving at verse. But I don't think so. Prose can be a laboratory for metrics. It is lower in the literary scale. But it throws up jewels which may be cleaned and grouped.

I don't think any poetry ever originated in any other way. It must have been inherent in the language, Greek, Latin, Italian, English, French or Chinese.

And this should blast that occasionally pushing notion that the form of poetry (as that of any art) is social in character. Such an opinion is purest superficiality. The form of poetry is that of language. It is related to all art first, then to certain essential characteristics of language, to words then and finally to everything among all the categories of knowledge among which the social attributes of a time occur. The work of Einstein also merges into it, hardly a social phenomenon. It is not formed "like" the society of any time; it might be formed in a manner opposite to the character of the times, a formal rigidity of line in a period of social looseness. That is, the outstanding genius of such a time might, in his attic, be writing that sort of poetry. . . .

The Writer

To Horace Gregory

[Horace Gregory was a poet, critic, and friend of Williams; he was one of the judges when Williams won the National Book Award for Poetry in 1950.]

Tuesday [1948]

Dear Horace:

Glad to hear from you. The purpose of the long letter at the end [of *Paterson*, book 1] is partly ironic, partly "writing" to make it plain that even poetry is writing and nothing else—so that there's a logical continuity in the art, prose, verse: an identity.

Frankly I'm sick of the constant aping of the Stevens' dictum that I resort to the antipoetic as a heightening device. That's plain crap—and everyone copies it. Now Rodman. The truth is that there's an *identity* between prose and verse, not an antithesis. It all rests on the same time base, the same measure. Prose, as Pound has always pointed out, came after verse, not before it—No use tho trying to break up an error of that sort when it begins to roll. Nobody will attempt to think, once a convenient peg to hang his critical opinion on without thinking is found.

But specifically, as you see, the long letter is definitely germane to the rest of the text. It is psychologically related to the text—just as the notes following the *Waste Land* are related to the text of the poem. The difference being that is this case the "note" is subtly relevant to the matter and not merely a load for the mule's back. That it is *not* the same stuff as the poem but comes from below 14th St. is precisely the key. It does not belong in the poem itself any more than a note on— Dante would.

Also, in Book IV, the poem does definitely break out to the world at large—the sea, the river to the sea. This begins it.

And, if you'll notice, dogs run all through the poem and will continue to do so from first to last. And there is no dog without a tail. Here the tail has tried to wag the dog. Does it? (God help me, it may yet, but I hope not!)

I'm going with Floss to Atlantic City for a short time to try to get on my feet.

My best to you,
Bill

Excerpts from *Interviews with William Carlos Williams: "Speaking Straight Ahead"**

[The following is excerpted from a wide-ranging interview with Williams in June 1950, conducted by John Gerber at Williams's home at 9 Ridge Road, Rutherford, New Jersey.]

Interviewer: What I had in mind was simply having you talk about the problems of being a doctor and being a poet—

Williams: Oh. Yes, I see.

Interviewer: —and perhaps start by telling how you got to be a doctor and a poet.

Williams: Hmmm. Well you want me to begin way back [*laughs*].

Interviewer: Begin way back.

Williams: Well all right, I was born—that's where we begin usually—born right in Rutherford of parents who were themselves born out of the country. My father was born in England and didn't come here till he was brought here by his mother, having lost his father at the age of five. And, well, switch to Mother, she was born in Mayagüez, Puerto Rico, of mixed parentage she was, her mother coming originally from Martinique, a Frenchwoman, and her father being a Puerto Rican. So, they came here. My father came here because the advantages there for a young man going into business were not great, came to New York, moved to Rutherford, and here I was born— [*laughs*] that's the way it begins. I have one brother. We were both born here.

When it came to a decision about what I should do in life to earn a living, which was of course very distasteful to me that I should have to earn a living, it was very very bad [*laughs*]. Never having had anything,

*From *Interviews with William Carlos Williams: "Speaking Straight Ahead,"* ed. Linda Wagner (New York: New Directions, 1976), 5–8, 12–14, 24–26, 59–60, 81–82, 84. ©1976 by the Estate of William Carlos Williams. Reprinted by permission of New Directions Publishing Corp.

it was quite natural that I should continue doing nothing [*laughs*] and still having nothing—I thought it would be all right. Well, my middle name is Carlos. My mother had one brother who was her *beau idéal*. He was Carlos too. He was her only brother, as I say, who became a physician, graduated from the University of Paris, and started to practice in the West Indies and became rather a good surgeon, and I was named after him, so that, well, I was rather pushed into medicine rather than choosing it myself. My own choice was to be a forester, strange to say. Yeah. I had no desire to be among people. I lived rather a solitary sort of life with one or two companions. I liked to be outdoors and had no intention of becoming a physician, at all.

I went to Horace Mann High School in New York City. My brother and I commuted from here, taking the 7:16 train every morning for the three years that I went there, taking the Chamber Street ferry, walking up Chambers or Warren Street, taking the Sixth or Ninth Avenue El, riding up to 116th or 125th Street, and walking up Morningside Heights, and getting to Horace Mann High School on Morningside Heights in time for the nine o'clock bell. That was quite a little stunt. The reason for connecting that up is that I'd been very athletic. I was never any good at anything, but I loved it, and that's what I wanted to do, to be outdoors and to go into baseball and track. And I went into track a little bit too much, without a coach. I remember that I was going to run in Madison Square Garden a 300-yard run. That's a queer distance, just between the 220 and the quarter mile. It was a handicap event and I was tutored to win it, if I ran according to my style and in my own class. And we were training at the 22nd Regiment Armory, and I ran around, put my sprint on at the end of the quarter mile, and then when we got to the end of it, somebody said, "You got one more lap to go," which was not bright. And being ambitious, I ran and probably continued my sprint all the way around, and came home sick at my stomach, with a headache, and was put to bed after that. And that knocked me out. I remember Dr. [Charles] Calhoun, our old family physician, said, "Well, you got a bad heart? You'll never be able to do anything but take long walks in the country."

All this is important because it determined my life thereafter, not to go into athletics or to do anything strenuous. And I had to give up forestry, the idea of being outdoors, and Mother said, "Well, why don't you become"—not a doctor yet, that hadn't come up—"be a dentist?" So I got into the University of Pennsylvania and enrolled for a course, a five-year course, by which I was to get two degrees, the D.D.S. of dentistry and the M.D. of medicine, and go into oral surgery, which was a bright idea [*laughs*]. After the first year of the combined course, I quit dentistry and went on with medicine, and so, largely because of my mother's remembrance of her brother who was a distinguished surgeon, and because there I was, I didn't know what else to do, and it was put into my head, I became a doctor. Lucky, too, for me, because it forced me to get used to people of all sorts, which was a fine thing for a writer or a potential writer.

Interviewer: It was at Pennsylvania that you started writing poetry, wasn't it?

Williams: No, I had started before that. I had started a short time before that. I wrote—not poetry and I never pretended that I was writing poetry—I was interested in writing. I kept notebooks. I remember it must have been twenty-three (it may have gone up to twenty-eight because eight and three are somewhat alike, and I can't remember them as between twenty-three and twenty-eight) notebooks, and I wrote my immortal thoughts in those books [*laughs*], whatever they were. If I had an opinion about things about me, I'd jot it down, and occasionally it would take the loose form of verse. I was reading Keats at the time. Keats was my favorite.

Interviewer: This was while you were still in Horace Mann?

Williams: While I was getting through, yes. I had some very good English teachers at Horace Mann. There was an Uncle Billy Abbott, who later went to Smith I think, one of the Abbott family of New York, the Lyman Abbotts and others—I don't know who the original was, but they were very interesting people. And I believe that Uncle Billy Abbott was the first one who really led me toward English, toward writing, toward the satisfaction of externalizing my sorrows and distresses. And believe me, that's the way writing often starts, a disaster or a catastrophe of some sort, as happened to me, and you're a child not knowing where to go or what to do or what to think. He's thrown back so much on himself that he's really in distress. And if someone can teach him, through an art or through an interest in whatever it may be, to externalize his sorrows [*laughs*], like *The Sorrows of Werther*, he immediately is put on a good basis for life, if he can continue it. And I think that's the basis for my continued interest in writing, because by writing I rescue myself under all sorts of conditions, whatever it may be that has upset me or some trouble that I've got myself into [*laughs*] through my excessive energy, let's say, if there is any at times, then I can write and it relieves the feeling of distress. I think quite literally, psychologically, speaking as Freud might think [*laughs*], that writing has meant that to me all the way through.

I started to write! I even remember the first thing I ever wrote, because it was a sudden . . . it was a crisis. It was shortly after I had been forbidden to go into athletics, told that I shouldn't undertake anything too strenuous in life. I spontaneously said to myself:

> A black black cloud
> flew over the sun
> driven by fierce flying
> rain.

Well, immediately I thought, "That's the most stupid thing I've ever said because, after all, the rain doesn't drive the clouds," so at the same moment I was born a poet and a critic instantly [*laughs*]. And I've never forgotten either one. But the outstanding thing was that when I said that, I experienced a pleasure, a real pleasure, a delightful feeling as if I had done something outstanding. I had no idea what I'd done. I did plenty [*laughs*]—ruined myself for life! [*laughs*] From being a regular guy, I became a poet, that horrible thing! But it was a satisfaction, and it's continued ever since. . . .

Interviewer: I wanted to ask you about that poem ["Danse Russe"], a couple of things. Many many poets have talked about being lonely.

Williams: Hmmm. Well I think the artist, generally speaking, feels lonely. Perhaps his very recourse to art, in any form, comes from his essential loneliness. He is usually in rebellion against the world, I think. I think that's a rule. I have thought myself that that's rather a snide thing to day—here I am living with my wife and [*laughs*] child and saying, "I'm lonely." It merely records a fact.

Interviewer: Yes, but you, more than most artists, are also living in a community and doing a job in a community.

Williams: Yes, it's true. But if you do your job, you're sometimes most lonely, strange as it may seem, because in your ordinary work— and there's your incentive for art all the way through—you yourself, as a man, as a woman, as an individual, are very seldom completely involved in your own work, and that answers to some extent the question, "How do you find time for writing?" It's a necessity! Because the essential "I," the person himself, does his work, but remains—after the work is finished, there he stays. Like a man who arrives at the age of sixty-five and retires, or is retired by his firm, and when he gets all through, he finds that he doesn't exist and never has existed, poor guy. He never knew it before. He thought that the job was everything in his life. Well, he's finished. He's absolutely finished! He goes out and shoots himself very often. There is nothing left of him. And I wanted to make very sure that that was *not* going to happen to me, baby, no sir! I knew that if I lived long enough I was going to be old, and after I became old, then life really would begin, as I've said over and over again. Then I would be retired because I've served. I've done my stuff for society, and what's left is my time. . . .

But a man, an artist, wants a world to be different from what he finds it. So he finds himself lonely. Just the other day, in one of the New York magazines I saw (one of the smaller magazines, I can't recall what its name was. . . . A. P., I think, or A. D.—oh [*laughs*], A. P. is good!— A. D. *1950*) [*laughs*], there was an article by Cocteau in which he said: The revolution, which every man experiences when he becomes fully aware of life in his own mind, among artists is always at least twenty years before the popular revolution. He sees, inevitably, as an artist or any . . . I won't say any thinking person, but any honestly thinking person (that excludes financiers and economists, those who profit by their careful errors), that anyone who really thinks and knows what goes on in the world, has already been through the revolution in his own spirit, as artists must—they embody it in their technique, and there we come back to my whole reason for being alive.

I believe certain things. I feel that certain things, disastrous things, are happening in the world because of man's stupidity, definite stupidity. I can't do anything about it. Personally, either as a physician or as a citizen, I can do very little but vote, which is a mechanical gesture of some value, of course—I acknowledge it, and I always vote. But in my mind, I've so far gone beyond any of the formal pretexts of politics (whether I'm entirely right or not is another thing) that they seem old hat, most of it. I mean humanly, they are! Every man of any sense knows that the brutality of the world has to be outgrown, that's all. And we outgrow it in our art, in the technique of our art, in the way the line is put down, in the way the colors are applied. I think that the artist really, basically, within himself, is always among the most advanced men of any period. They are the ones who symbolize their thought in their works, and so are always laughed at, inevitably too, because our first reaction is laughter to anything we don't know, laughter or murderous designs. The artist is way ahead of his age in his general thought. And so he's *lonely, lonely*. That's where the loneliness comes from. . . .

Interviewer: Well, what do you think there is about the American language that is so different? You've done more in American than anybody.

Williams: Well, our lives are lived according to a certain rhythm, whether we know it or not. There is a pace to our lives, which largely governs our lives. There's no question about it. You take a young man who is employed by Standard Oil. Well his life is set to the pace of Standard Oil. He may deny it and think that's a lot of baloney, but it ain't! That's its pace, and the language they speak is his language. I'm not going to fight with him. I'm going to say, that's your language, that's the way you live. It's my job to take it as I find it. I'm no reformer. I take what I find, I make a poem out of it. I make it into a shape which will have a quality which is no longer you. It's come out of you, but I've objectified it. I've given it a form, a human habitation and a place—you know, the Shakespeare stuff.

And it is so. You have to objectify your life, as I've said over and over again. The pianist sits in front of the piano and plays it. He doesn't fall into the strings. He sits there apart and makes a melody of it. So it's up to me. These people are human. I don't fight with them because I don't agree with their ideas. I accept them because they're my friends, because I like their qualities, and because they have an overall quality which is American which they can never recognize unless the artist or the philosopher, but I think largely the artist, presents it as an entity to them, gives them something to believe in, which the artist must do.

We don't know what to believe in. We divide over our religious tenets, unfortunately, unhappily, so that, largely speaking, I never attempt to touch that. I don't attempt to do what Eliot did, go over and take the British religion and make that as his great tenet of life. That's not my business. I'm not that. I'm an artist, if I am anything at all, and so I take the American language as I find it, because in the English language, from which our language is derived, the conventions of speech and the conventions of art, of the poetic line—let's be specific—carry over not only the traditional, which is good (I mean, after all, who can escape the great tradition of the British language?), but they carry over the restricting formulations of that language. They even modify the thought of the language. The forms modify the thought.

That's why the priests of all sorts, the priest, generally speaking, whether Christian or otherwise, sticks to ritual, because he knows if he can get those people to repeat that ritual, they are caught. They are snared, for life, for good or for evil, whatever it may be, but they are snared. And I feel that in a democracy, in a [*sighs*] life that the paleontologists tell us has only existed consciously 700,000 years or something of that sort—a very brief thing—there's a lot yet to discover in the way we behave and what we do and what we think. And the way to discover it is to be an iconoclast, which means to break the icon, to get out from inside that strictly restricting mold or ritual, and get out, not because we want to get out of it, because the secret spirit of that ritual can exist not only in that form, but once that form is broken, the spirit of it comes out and can take again a form which will be more contemporary. So, I think it is our duty as Americans, our devotional duty, let's say, to take out the spirit that has made not only Greek and Latin and French poetry but British poetry also, and which restricts us when we're too stern about following their modes, and put it into something which will be far more liberating to the mind and the spirit of man, if I'm going to be philosophic in that sense. Back of it all, that is the theory. And for that, you have to go into structure, the structure of the line itself.

And you have to build your little model and finally try it out, here and there, and if at the age of sixty-seven, you get a little publicity in the *New York Times Books*, why you're a great man [*laughs*]. You see how important it is [*laughs*]. But the basic thing has nothing to do with that, God help us! Nothing in the world! It's nice to get a prize, it's a little tickling, it's embarrassing, but it's a little bit silly, if I *must* say it [*laughs*], with due respect to my benefactors [*laughs*]. . . .

On the American Idiom

[Williams:] This seemed to me to be what a poem was for, to speak for us in a language we can understand. . . . We must know it as our own, we must be satisfied that it speaks for us. And yet it must remain a language like all languages, a symbol of communication (*ND 17*, p. 254)

The Writer

Obviously the first thing to do is to extablish a department of the American language: a Chair, that is, of our language which would have primacy over the teachings of all other languages at the university. Under this would come other languages bearing on our own: German, French, Spanish, Portuguese, and of course, English.

Second, we should have to differentiate a modern prosody or method of construction of the poem from the conventional English and French modes which are standard for those languages. We should have to insist that English prosody as established by English custom . . . is a purely arbitrary matter wholly unrelated to our own language or necessity.

This is most important, for until we disabuse ourselves of the notion that English prosody is an inevitable and God-given rule for us as for the English, we shall remain impotent.

Next we must establish in our minds the historical fact that the American Language invaded both English and French in the nineteenth century. . . .

The invasion, the modification of Yeats' corpus by the direct criticisms of Ezra Pound, Joyce (who never failed to read his Paris edition of the *Herald-Tribune* lest he miss the sayings of Andy Gump), Gertrude Stein, Hemingway, etc., etc. The thing to bear in mind is that it is the American language penetrating the European literary modes which should be studied. (*GG, U*)

Poetry is in a chaotic stage. We have to reject the standard forms of English verse and put ourselves into chaos on purpose, in order to discover new constellations of the elements of verse in our time. We have to break down poetry into its elements just as the chemists and physicists are doing. In order to realize ourselves. In order to reform the elements. (*B*). . .

On Short Stories

Interviewer: Did you write the short stories on a different "level" than the poems—as a kind of interlude to them?

Williams: No, as an alternative. They were written in the form of a conversation which I was partaking in. We were in it together.

Interviewer: Then the composition of them was just as casual and spontaneous as you have suggested. You would come home in the evening and write twelve pages or so without revising?

Williams: I think so. I was coming *home*. I was placing myself in continuation of a common conversation. . . .

On Writing

Q: What would you say about the mental and physical condition of the poet? What is his condition when he writes his best work?

A: It doesn't make any difference where he is—whether he's alone, as some might like to be, or whether he's in the next room, as Mozart liked to be with a dance going on, writing independently, and feeling alone. Certainly when he writes, he is feeling intensely himself, in whatever place he happens to be. And, I'm sufficient of a doctor to know that no one can do any good work unless the supply of oxygen to his brain is so intense that he can do his best work. In my case it's not in a dreamy, relaxed state whatever, but in a tense state, that the best work occurs. It might be when you're fatigued. Perhaps fatigue is an anesthetic, lets the body go to some unimportant place, lets the faculties come out sharply and dominate the whole psychosomatic picture. I think the psychic element must dominate, and your body be secondary, but tense. . . .

Paris Review Interview with Williams*

Williams: Well, what's to be done?

Interviewer: I would like to ask you about this new measure that I see here—

Williams: If I could only talk.

Interviewer: Perhaps we might begin with Rutherford, whether you thought it was a good environment for you.

Williams: A very—bad environment—for poets. We didn't take anything seriously—in Ruth—in Rutherford. We didn't take poetry very seriously. As far as recording my voice in Rutherford—I read before the ladies, mostly.

Interviewer: You mean the Women's Club? How did they like it?

Williams: Very much: they applauded. I was quite a hero [*Picking up a volume*] I remember "By the Road to the Contagious Hospital" was one of the ones I read. The hospital was up in Clifton. I was always intent on saying what I had to say in the accents that were native to me. But I didn't know what I was doing. I knew that the measure was intended to record—something. But I didn't know what the measure was. I stumbled all over the place in those earlier poems. For instance, in this one here [*"Queen-Anne's Lace"*]. I would divide those lines differently now. It's just like the later line, only not opened up in the same way.

Interviewer: You were saying that Rutherford was a bad environment for poets.

Williams: Yes. But except for my casual conversations about the town, I didn't think anything of it at all. I had a great amount of patience with artisans.

*From "William Carlos Williams," in *Writers at Work: The Paris Review Interviews*, third series, ed. George Plimpton (New York: Viking Penguin, 1967), 7–17. ©1967 by the Paris Review, Inc. All rights reserved. Reprinted by permission of Viking Penguin Inc.

Interviewer: Did you mean it when you said medicine was an interference which you resented?

Williams: I didn't resent it at all. I just wanted to go straight ahead.

Interviewer: And medicine was not on the way?

Williams: I don't know whether it would be. I used to give readings at the high school and Fairleigh Dickinson. I was sympathetic with these audiences. I was talking about the same people that I had to do with as patients, and trying to interest them. I was not pretending: I was speaking to them as if they were interested in the same sort of thing.

Interviewer: But were they? Perhaps they felt the double nature of your role, as both poet and doctor, was something of a barrier.

Williams: No, no. The language itself was what intrigued me. I thought that we were on common territory there.

Interviewer: Did you write the short stories on a different "level" than the poems—as a kind of interlude to them?

Williams: No, as an alternative. They were written in the form of a conversation which I was partaking in. We were in it together.

Interviewer: Then the composition of them was just as casual and spontaneous as you have suggested. You would come home in the evening and write twelve pages or so without revising?

Williams: I think so. I was coming *home.* I was placing myself in continuation of a common conversation.

Interviewer: You have insisted that there cannot be a seeking for words in literature. Were you speaking of prose as well as poetry?

Williams: I think so. Not to choose between words.

Interviewer: Certainly the word does matter though.

Williams: It does matter, very definitely. Strange that I could say that.

Interviewer: But when you had come home, and were continuing the experience of reality—

Williams: Reality. Reality. My vocabulary was chosen out of the intensity of my concern. When I was talking in front of a group, I wasn't interested in impressing them with my power of speech, but only with the seriousness of my intentions toward them. I had to make them come alive.

Interviewer: You have said you felt trapped in Rutherford, that you couldn't get out, never had any contact with anyone here. Do you still feel that Rutherford hasn't provided enough of the contact you managed to find during the twenties, in New York, with the Others group? Was that a genuine contribution to your development?

Williams: That was not a literary thing exactly. But it was about writing—intensely so. We were speaking straight ahead about what concerned us, and if I could have overheard what I was saying then, that would have given me a hint of how to phrase myself, to say what I had to say. Not after the establishment, but speaking straight ahead. I would gladly have traded what I have tried to say, for what came off my tongue, naturally.

Interviewer: Which was not the same?

Williams: Not free enough. What came off in this writing, finally— *this* writing [*pointing to "The Descent"*]–that was pretty much what I wanted to say, in the way I wanted to say it, then. I was searching in this congeries. I wanted to say something in a certain tone of my voice which would be exactly how I wanted to say it, to measure it in a certain way.

Interviewer: Was this in line with what the others in the group were trying to do?

Williams: I don't think they knew what they were trying to do; but in effect it was. I couldn't speak like the academy. It had to be modified by the conversation about me. As Marianne Moore used to say, a language dogs and cats could understand. So I think she agrees with me fundamentally. Not the speech of English country people, which would have something artificial about it; not that, but language modified by *our* environment; the American environment.

Interviewer: Your own background is pretty much a mixture of English and Spanish, isn't it? Do you think the Spanish has had any influence on your work?

Williams: There might have been a permanent impression on my mind. It was certainly different from the French. French is too formal; the Spanish language isn't. They were broad men, as in *El Cid*, very much broader than the French. My relation to language was a curious thing. My father was English, but Spanish was spoken in my home. I didn't speak it, but I was read to in Spanish. My mother's relatives used to come up and stay two or three months.

Interviewer: You have said you equated Spanish with the "romantic." Is that a designation you would shrink from?

Williams: No, not shrink from.

Interviewer: What I was getting at is that you have kept the name "Carlos."

Williams: I had no choice but to keep the "Carlos."

Interviewer: I understand Solomon Hoheb, your mother's father, was Dutch.

Williams: Maybe. The Spanish came from the Sephardic Jews. Though the English was strong indeed, through my grandfather.

Interviewer: You've been more conscious of the Spanish, then, than of the other.

Williams: Yes! I've insisted on breaking with my brother's memory of the Williamses as English. All one needs to do is look at my nose. Flossie says, "I love your nose." And the hell with my nose, after all. The thing that concerns me is the theory of what I was determined to do with measure, what you encounter on the page. It must be transcribed to the page from the lips of the poet, as it was with such a master as Sappho. "The Descent" was very important to me in that way.

Interviewer: You mean that is where it finally happened?

Williams: Yes, there it happened; and before that it didn't. I remember writing this (*trying to read*):

The descent beckons
     as the ascent beckoned.
          Memory is a kind . . .

Interviewer: . . .*of accomplishment.*

Williams: *A sort of renewal*
               even
an initiation, since the spaces it opens are new places.

You see how I run that line? I was very much excited when I wrote this. I had to do something. I was sitting there with the typewriter in front of me. I was attempting to imitate myself (I think I can't even see it at all) but it didn't come alive to me.

The Writer

Interviewer: It seems to me you were reading it just now.

Williams: More or less. But something went wrong with me. I can't make it out any more. I can't type.

Interviewer: Would a tape recorder or a dictaphone be uncongenial?

Williams: No, anything that would serve me I'd gladly adopt.

Interviewer: The appearance of this poem on the page suggests you were conscious of it as a thing—something for the eye.

Williams: Yes, very good. I was conscious of making it even. I wanted it to read regularly.

Interviewer: Not just to please the eye?

Williams: The total effect is very important.

Interviewer: But the care in placing the words—did you ever feel you would be as happy painting?

Williams: I'd like to have been a painter, and it would have given me at least as great a satisfaction as being a poet.

Interviewer: But you say you are a "word man."

Williams: Yes, that took place early in my development. I was early inducted into my father's habit of reading—that made me a poet, not a painter. My mother was a painter. Her brother Carlos won the Grand Prix—the Gros Lot it was called—then he financed her to go to Paris, to study painting. Then the money ran out.

Interviewer: And she met your father through Carlos, whom he knew in—

Williams: —Puerto Plata. My father was a businessman, interested in South America. But he always loved books. He used to read poetry to me. Shakespeare. He had a group who used to come to our house, a Shakespeare club. They did dramatic readings. So I was always interested in Shakespeare, and Grandmother was interested in the stage—my father's mother, Emily Dickinson, her name was. Isn't that amazing?

Interview: Quite a coincidence: I notice a picture of her namesake over the desk.

Williams: Emily was my patron saint. She was also an American, seeking to divide the line in some respectable way. We were all of us Americans.

138

Interviewer: Than you did read a good bit of her at some stage, with your father?

Williams: My father didn't know anything about Emily Dickinson. He was sold on Shakespeare. [*Doorbell rings. WCW makes his way downstairs to answer it.*]

Interviewer [*As he returns*]: You say you were hoping it might be the new volume?

Williams: Yes. I am keenly disappointed. But that's always the way it is with me—my life's blood dripping away. Laughlin has been a wonderful friend, but it's always so goddam *slow*! I have still the illusion that I will be able to talk when I make these connections. It's possible, because I am an emotional creature, and if I could only talk, to you for instance. Here is a person well-intentioned toward me, meaning yourself, and I can't talk to him. It makes me furious.

Interviewer: It's good of you to put up with this business at all. We were talking about painting and the theater and poetry. Was that a natural progression for you?

Williams: More or less; stemming from frustration. I was wondering—I was seeking to be articulate.

Interviewer: At one point you wanted to be an actor.

Williams: I had no skill as an actor. But through Dad's reading, the plays of Shakespeare made an impresson on me. He didn't *want* them to necessarily, just to read them—as words, that came off as speech.

Interviewer: How did this interest in words make you interested in poetry as opposed, say, to writing novels?

Williams: That didn't have any connection.

Interviewer: The words weren't sufficiently important in prose?

Williams: No. I never thought I was a very good prose writer anyway. But when I speak of Emily Dickinson—she was an independent spirit. She did her best to get away from too strict an interpretation. And she didn't want to be confined to rhyme or reason. (Even in Shakespeare, the speech of the players: it was annoying to him to have to rhyme, for Godsake.) And she followed the American idiom. She didn't know it, but she followed it nonetheless. I was a better poet.

Interviewer: You are speaking about language now, not form.

Williams: Yes, her native speech. She was a wild girl. She chafed against restraint. But she speaks the spoken language, the idiom, which would be deformed by Oxford English.

Interviewer: This new measure of yours, in the later poems, is meant then to accomodate the American speech rhythms.

Williams: Yes. It's a strange phenomenon, my writing. I think what I have been searching for—

Interviewer: You were suggesting that Emily Dickinson had something to do with it; and her objection to rhyme. But that you were a better poet.

Williams: Oh, yes [*laughing*]. She was a real good guy. I thought I was a better poet because the American idiom was so close to me, and she didn't get what the poets were doing at that time—writing according to a new method, not the English method, which wouldn't have made much sense to an American. Whitman was on the right track, but when he switched to the English intonation, and followed the English method of recording the feet, he didn't realize it was a different method, which was not satisfactory to an American. Everything started with Shakespeare.

Interviewer: Because it was meant to be spoken?

Williams: Yes. But when the Shakespearean line was recorded, it was meant to be a formal thing, divided in the English method according to what was written on the page. The Americans shouldn't tolerate that. An Englishman—an English rhetorician, an actor—will speak like Shakespeare, but it's only rhetorical. He can't be true to his own speech. He has to change it in order to conform.

Interviewer: You think it is easier for the English to conform, in poetry, to their kind of speech pattern than it is for an American? You don't think for example that Frost is as true to the American idiom as you are trying to be?

Williams: No, I don't think so. Eliot, on the other hand, was trying to find a way to record the speech and he didn't find it. He wanted to be regular, to be true to the American idiom, but he didn't find a way to do it. One has to bow down finally, either to the English or to the American.

Interviewer: Eliot went to England; you stayed here.

Williams: To my sorrow.

Interviewer: To your sorrow? What do you mean by that?

Williams [*yielding, perhaps*]: It is better to stick to something.

Interviewer: It's rare to find someone who has. Eliot says he would not be the same if he had stayed. You have said there was a great virtue in the kind of isolation you experienced here.

Williams: A key question.

Interviewer: And you have been called our most valuable home spun sensitivity.

Williams: "Homespun sensitivity." Very good.

Interviewer: But you still feel it was a bad environment.

Williams: It was native, but I doubt that it was very satisfactory to me personally. Though it did provide the accent which satisfied me.

Interviewer: Do you think you could have picked a better one? Do you think you would have been happier in Boston, or Hartford, or New York, or Paris?

Williams: I might have picked a better one, if I had wanted to—which I did. But if I lived there—if its language was familiar to me, if that was the kind of conversation which I heard, which I grew up with—I could tolerate the vulgarity because it forced me to speak in a particular manner. Not the English intonation.

Interviewer: Do you still feel that the English influence on Eliot set us back twenty years?

Williams: Very definitely. He was a conformist. He wanted to go back to the iambic pentameter; and he did go back to it, very well; but he didn't acknowledge it.

Interviewer: You say that you could never be a calm speaker, so that this unit you use, which isn't either a foot or a line necessarily, and which works by speech impulses, this is meant to reflect also your own nervous habit of speech—in which things come more or less in a rush.

Williams: Common sense would force me to work out some such method.

Interviewer: You do pause, though, in the midst of these lines.

Williams: Very definitely.

Interviewer: Then what is the integrity of the line?

The Writer

Williams: If I was consistent in myself it would be very much more effective than it is now. I would have followed much closer to the indicated divisions of the line than I did. It's too haphazard.

Interviewer: The poetry? You admit that in prose, but—

Williams: —in poetry also. I think I was too haphazard.

Interviewer: In the later poems—like "The Orchestra" here—you think there is still some work to do?

Williams: It's not successful. It would be classical if it had the proper division of lines. "Reluctant mood," "stretches and yawns." What the devil is that? It isn't firmly enough stated. It's all very complicated—but I can't go on.

Interviewer: You mean you can't find a theory to explain what you do naturally.

Williams: Yes. It's all in the ear. I wanted to be regular. To continue that—

Interviewer [*picking up a copy of* Paterson V, *from which some clippings fall to the floor*]: These opening lines—they make an image on the page.

Williams: Yes, I was imitating the flight of the bird.

Interviewer: Then it's directed—

Williams: —to the eyes. Read it.

Interviewer: "In old age the mind casts off. . ."

Williams: *In old age*
                the mind
                        casts off
                    rebelliously
                an eagle
        from its crag

Interviewer: Did you ever think of using any other city as subject for a poem?

Williams: I didn't dare any mention of it in *Paterson*, but I thought strongly of Manhattan when I was looking about for a city to celebrate. I thought it was not particularized enough for me, not American in the sense I wanted. It was near enough, God knows, and I was familiar enough with it for all my purposes—but so was Leipzig, where I lived

142

for a year when I was young, or Paris. Or even Vienna or even Frascati. But Manhattan escaped me.

Interviewer: Someone remarks in one of these clippings that there is no reason the poem should ever end. Part Four completes the cycle, Five renews it. Then what?

Williams [*laughing*]: Go on repeating it. At the end—the last part, the dance—

Interviewer: "We can know nothing but the dance. . ."

Williams: *The dance.*

> *To dance to a measure*
> *contrapuntally,*
> *Satyrically, the tragic foot.*

That has to be interpreted; but how are you going to interpret it?

Interviewer: I don't presume to interpret it; but perhaps the satyrs represent the element of freedom, of energy within the form.

Williams: Yes. The satyrs are understood as action, a dance. I always think of the Indians there.

Interviewer: Is anything implied, in "contrapuntally," about the nature of the foot?

Williams: It means "musically"—it's a musical image. The Indians had a beat in their own music, which they beat with their feet. It isn't an image exactly, a poetic image. Or perhaps it is. The beat goes according to the image. It should all be so simple; but with my damaged brain—

Interviewer: We probably shouldn't be trying to reduce a poetic statement to prose, when we have *The Desert Music* here: "Only the poem. . ."

Williams: "The counted poem, to an exact measure."

Interviewer: You think it should be more exact then, than you have yet made it.

Williams: Yes, it should be more exact, in Milton's sense. Milton counted the syllables.

Interviewer: "And I could not help thinking of the wonders of the brain that hears that music."

Williams: Yes.

Part 3

THE CRITICS

Introduction: El Hombre

Williams invited his short story workshop students to "go ahead and dig," see what they could haul up with their buckets or thumb. As Williams scholarship has shown over the past fifty years, and particularly the last twenty-five years since his death, the "mother-lode" shows no sign of running out. As the partial survey of criticism in part 1 shows, and as Paul L. Mariani discusses fully in *William Carlos Williams: The Poet and His Critics* (Chicago, 1975), the vein of Williams's poetry is so rich that only a relative few have started to mine the riches of his fiction—short and long.

As the following selections demonstrate, however, attention is being paid to Williams's short stories, and by some very imaginative, insightful and caring critics. Robert Coles and Richard E. Peschel give especially intriguing evidence of Williams's presence as a physician/writer among his physician/writer colleagues; Joseph E. Slate, James E. B. Breslin, and Warren Tallman lay claim to some of the earliest commentary about Williams's stories and establish the standard of excellence that subsequent critics like George Monteiro, Marjorie Perloff and others meet—and continue. Philip Rahv remains provocative decades after he first tried to find and identify Williams *in* his short stories. All of these critics give hard-headed, clear-eyed respect and finally homage to "El Hombre," who like the ancient star shining luminously in his poem of that title gives "strange courage" to the critic who, perhaps, needs it most of all.

Doctor Stories

*Robert Coles**

"Outside / outside myself / there is a world," the poet of *Paterson* declares himself to have "rumbled," and then notes that such a world was
"subject" to his "incursions," and was one he made it his business to
"approach concretely." No question he did, with all the directness,
earthiness, and urgent immediacy of a doctor who knows life itself to
be at stake—someone else's, and in a way (professional, moral) his own
as well. I remember the doctor describing his work, telling stories that
were real events, wondering in retrospect how he did it, kept going at
such a pace, hauled himself so many miles a day, got himself up so
many stairs, persisted so long and hard with families who had trouble,
often enough, using English, never mind paying their bills. And as he
knew, and sometimes had to say out loud, even mention in his writing,
it wasn't as if he was loaded with money, or a writer who took in big
royalties.

America's Depression was a disaster for Dr. Williams' patients, and
many of them never paid him much, if indeed, anything at all. America's Depression was also a time when a marvelously versatile, knowing, and gifted writer who happened to be a full-time doctor was not
having any great success with critics, especially the powerful ones who
claimed for themselves the imprimatur of the academy. No wonder this
writing doctor was glad to go "outside" himself, greet and try to com-
prehend a world other than that of literary people. No wonder, too, he
shunned the possibility of a relatively plush Manhattan practice—the
doctor to well-known cultural figures. His patients may have been obscure, down and out, even illiterate by the formal testing standards of
one or another school system, but they were, he had figured out early
on, a splendidly vital people—full of important experiences to tell,
memories to recall, ideas to try on their most respected of visitors, the
busy doc who yet could be spellbound by what he chanced to hear,

*Excerpted from the introduction to *William Carlos Williams: The Doctor Stories*, compiled by Robert Coles (New York: New Directions, 1984), x–xvi. ©1984 by Robert
Coles. Reprinted by permission of New Directions Publishing Corp.

and knew to keep in mind at night when the typewriter replaced the stethoscope as his major professional instrument.

I remember asking Williams the usual, dreary question—one I hadn't stopped to realize he'd been asked a million or so times before: how did he do it, manage two full-time careers so well and for so long? His answer was quickly forthcoming, and rendered with remarkable tact and patience, given the provocation: "It's no strain. In fact, the one [medicine] nourishes the other [writing], even if at times I've groaned to the contrary." If he had sometimes complained that he felt drained, overworked, denied the writing time he craved, needed, he would not forget for long all the sustaining, healing, inspiring moments a profession—a calling, maybe, it was in his life—had given him: moment upon moment in the course of more than four decades of medical work.

Such moments are the stuff of these "doctor stories"—the best of their kind since Dr. Anton Chekhov did his (late nineteenth-century) storytelling. As one goes through Williams' evocation of a twentieth-century American medical practice, the sheer daring of the literary effort soon enough comes to mind—the nerve he had to say what he says. These are brief talks, or accounts meant to register disappointment, frustration, confusion, perplexity; or, of course, enchantment, pleasure, excitement, strange or surprising or simple and not at all surprising satisfaction. These are stories that tell of mistakes, of errors of judgment; and as well, of one modest breakthrough, then another—not in research efforts of major clinical projects, but in that most important of all situations, the would-be healer face-to-face with the sufferer who half desires, half dreads the stranger's medical help. As I heard Dr. Williams once say: "Even when the patients knew me well, and trusted me a lot, I could sense their fear, their skepticism. And why not? I could sense my own worries, my own doubts!"

He has the courage to share in these stories such raw and usually unacknowledged turmoil with his readers—even as he took after himself in an almost Augustinian kind of self-scrutiny toward the end of the second book of *Paterson*. In almost every story the doctor is challenged not only by his old, familiar antagonist, disease, but that other foe whose continuing power is a given for all of us—pride in all its forms, disguises, assertions. It is this "unreflecting egoism," as George Eliot called it, which the doctor-narrator of these stories allows us to see, and so doing, naturally, we are nudged closer to ourselves. Narcissism, as we of this era have learned to call the sin of pride, knows no barriers of race or class—of occupation or profession, either. But as ministers and doctors occasionally realize, there is a sad, inevitable irony at work in their lives—the preacher flawed in precisely the respect he denounces during his sermons, the doctor ailing even as he tries to heal others.

Williams knew the special weakness we all have for those who have a moral hold on us, for those who attend us in our life-and-death times. Williams knew, too, that such a vulnerability prompts gullibility, an abject surrender of one's personal authority—and the result is not only the jeopardy of the parishioner or the patient, but the priest or the physician. Arrogance is the other side of eager acquiescence. Presumptuousness and self-importance are the wounds this life imposes upon those privy to the wounds of others. The busy, capable doctor, well aware of all the burdens he must carry, and not in the least inclined to shirk his duties, may stumble badly in those small moral moments that constantly press upon him or her—the nature of a hello or good-bye, the tone of voice as a question is asked or answered, the private thoughts one has, and the effect they have on our face, our hands as they do their work, our posture, our gait. "There's nothing like a difficult patient to show us ourselves," Williams once said to a medical student, and then he expanded the observation further: "I would learn so much on my rounds, or making home visits. At times I felt like a thief because I heard words, lines, saw people and places—and used it all in my writing. I guess I've told people that, and no one's so surprised! There was something deeper going on, though—the *force* of all those encounters. I was put off guard again and again, and the result was—well, a descent into myself."

He laughed as he said that, and worried about a comparison he nevertheless proceeded to make—with the achievement of "insight" in psychoanalysis. I say "worried" because he knew rather well that he had in mind a moral as well as psychological or emotional confrontation, and he'd been hearing a lot in those last years of his life (to his amazement and chagrin) about a supposedly "value-free" psychoanalysis or social science. Not that he couldn't put aside his anger and disgust and simply laugh at his own pretensions and spells of blindness, at those of others. These stories abound with such self-mocking gestures—parody turned on the parodist, words used to take the stern (but also compassionate) measure of the doctor who dispensed (among other things) words, and then went home to dish them out—well, "in the American grain." It is important to emphasize the humorous and tolerant side of this storytelling self-arraignment of a singular New Jersey doctor: even the terribly hurt, driven, melancholy "Old Doc Rivers" is not without his spirited decency—a dizzying mix of selfless honor, passionate concern, and alas, the unrestrained demonic constantly at work.

These stories are, really, frank confidences extended to the rest of us by one especially knowing, dedicated physician who was willing to use his magical gifts of storytelling in a gesture of—what? We all require forgiveness, and we all hope to redeem our own missteps—hope, through whatever grace is granted us, to make every possible reparation. Words were the instrument of grace given to this one doctor, and words are the instrument of grace, also, for the rest of us, the readers who have and will come upon these marvelously provocative tales. As Dr. Williams' beloved wife Flossie (she appears now and then in these medical fictions) once said to me: "There's little in a doctor's life Bill didn't get at when he wrote." She'd been there with him, of course, all along, and she knew: the periods of irritability and impatience; the flashes of annoyance and resentment; the instance of greed, or just plain bitterness that "they" can't, don't, won't pay up; the surge of affection—even desire, lust; the assertion of power—a fierce wish to control, to tell in no uncertain terms, to win at all costs; the tiredness, the exhaustion, the despondency. The rush of it all, the fast-paced struggle, again and again, with all sorts of illnesses—and the victories over them, the defeats at their hands, and not least, the realization (postmortem) of one's limitations, one's mistakes.

For years I have been teaching these doctor stories to medical students, and during each class we all seem newly awakened—encouraged to ask the important whys, consider the perplexing ifs. The stories offer medical students and their teachers an opportunity to discuss the big things, so to speak, of the physician's life—the great unmentionables that are, yet, everyday aspects of doctoring: the prejudices we feel (and feel ashamed of), the moments of spite or malice we try to overlook, the ever loaded question of money, a matter few of us like to discuss, yet one constantly stirring us to pleasure, to bedeviling disappointment in others, in ourselves. What, in fact, that is really important has Williams left out? Nothing, it seems. He gives us a chance to discuss the alcoholic doctor, the suicidal doctor. He prompts us to examine our ambitions, our motives, our aspirations, our purposes, our worrying lapses, our grave errors, our overall worth. He gives us permission to bare our souls, to be candidly introspective, but not least, to smile at ourselves, to be grateful for the continuing opportunity we have to make recompense for our failures of omission or commission.

He extends to us, really, moments of a doctor's self-recognition—rendered in such a way that the particular becomes the universal, and the instantly recognizable: the function, the great advantage of all first-rate art. And not to be forgotten in this age of glib, overwrought formulations, of theories and more theories, of conceptualizations meant to explain (and explain away) anything and everything, he brings to us ironies, paradoxes, inconsistencies, contradictions—the small vignette which opens up a world of pleasurable, startling, or forbidden mystery. Doc Williams becomes William Carlos Williams the accomplished fabulist, anecdotist—and as well, the medical and social historian who takes the risks of autobiography. . . .

. . . On a few occasions physicians invited him to come speak at their conferences, their grand rounds, but he was shy, modest—afraid he had little to say directly to his colleagues, no matter how much he'd offered the world in general through his many and varied writings. But he was dead wrong; he had everything to say to us. He opens up the whole world, our world, to us—and so, once again, as many in New Jersey had occasion to say during the first half of this century, say and say again: thank you, Doctor Williams.

When a Doctor Hates a Patient: Case History, Literary Histories

*Richard E. Peschel, M. D., and Enid Rhodes Peschel**

Generally, physicians have a variety of emotions about their patients. Some they really like; others they may not like but still regard sympathetically because of their illnesses. In a few rare instances, however, a doctor actually hates a patient and yet is forced to take care of that patient. That is what happened to me (R.E.P.) in one case when I was an intern.

*From the *Michigan Quarterly Review* 23, no. 3 (Summer 1984):402–7, 410. Reprinted by permission.

Richard E. Peschel, M.D. and Enid Rhodes Peschel

Case History: "Queenie"

Over a period of several years, one of the most infamous patients in our hospital was "Queenie." "Queenie," in fact, was the nickname the hospital staff had given her. A fifty-two-year-old female who suffered from chronic kidney failure, "Queenie" was on peritoneal dialysis. Not only does peritoneal dialysis demand very careful medical management by doctors, it also requires a lot of cooperation from patients who must monitor their diet and fluid intake. Patients on peritoneal dialysis come to the hospital to be dialyzed as out-patients several times a week; they only have to become in-patients when they get in trouble. Without their dialysis, they would die within a matter of days.

When patients on dialysis don't pay strict attention to their diet, they often need immediate hospitalization with around-the-clock dialysis and meticulous medical monitoring in order to correct their fluid over-load and metabolic status. Since "Queenie" habitually broke all the rules of her diet (for instance, she would eat enormous quantities of salt), she required periodic hospitalization.

Some time during my second month as an intern, "Queenie" was admitted to my service. At that time I was working in the Intensive Care Unit (ICU). Naturally all the nurses there knew "Queenie." In fact, when I was going down to the Emergency Room (ER) to pick her up, all the nurses warned me that she was one of the most difficult and obnoxious patients anyone could ever have.

But I wasn't really prepared for just how bad she was.

The first thing I noticed after "Queenie" settled into the ICU was that she was chewing a big plug of tobacco and periodically spitting tobacco juice on the bed. Being naive, I asked the nurses to take her tobacco away. They told me that they knew from past experience that if "Queenie" didn't have her tobacco she would refuse to let anyone do anything. In fact, they said, when they had taken her tobacco away in the past, she had sat on her bed and screamed and cursed and re-fused to let any doctor examine her or even come near her. And so they advised me, one had to bribe her with tobacco in order to try to take care of her. I, therefore, had to agree to let "Queenie" keep chewing tobacco and spitting tobacco juice on the bed so that I could examine her.

Meeting her was something less than a pleasure. Because of her fluid overload, she was in congestive heart failure and therefore very short of breath. But even though she could barely breathe, she insisted upon chewing tobacco and firing out its juice like venom or a barrage of gunfire.

Examining her was all but impossible. Because she refused to co-operate, I could not listen to her lungs properly. The few times I gently tried to force her to do something—like roll onto her side—she made a fist and threatened to hit me.

"Queenie" would not even cooperate verbally. Whenever I asked a question, she would refuse to answer, but not because she was short of breath, for at random intervals she fired out volleys of the vilest obscenities. Although initially I had felt a great sympathy for this woman and her condition, after several rounds of her obscenities, I began to feel a rage within me which I had to struggle to control.

Finally I gave up trying to examine her properly (I had done all I could) and told the ICU nurses to begin her intensive peritoneal dialysis. They were very reluctant to proceed because during the past year "Queenie" had sent two ICU nurses to the ER: she had bitten them and had broken through their skin. (An adult mouthbite can produce a serious infection.) Naturally, all the nurses were frightened of her and did not want to take care of her. But they had no choice.

Over the next few days, I came to hate taking care of this obnoxious patient. I found that the only way "Queenie" would let me do anything at all was if I threatened to take away her tobacco.

After three days we finally discharged her. That was about all I could stand of her anyway.

Some three weeks later, "Queenie" was admitted again for the same problem. On this occasion, when I was drawing blood from her, she tried to bite me. After that, she tried to pull the needle from my hand and in so doing, knocked down all the samples I had already drawn. The tubes broke and blood splattered on the floor. Which meant that I had to draw her bloods all over again. . . .

A few weeks later, "Queenie" was admitted again for the same problem. Because she was in the hospital, she had to adhere to a very low salt and fluid-restricted diet. (She was supposed to be on that kind of diet all the time anyway.) But she obviously hated her diet, and so when the people from the diet service came to remove her tray after each meal, she would either spit at them or hurl a fork or knife their way.

Needless to say, taking care of someone like that was very trying. Your natural urges were to choke her to death. In fact, it gave me a lot of relief to fantasize how I would kill her.

Over the year, I had to minister to "Queenie" about four times. Each time was an indescribable ordeal of exercising patience and self-control to prevent my anger from surfacing. Always I had to smother my rage in order to maintain an objective approach to her medical problems. Still, every time she was admitted to our hospital, "Queenie" got from all of us the best of modern medical care that carried her through another crisis. As professionals, the doctors and nurses refused to let personal feelings interfere with the proper medical management of her case. But each time, each one of us must have secretly been imaging her murder thousands of times over.

After my internship, I never had to take care of "Queenie" again. About two years later, I learned from the medical housestaff that she had finally died. I guess my predominant feeling was one of frustration, as though I had been thwarted in my desire for revenge.

Do other doctors sometimes hate their patients?

We find [a] fascinating [case] recounted by . . . William Carlos Williams. . . .

Literary History . . .: William Carlos Williams

The eminent poet William Carlos Williams (1883–1963) received his M.D. from the University of Pennsylvania in 1906. Four years later, he returned to his home town of Rutherford, New Jersey, to practice medicine—and writing. "When they ask me . . . how I have for so many years continued an equal interest in medicine and the poem, I reply that they amount for me to nearly the same thing," he wrote in his *Autobiography*. Williams stayed in active medical practice until 1951, when a stroke forced him to stop.

Williams spent part of his internship at Nursery and Child's Hospital ("Sixty-first Street and Tenth Avenue . . . just across Tenth from the most notorious block in the New York criminal West Side, San Juan Hill or Hell's Kitchen, as you preferred to call it"). There he did a lot of pediatrics. "I was fascinated by it and knew at once that that was my field," he said. In his works we sense his fascination for children, even—and perhaps even especially—for the most difficult and obstreperous ones. Mathilda in "The Use of Force," from his collected stories, *The Farmers' Daughters*, is such a case.

In this story, the doctor-narrator goes to the patient's house. The mother, father and girl, "an unusually attractive little thing, and as strong as a heifer in appearance," are huddled in the kitchen for warmth. Just from looking at Mathilda the doctor knows that she has a high fever. She has been sick for three days but has been denying that her throat hurts. The doctor and Mathilda's parents are concerned because they know there have been several cases of diphtheria in Mathilda's school. But Mathilda absolutely refuses to let the doctor examine her throat. Not only that: when he moves his chair closer to her, she tries to claw his eyes and, in so doing, knocks his glasses onto the floor. It becomes a battle.

> If you don't do what the doctor says you'll have to go to the hospital, the mother admonished her severely.
> Oh yeah? [the doctor thought.] I had to smile to myself. After all, I had already fallen in love with the savage brat.

Despite his "love" for Mathilda, the doctor finally grows furious with her.

> I grasped the child's head with my left hand and tried to get the wooden tongue depressor between her teeth. She fought, with clenched teeth, desperately! But now I also had grown furious—at a child. I tried to hold myself down but I couldn't.

When he finally gets the tongue depressor behind Mathilda's last teeth, she bites down so hard that she reduces it to splinters. He orders the mother to give him a smooth-handled spoon.

The doctor's anger is now beyond control. Rationally he knows that if he leaves and returns in about an hour, he'll probably be able to examine the girl. But he also realizes that he now relishes his anger and hate: "the worst of it was that I too had got beyond reason. I could have torn the child apart in my own fury and enjoyed it. It was a pleasure to attack her. My face was burning with it." Naturally, the physician tries to rationalize his behavior to himself. "The damned little brat must be protected against her own idiocy, one says to one's self at such times. Others must be protected against her," etc. But he knows that there is more: not only his own fury and desire for muscular release, but also his shame at being defeated by a child.

> [A] blind fury, a feeling of adult shame, bred of a longing for muscular release are the operatives. One goes on to the end.

Richard E. Peschel, M.D. and Enid Rhodes Peschel

> In a final unreasoning assault I overpowered the child's neck and
> jaws. I forced the heavy silver spoon back of her teeth and down her
> throat until she gagged.

And there he sees it: her tonsils covered with membrane, the terrible
sore throat she had been hiding and denying for days.

In the end, the doctor is glad of his victory, yet he also feels com-
passion for the child's defeat. In his final words, we sense his triumph
as well as his sympathy for Mathilda: "She had been on the defensive
before but now she attacked. Tried to get off her father's lap and fly at
me while tears of defeat blinded her eyes."

For several reasons, Williams's hatred toward his pediatric patient
does not remain. First, he has conquered this seemingly unconquer-
able creature. Second, though he has vented his anger on her, he has
the satisfaction of finding her unhealthy. Thus the negative implications of an act potentially comparable to rape (the story's title alerts us
to this hideous violation) are safely dissipated. Third, his feelings
about her are ambivalent: a combination of hate and love, resentment
and admiration. The doctor always reminds himself that this patient is
just a child, smaller and weaker than he. We sense that the doctor-
narrator likes this patient's wildness, willfulness and stubborness as
much as—or maybe even more than—he hates it. Perhaps it reminds
him of something fierce and persistent in himself: of that very fierce-
ness and persistency by which he eventually conquers his patient. . . .

Reflections

William Carlos Williams, who felt love and hate for the fierce-fighting
Mathilda, vented his anger on her and conquered her. . . . [He] could
feel ambivalent or guilty about [his] anger precisely because [he] had
expressed it.

My own case is different. Since I never did vent my anger on
"Queenie" (except in my multitudinous private fantasies), I do not
feel guilty for having hated her and for continuing to hate her even
now, years after her death. But I do feel sad about it and wish my
recollections could be otherwise.

Naturally, I do feel sympathy for other people on dialysis and for
other patients suffering from a variety of medical, sociological or psychological ills. But not for "Queenie," who always received the best of

modern medical care and who always tried to disgrace, disgust or destroy the medical staff assigned to care for her.

It is distasteful to think that a physician can hate a sick patient. But
a doctor—like any other person—is also a human being who sometimes, when pushed to the extreme, returns hate for hate. It is not a
praiseworthy reaction, but perhaps an understandable one. In fact, on
those rare instances when a doctor is forced to take care of a particularly
abusive patient, hate may be the only refuge or defense the physician
has left. And actually on those occasions the doctor's hate may be
strangely healing because it enables him to face, and not to reject or
refuse to treat, his patient. Still, this curiously healing hate, whether
expressed toward the patient or suppressed by the doctor (but nonetheless just as keenly felt) is—as hate always is—a kind of wound itself.
For it mars the physician with scars of guilt or sadness that not even
an abundance of years can erase, or ease from the memory.

Dr. Williams in His Short Stories
Philip Rahv*

In his prose as in his poetry William Carlos Williams is too hardy a
frontiersman of the word to permit himself the idle luxuries of aes-
theticism. There are too many things to be seen and touched, too many
cadences of living speech to be listened to and recorded. Kenneth
Burke once said of Williams that he was engaged in "discovering the
shortest route between subject and object." Perhaps that explains why
in *Life on the Passaic River* [sic], a collection of nineteen short stories,
not one imitates in any way the conventional patterns of the genre.
The directness of this writer's approach to his material excludes its
subjection to the researches of plot and calculated form. What Williams
tells us is much too close to him to lend itself to the alienation of
design; none of his perceptions can be communicated through the
agency of invented equivalents. The phenomena he observes and their
means are so intimately involved with one another, the cohabitation of

*From *Literature and the Sixth Sense* by Philip Rahv (Boston: Houghton Mifflin, 1969),
316–18. Reprinted by permission of Houghton Mifflin Co. Copyright 1938, ©1969 by
Philip Rahv.

Philip Rahv

language and object is so harmonious, that formal means of expression would not only be superfluous but might actually nullify the incentive to creation.

These notations in a doctor's notebook, these fragments salvaged from grime and squalor, these insights gained during the routines of humble labor—such would only be given the lie by the professional mannerisms of authorship, its pomposities and braggadocio. Where a writer usually takes the attitude of an impresario toward his themes, calculating each entrance and exit, Williams will begin or end his story as the spirit moves him; pausing to face his reader, he will take him into his confidence and speak his mind without recourse to stratagems of ingratiation. Elliptical in some passages and naturalistic in others, Williams is perfectly conscious of writing but hostile to "literature." Out of "a straight impulse, without borrowing, without lie or complaint," he puts down on paper that which stirs him. His subjects are few and often minute, their scope is sharply circumscribed by his personal experience and by his voluntary seclusion within the local and immediate, he repeats himself frequently—yet these stories are exceptional for their authenticity and told not to provoke but to record. It is pain which is the source of values here. The dread of annihilation is ever present. "Christ, Christ! . . . How can a man live in the face of this daily uncertainty? How can a man not go mad with grief, with apprehension?" No grand conceits, no gratuitous excitements, no melodrama. There is no doing away with the staples of existence; no gallivanting on the banks of the Passaic River.

For what could be more dismal than life in these small industrial towns of New Jersey? The mills are worked by immigrant laborers, and their youngsters are "all over the city as soon as they can walk and say, Paper!" The doctor visits these uprooted households, often angry at himself because of the tenderness in him that reaches out to these people, quite as often resigned to doing his job, to immersing himself in the finalities of human life. "To me," he writes, "it is a hard, barren life, where I am alone and unmolested (work as I do in the thick of it), though in constant danger lest some slip send me to perdition but which, being covetous not at all, I enjoy for the seclusion and primitive air of it."

The little girl, both of whose tonsils are covered with membrane, fights furiously to keep him from knowing her secret. Another one, a lank-haired girl of fifteen, is a powerful little animal upon whom you can stumble on the roof, behind the stairs "any time at all." A whole

159

gang is on her trail. Cured of her pimples, how will this tenacious creature ever slash her way to the bliss recited on the radio? "The pure products of America go crazy," Williams once wrote in a poem. And these stories are familiar images of the same, released by that active element of sympathy which is to be prized above all else in the equipment of an artist. But this writer has no hankering for consistent explanations, for the constancy of reason; he seldom permits himself to ask why. "What are you going to do with a guy like that. Or why want to do anything with him. Except not miss him," he says of one of his characters. This last is the point. He is content with grasping the fact, with creating a phenomenology; but the relations, social and historic, that might unify these facts and significate them on a plane beyond sensation or nostalgia or pathos he has no mind for. And this absence of what one might call, in his terms, ideological presumptuousness, while admirable in its modesty, also constitutes his defeat. However much of value there is in these facts of "hard history" and in the scrupulous gathering of their detail, the larger implications are systematically neglected. Thought is proscribed as anti-aesthetic. Yet, though habitually confined to the suggestive and purely descriptive, this prose nevertheless holds within itself some of the raw elements of a comprehensive consciousness. . . .

William Carlos Williams and the Modern Short Story
J. E. Slate*

William Carlos Williams' "The Use of Force" needs no defense in academic circles. Endorsed by the critics and teachers who print it in anthologies, "The Use of Force" now indisputably belongs. Though the other fifty-one stories in Williams' largest collection are still relatively unknown, fifteen years in the right circles have established this single piece of fiction. Success is always paradoxical for an artist, but Williams' success with "The Use of Force" contains an especially sharp

*From the *Southern Review* 4, no. 3 (July 1968):647–52, 659–64. Reprinted by permission.

self-contradiction: Williams was an esthetic revolutionary who never stopped thinking of himself as a dangerous outsider or—at the very least—a subversive agent. He usually wrote to attack academic assumptions about the short story and continually questioned the premises of successful fiction.

"The Use of Force" conceals Williams' intentions better than his other stories; and it is not surprising that Williams' destructive role escaped notice, for he often pretended sympathy for the intellectual establishments in order to undermine them from within. When they finally listened to him, though never as they had listened to T. S. Eliot, he was happy to speak to groups of young writers about the need for formal revolution. His lecture at the University of Washington, published in 1950 as *A Beginning on the Short Story*, is typical in its contrast between the classic, which aspires to the timeless, and the modern, which formally reflects its own time. Although his words openly urged undergraduates to revolt, they were either ignored or misunderstood, because "The Use of Force" was enshrined in a college text that same year.

The brief analysis of the story in Robert Heilman's *Modern Short Stories* ignored Williams' theories but was notable for its refusal to categorize Williams as a primitive or proletarian writer. This error had been encouraged by Williams himself, who not only published five of his best stories in a magazine called *Blast: Proletarian Short Stories* but also acted as its advisory editor. Nevertheless, even in 1934, the idea of Williams as a primitive was so ridiculous that Ezra Pound could enjoy the irony of naming him "the Communists' white-haired boy" while reporting that one story had been rejected by a doctrinaire Communist magazine as lacking in class consciousness. "One of the editors pointed out that the 'doctor' seemed unaware of the implications of giving the girl a prescription that would cost not less than fifty cents, when her father was receiving ten dollars a week."

Philip Rahv knew better than to expect party orthodoxy of Williams, but he, too, missed the point when he reviewed the collection containing these stories in 1938. He described Williams as the kind of writer who rejects all ideas ("thought is proscribed as anti-aesthetic") and merely wants to record facts ("the relations, social and historic, that might unify these facts and significate them on a higher plane beyond sensation or nostalgia or pathos he has no mind for"). By 1950 the ideas implicit in Williams' "facts" were beginning to emerge, so that Heilman stressed the "symbolic value" of "The Use of Force." Yet its values for him turn out to be moral rather than esthetic and not at all revolutionary. Although "it would be a mistake . . . to read the story as a treatise against the use of force," it illuminates "the kind of hostility, love of conquest, and madness that the use of force brings into play, whatever the apparent justification for vigorous action." As a matter of fact, violence has no more moral value than it has political meaning in Williams' world, though its broad metaphoric use makes it a valuable key for discovering what sort of esthetic blast Williams wanted to set off with stories like "The Use of Force."

In Williams' *Beginning on the Short Story,* the basic problem of the writer in twentieth-century America is clearly articulated. "How shall we write today? The hero? Who is a hero? The peasantry? There is none. Men and women faithful to a belief? What belief?" In the past there were heroes, whole men, and traditional systems of values; but today, and especially in America, "we are no one of us 'all' of anything." We are still too new to have inherited any of the old values, yet we are too frightened by our new world to live independent of the past. In art we still value the old forms for the stability implicit in them, paying the commercial artist to produce familiar shapes. But if our world is actually new—modern, American, or both—we must face the terror of the unfamiliar and find our values in it rather than in the past or in distant places. Valueless, offering as yet no perfect art, the new world is all we have that is truly ours.

In the new and terrifying world of the imagination, cut off from the comfortable certainties of the past, the serious artist creates in the fullest sense of the term. "You do not *copy* nature, you make something which is an *imitation* of nature," Williams told the Washington students. In the imagination, the artist, like nature, evolves new forms out of his new material; or, in terms closer to the center of Williams' theory, the artist faces the poverty and isolation of his world and embraces it violently, shaping it formally in its own terms while rejecting the alien and the old.

The distinction between *copying* and *imitation* appears as early as 1925 in the contrast between Hawthorne and Poe developed in Williams' *American Grain.* Despite Hawthorne's "willing closeness to the life of his locality in its vague humors; his lifelike copying of the New England melancholy; his reposeful closeness to the town pump," his tales are formally too old to have much value for a new world. Poe,

J. E. Slate

Williams argued, is actually much more valuable, though he might at first seem to have fled the scene before him by refusing to write about "trees and Indians." Poe not only used new materials—his language was American, not English—and expressed the terror of life in a new world over and over again, but he also kept in mind "a beginning literature . . . that must establish its own rules, own framework." Behind the appearance of a wealth of new material, an illusion which trapped most of his contemporaries, Poe recognized a world lacking in value but so stubborn and savage in character that only the greatest formal skill, employed with imitative savagery, could allow the artist to survive and create. Williams imagined Poe as a frontiersman who survived by refusing to trust "the great natural beauty of the New World," by relying on his murderous skill as Boone had done, and by losing his alien ways in the violence of our new world. Because Poe understood the need for violence, "in all he says there is a sense of him *surrounded* by his time, tearing at it, ever with more rancour, but always at battle, taking hold."

Williams' new world is as violent as Poe's because it is still a wilderness violently resisting all efforts to cultivate it, and because, in its violently accelerated change, it is even more difficult to grasp than before. For Doctor Williams, daily faced with poverty-stricken patients too ignorant to help themselves, the available material was indeed raw. Instead of complete actions he found isolated moments; instead of whole persons he found unrelated parts. These materials and the temporal situation, he says, "dictated the terms" in which they must be shaped, while the short story specifically had to "accommodate itself to the heterogeneous character of the people, the elements involved, the situation in hand."

Inventing truly new forms demands involvement in our time. Writing what Pound called "'histoire morale contemporaine,'" Williams was so deeply involved in his time that his active political concerns could have no place in his short stories: to him, being a "proletarian writer" meant imitating the antisocial attitude of the deprived citizen, a man who clings to the myth of the self-made man so stubbornly that he cannot conceive of a revolutionary social movement which will not threaten his freedom. The central idea of the story and the collection called *Life Along the Passaic River* is "Nobody's gonna teach it to you; you got to learn it yourself." This is a significant statement of Williams' artistic creed made more significant because it is spoken with the accents of the poor. He is so determined to save them from cultural poverty that he becomes them, sharing their language and its limitations, their stubborn ignorance and their violence.

In theme, language and physical detail, "The Use of Force" is unquestionably modern, reflecting its time exactly as Williams' theory demands. Its broad outlines, however, are more classic than modern, and this fact explains why the story has been more popular with critics than with Williams himself, who identified another story written the same year as his favorite. "The Use of Force" suggests classical tragedy, as one 1965 textbook explains, because the protagonist fights against overwhelming forces so well that her courage and determination take on values which outlast her ultimate defeat. Even though Mathilda Olson is not Antigone but a little girl lacking in real tragic stature, there is enough of the heroine in her to make the doctor into a kind of scientific Creon: his sense of social responsibility and his personal passion combine in a familiar pattern. Yet the story is more than a miniature tragedy in modern dress. In "The Use of Force" classical form is joined—though not successfully in my opinion—to a number of modern themes which, like violence, are characteristic of Williams' fiction in general. Ironically, the presence of the classic formula does not prevent the story from functioning as a good introduction to Williams' theory of modern fiction.

In all Williams' fiction, but most fully in his novel *White Mule*, children and childish adults represent modern or American man. As in "The Use of Force," the child's helpless struggle to retain her independence often generates admiration and other powerful emotions, but her character remains incomplete, material too raw to be valuable in itself. The central figure of "Jean Beicke," Williams' favorite story, is an infant resembling Mathilda in her resistance and her hidden disease. "A worthless piece of humanity," Jean dies despite the affection of the nurses and the intense professional interest of two good doctors. They attempt to make sense out of the child's condition but are left "dumb," defeated by their lack of knowledge and of words to express their feelings.

Jean, Mathilda, and the Flossie Stecher of *White Mule* share a capacity for self-destruction, irrational behavior, and violence. Jean's death spurs the narrator to say, "Vote the straight Communist ticket," suggesting—among other things—a revolutionary new view of life; and the little girl called "white mule" or moonshine is irrationally stubborn and as violent as a shot of raw whisky. Commenting on *White Mule*, Williams said, "I was crazy about babies, the contempt that all babies have for adults. They don't give a damn what goes on." In other words, the emotions associated with children are in themselves not only worthless but even self-destructive; yet these violent emotions are all we as new or unformed men have to give. The artist's social function is to invent forms for these emotions, to arrest the suicidal movement and to give the subjective emotion objective value.

Just as the child replaces the whole man or hero in Williams' fiction, circular movement or anticlimax often replaces a classical resolution of the plot. The last paragraph of "The Use of Force" imperfectly illustrates the difference, for after the doctor finally defeats the child and seems to resolve the conflict, the child attacks him again as if to renew the struggle. To invent a new ending suitable for his time, Williams has to make the ending a beginning, returning the plot from the movement of peace—a kind of death—to violence and life. Because defeat and death are the major premises of classical tragedy, the new form must go beyond it, suggesting a larger view in which life, though lacking in real value, goes on.

In his lecture on the short story Williams declared, "Murder is nothing at all but death—and what's new about death? Violence is the mood today." He sincerely admired the classic use of death as a means of defining life and intensifying human values, from Aeschylus ("a son cuts his mother's throat") to Hemingway ("a woman shooting her husband's head off"). But he suspected this was already old to the Hellenistic Greeks. "Maybe Plato was a bit fed up on the Sophocles" and invented the new form of the dialogue as a way of replacing murder with verbal violence. Williams notes that Plato's dialogues have arguments rather than deaths for endings, though he finally gave Socrates, his hero, the hemlock as well as a wife who could outtalk him. . . . The short story, Williams says "must be written so well that that in itself becomes its truth while the deformity informs it.". . .

. . .Once again, "The Use of Force" may be read as a dramatization of a critical principle. Mathilda's lies about her throat fail, forcing her to violence that reveals her true worth; the doctor's false smile—in his "best professional manner"—fails, forcing him also to violence. However, he would still prefer to achieve his goal in some less physical manner, and his familiarity with successful lies makes him furious with Mrs. Olson's unsuccessful "He won't hurt you." "If only they wouldn't use the word 'hurt' I might be able to get somewhere." Of all the characters, only Mrs. Olson fails to realize that her lies are lies, so that she remains ignorant to the end and refuses to give up her interjections of "nice" and "kind" for the crude action which is an admission of failure and a deformed kind of success.

"I lived among these people," Williams said of the patients who were the chief characters of his stories. "I was involved." Involvement, of course, meant lack of esthetic distance or a point of view, a technical deformity Williams was conscious of almost to the point of "shame." But as usual, he attempted to exploit this flaw, to make the deformity inform his work. Since the fictional narrator belonged to the past and a modern substitute had not yet appeared, he had nothing from which to invent a new form except his own shameful involvement. Thus "The Use of Force" and most of Williams' other stories might be described as fictions in which Williams involves himself as the narrator, but they are more accurately stories in which the point of view is missing, formal structures in which the flaw functions as part of the whole, giving it its meaning. His closeness to the action of the story must appear as a deformity, a failure to invent, until the meaning of the story becomes radiantly clear. Then the form is seen as new rather than old and the imperfection becomes a kind of refinement.

The technical refinements in Williams' stories like "The Use of Force" are so new that they can seldom be described except in terms of the old. In language, for example, Williams' stories appear careless, crude or unfinished. One, called "Verbal Transcription: 6 A.M.," pretends to be nothing more than a crude set of notes, and its material, like Frankie's joke, is often cliché. But the language is not copied; instead, it imitates the rough talk of the new world, recreating that world in its own terms. The careless effect of the first paragraph of "The Use of Force" comes from two sentences combining inaccurate statement with loose and illogical connections of ideas. And although one sentence is spoken by one of the Olsons and the other by the doctor, the speaker's individuality seems to be denied by the stylistic flatness of both. Yet in the end, we see that the whole family *are* patients, that the two speakers are close-knit in speech because they are related in several significant ways, and that subtle distinctions between parental nervousness and professional calm are present in the two speeches.

Similarly, the diction of "The Use of Force" appears flat and its metaphors seem clichés. The words and phrases describing Mathilda—

eating me up, strong as a heifer, with one cat-like movement, clawed, savage, wild, damned—do not call attention to themselves; lacking commercial beauty or obvious newness, they generate meaning through their arrangement within individual sentences and within the story. *Damned,* the climactic word, is probably the best of all the calculated failures. It does, of course, fail to convey the doctor's frustration or his need to express himself violently; a banal blasphemy, it expresses only failure. But attached to a child who contains all the new world, it takes on the solid new meanings of *doomed* and *lost.*

Looking back, Williams said of his stories, "I kept the literary thing to myself. No one knew I felt that the stories might be literary." It is this attitude which distinguishes Williams from his contemporaries, Gertrude Stein, Sherwood Anderson, and Ernest Hemingway, each of whom shared some part of his theory of modern fiction. All these others refined their materials in the classical manner: their writing quickly became independent of its sources in everyday diction, the rhythms of the spoken language, the mind of the nonliterary and anti-intellectual citizen. Hemingway, Williams complained to Pound in 1928, misused the formal qualities implicit in conversation: "I am afraid Hem doesn't at all understand, since it is rarely as expressive as he makes it and twice as succinct." Later Williams returned to the same point to say "Hemingway's not a bad poet and might have been a better one." Both comments seem to be references to the techniques of refinement which made Hemingway a successful and even salable writer. Prose so obviously patterned that it became poetic was for Williams a betrayal of the new and its inherent deformity; it was neo-orthodox writing, the old masquerading as something new.

Like Williams' famous but misunderstood criticism of T. S. Eliot's neo-orthodoxy, his opposition to Hemingway's style was an outgrowth of his theory more than it was jealousy of one more successful than himself. Williams' theory of the new could not accommodate a successful writer, even one whom he had helped and who had arrived only after years of neglect. Williams assumed the existence of a new world always new and therefore never wholly conquered; its writers must always be on the way, in the midst of their work, and never in a position of having arrived. Furthermore, Williams' world of perpetual change claims the artist's whole attention, leaving him no time to compare himself with the great men of the past as Hemingway was so fond of doing. For all these reasons, Williams' approach will appeal strongly to the young or unsuccessful writer even where its appeal to basic American prejudices does not touch him. It was entirely appropriate that Williams' fullest statement of his theory of fiction be made to college students, and that it be called *A Beginning on the Short Story.*

William Carlos Williams demanded so much of the modern artist that he could not always satisfy his own demands. A few of his stories, like "The Dawn of Another Day," cannot be distinguished from the commercial formulas he said he was attacking; a great many more, like the ones mentioned through this essay, are fascinating attempts to make the deformity inform the modern short story. "The Use of Force," however, stands out. Its critical and commercial success calls attention to its failure as a modern work, its failure to deal with the people and the times completely in the contemporary patterns of deformity and failure.

The deficiencies of "The Use of Force" as a modern short story become apparent when it is contrasted with a more anecdotal fragment like the following narrative from Williams' *Autobiography*. "One day I was examining a fifteen-year-old white girl—a cute kid who had been brought into the clinic for diagnosis by her mother who wanted to know what made her belly so big. The kid was not dumb and fought us every step of the way. Finally after threats by her mother and persuasion on my part, we got her dress off, but at that point she flew at us all and in her underwear dashed out the door and up the street like a young doe. That's the last I saw of her." Like some of *Kora in Hell: Improvisations* and all of the miniature narratives that make up the story "World's End," this expresses the fragmentary nature of Williams' world more clearly than "The Use of Force," as well as avoiding the suggestion of any classic pattern. Her escape is not the comic success of the underdog, for her secret can be concealed even less successfully than Mathilda's; and her deformity is full of human meaning which has no relationship to her rather temporary escape. In escaping the doctor's clutches, she is also life escaping the artist no matter how many times he tries to bring his work to perfection. The diagnosis is incomplete and the "cure" for pregnancy is such an unlikely possibility that it is not mentioned in the narrative.

As this example suggests, Williams' theory and practice both make it necessary to redefine the term *fiction*, at least for him, to include almost all his prose: novels, short stories, improvisations, autobiographical works. . . .

The critical problem of Williams' basic assumption of a perpetually new world, of course, remains, for understanding of the importance of the assumption to him should precede any attack on this problem. It is certainly far from the simple primitivism which a number of critics have claimed. I have tried to show how much misunderstanding exists in spite of Williams' coherence and consistency. I have been especially eager to correct the confusion between traditional morality, for which Williams has no artistic use, and the morality of art that operates in all of Williams' work. His dedication to art was as single-minded as that of his "saint" Edgar Allan Poe, and his dedication to the new world was as great as that of his other guide and patron, Walt Whitman.

The Doctor's Bag: William Carlos Williams' Passaic River Stories

George Monteiro*

In "Jean Beicke," a second story from his collection *Life Along the Passaic River,* the relationship between the physician and his patient is all on the side of the physician. Perhaps the best place to begin discussing "Jean Beicke" is the end of the story: the account of the autopsy. The child with the too long legs, with an omnivorous appetite that compelled her to eat everything given her, has succumbed at last, having first won the emotional support of her nurses and doctors. So much so, in fact, that her nurse, despite the doctor's attempts, has not gone down to the postmortem. "I may be a sap, she said, but I can't do it, that's all. I can't. Not when I've taken care of them. I feel as if they're my own." It is important that we hear this, for the nurse's behavior, with her attendant explanation, serves as a necessary prelude to the doctor's account of the autopsy.

> I was amazed to see how completely the lungs had cleared up. They
> were almost normal except for a very small patch of residual pneu-

*From *Modern Language Studies* 13, no. 1 (Winter 1983): 79–84. ©1983 by Northeast Modern Language Association. Reprinted by permission. All quotations are from *Make Light of It* (New York: Random House, 1950).

monia here and there which really amounted to nothing. Chest and abdomen were in excellent shape, otherwise, throughout—not a thing aside from the negligible pneumonia. Then he opened the head. It seemed to me the poor kid's convolutions were unusually well developed. I kept thinking it's incredible that that complicated mechanism of the brain has come into being just for this. I never can quite get used to an autopsy.

The first evidence of the real trouble—for there had been no gross evidence of meningitis—was when the pathologist took the brain in his hand and made the long steady cut which opened up the left lateral ventricle. There was just a faint color of pus on the bulb of the choroid plexus there. Then the diagnosis all cleared up quickly. The left lateral sinus was completely thrombosed and on going into the left temporal bone from the inside the mastoid process was all broken down.

As one would expect, the doctor, who had been so solicitous, always looking for signs of progress and dreading the possibility of deterioration, even to the point of rooting like a fan for the scrappy kid, is now coolly clinical. Look at what he notices, and remember that the child is dead. "The lungs had *cleared up*. They were *almost normal.*" The patch of pneumonia that remains "really *amounted to nothing.*" Chest and abdomen are in "*excellent* shape." Then the doctor opens the head. As for its convolutions, they were "unusually *well developed.*" Then the coolness falters, when he admits that he kept thinking that it was incredible "that that complicated mechanism of the brain has come into being just for this," an autopsy. It is in the head that the doctors succeed in their quest—their inquest—as the pathologist takes up the brain. Here Williams describes his next professional move. He "made the *long steady cut* which opened the left lateral ventricle." Only at second or third thought, perhaps, does one realize the violence of the pathologist's act and its attending violation of the child's brain. But the clinical cut "opens" that part of the brain, and reveals the mystery. "The left lateral sinus was completely thrombosed and on going into the left temporal bone from the inside the mastoid process was all broken down." The breakdown is exposed, and the "diagnosis" cleared up. It should be noted that diagnoses are usually in the service of life and potential health, and therefore patient-oriented. But here there is no longer a patient, merely a cadaver for which all diagnoses are bootless. In what sense is it still a satisfying diagnosis? And in what sense is it still health-oriented? Uncovering the breakdown of the mastoid process, discovering the logic of the disease, serves the doctors, of course. When a third physician, the "ear man," is called down to see for himself what has been found, he conjectures that they made a mistake. "A clear miss, he said. I think if we'd gone in their earlier, we'd have saved her." But the narrator-physician will have none of such talk. The autopsy has apparently served its neutralizing purpose. The doctor dismisses the "ear man's" comment with a political quip. "For what? said I. Vote the straight Communist ticket." To which the ear man counters: "Would it make us any dumber?" Satisfaction has come with postmortem knowledge. The child has disappeared into the inquest. The physician's faith in his science and craft is intact. And besides, who needs another unwanted child, let alone an unwanted voter? The doctor, after his infatuation with the child ("we all got to be crazy about Jean"), has reverted to the self who, making rounds in the morning, would tell the nurses that the "miserable specimens" who would survive would "grow up into a cheap prostitute or something." Of course, what gives this story its power is that the wisecracking and the running diagnosis cum treatment cannot eradicate the narrator's affections. They can, from time to time, encapsulate them.

Collected in *Make Light of It* (1950), "A Night in June," set in that fabled month for love and marriage, calls for a doctor to attend a woman at term. Settling in for a night of waiting for the delivery of what will be the woman's ninth baby, the doctor falls asleep. He sleeps at the kitchen table in a pleasant and comfortable position. He dreams; and in his half sleep he begins to argue with himself—"or some imaginary power." The argument turns on a conflict between "science and humanity." The dream, as the doctor describes it, runs like this:

> Our exaggerated ways will have to pull in their horns, I said. We've learned from one teacher and neglected another. Now that I'm older, I'm finding the older school.
> The pituitary extract and other simple devices represent science. Science, I dreamed, has crowded the stage more than is necessary. The process of selection will simplify the application. It touches us too crudely now, all newness is over—complex. I couldn't tell whether I was asleep or awake.
> But without science, without pituitrin, I'd be here till noon or maybe—what? Some others wouldn't wait so long but rush her now. A carefully guarded shot of pituitrin—ought to save her at least much exhaustion—if not more. But I don't want to have anything happen to her.

Within the dream the doctor's options take the form of conflict. Shall he use a substance that will speed up the processes of labor or shall he wait patiently for nature's course? Shall he risk injecting pituitrin in the case of a woman whose uterus after eight deliveries is more than commonly susceptible to tearing to save them both time and fatiguing effort, and in her case possibly something "more," a something that he does not name? This conflict he sees as one between Science and Humanity. What makes its resolution into professional action difficult—after all, the doctor will choose to inject the pituitrin or he will choose not to do so—is that within the doctor another antagonism is playing itself out: the desire to act under the control of neutralized feelings in the face of emotions that threaten to break through the technique with which the doctor practices his artful science. In his dream the doctor sees such conflicts in terms of competing schools that are "older" and "newer." Significant, too, is his claim that as he gets older, he is finding "the older." It is the school of Humanity that is older, the school of Science younger. It has been hardly casual, one recalls at this point, that the doctor began his narrative with a two-paragraph summary of his failure years earlier—as a young man—to deliver successfully the woman's first baby. "It was a difficult forceps delivery"—of course that delivery would call for Science—"and I lost the child, to my disgust." Significant, as well, is the feeling that this failure engenders in the young doctor. He does not feel *disappointment*, which would be more neutral, more professional, nor *grief* or *pain*, which would be more humane. Rather, he feels *disgust*. He feels aversion, abhorrence; he is, perhaps, offended. If he feels that he is at all to blame for the failure, however, he quickly exonerates himself: "without nurse, anesthetist, or even enough hot water in the place, I shouldn't have been overmuch blamed. I must have been fairly able not to have done worse." In short, we are to infer, the doctor had done the best he could given limitations and circumstances outside his professional control. There was no failure of technique, obviously, and therefore no reason for disgust, at least not self-directed disgust.

But all this is preliminary to a story centering, years later, on still another delivery. And by this time the doctor is a seasoned professional. The story celebrates his preparation and judgment, and, in the end, his success. There runs through the narrative a strong sense of contentment and self-congratulation. For example, because seldom are women any longer delivered at home, the doctor must seek out that "relic" of a satchel he had tossed under a table "two or three years" before. Nevertheless, a check shows that it contains just about everything the doctor will need.

> There was just one sterile unbilical tie left, two, really, in the same envelope, as always, for possible twins, but that detail aside, everything was ample and in order. I complimented myself. Even the Argyrol was there, in tablet form, insuring the full potency of a fresh solution. Nothing so satisfying as a kit of any sort prepared and in order even when picked up in an emergency after an interval of years.

In the course of the early morning hours the doctor periodically examines the woman, assesses probabilities, and decides on procedures. All runs largely on course until the moment for delivery. "The woman and I then got to work," announces the doctor. Her "hands grabbed me at first a little timidly about the right wrist and forearm. Go ahead, I said. Pull hard. I welcomed the feel of her hands and the strong pull. It quieted me. . . ." No forceps are needed. There is no need for the doctor to resort to instrumental intervention. The delivery will be natural, becoming a collaboration of the woman and her doctor. The situation provides the doctor with a moment of quiet self-perception: "This woman in her present condition would have seemed repulsive to me ten years ago—now, poor soul, I see her to be as clean as a cow that calves." The head is born, and then the rest of the baby. There has been no injection of pituitrin, no need for forceps; it has been in every way, a natural delivery. It is as an afterthought that the doctor reminds himself: "Oh yes, the drops in the baby's eyes." But, he quickly decides, there is "no need. She's as clean as a beast." Yet, the professionalism within him reminds him that he can't know for sure. Again there is a professional conflict. "Medical discipline says every case must have drops in the eyes. No chance of gonorrhea though here—but—Do it." The resolution to the allegorical conflict between Science and Humanity—the claims of the younger school and those of the older—is that they can go hand-in-hand when united by the experienced, judicious doctor. There have been employed no "exaggerated ways"; the horns of Science have been pulled in. For once, all's right in Doctor Williams' medical world. Mother and baby are doing fine.

"A Night in June" had begun with a doctor's memory of a forceps-delivered child he had lost. Although he had rather quickly absolved himself of blame, he nevertheless was disturbed by his failure. And, of course, the infant was dead. In "Jean Beicke," the eleven-month child loses her fight, and she, too, is dead. If the Beicke autopsy serves to bring the doctors back to the right professional note, there is no sense that all's right with the world. Curiously enough, though, that is exactly the note sounded in William's "Comedy Entombed: 1930," also collected in *Make Light of It* (1950). The story is thoroughly comic, or would be if it were not for one thing: the culminating event of the story is the delivery of a dead fetus. On second thought, there is no exception to the story's comic thrust. Not only does everything turn out for the best but, in certain respects, rather well. It is, as the doctor says, "just a five months' miss." The fetus was a girl, information the mother uses to taunt her husband who, after several boys, wants a girl. It is the mother, as it turns out, who controls the emotional ambiance of the whole procedure, who "knew it was all right," and who laughs at her husband's bellyache. She taunts him about his couvade: "You'd be more famous than the Dionne quintuplets. . . . You'd get your pictures in the papers and talk over the radio and everything." In all likelihood the mother's sustained equanimity has given the doctor's narration its particular coloration and its sense of order-within-disorder. The story is about the discovery of that order, one unexpected and certainly unsuspected. The details of the house—its "greasy" smell to its "soiled sheets"—anticipate the potential messiness of a "birth" four months short of term.

> The whole place had a curious excitement about it for me, resembling in that the woman herself, I couldn't precisely tell why. There was nothing properly recognizable, nothing straight, nothing in what ordinarily might have been called its predictable relationships. Complete disorder. Tables, chairs, worn-out shoes piled in one corner. A range that didn't seem to be lighted. Every angle of the room jammed with something or other ill-assorted and of the rarest sort.

In a story in which a dead fetus occasions a mother's not-so-black humor, however, matters are not readily predictable, and the observant doctor does not stop with these observations. He has an insight, an artist's epiphany.

> I have seldom seen such disorder and brokenness—such a mass of unrelated parts of things lying about. That's it! I concluded to

James E. B. Breslin

myself. An unrecognizable order! Actually—the new! And so good-
natured and calm. So definitely the thing! And so compact. Excellent. And with such patina of use. Everything definitely "painty."
Even the table, that way, pushed off from the center of the room.

"An unrecognizable order! Actually—the new!" That new knowledge
will inform the doctor's experience with the collected mother and her
dead fetus of a daughter (it's 'born' "still in the sack . . . It all came
together. . . . the whole mass was intact"). Indeed, since death and
disorder are seen to be very much in the nature of things, it is almost
as if the whole thing were a joke on the comic father.

"Comedy Entombed: 1930" offers an unmatchable key into Williams Carlos Williams the physician-poet. Williams' aesthetic impulse
was in certain ways at odds with his doctor's scientific training. His
aesthetic was profoundly Dionysian ("a new order") but his profession
calls for an Apollonian temperament. The artist was always looking for
new order; the physician always trying to engender the known, predic-
tive, scientific order. As in the past—the scientist would say—so again,
so now. The artist: never so before, but now, anew, so.

For the physician the fear would always be that the order would
breed chaos, that it would be discovered that at the heart of order will
be a disorder (an unknown, unrecognized, unrecognizable disease).
The dream of the artist, and the artist's reward, is that his skill and
technique and vision will discover for him the new order, and that there
will always be such new orders. Williams displayed this most often and
most lyrically in his poetry. But these truths were also there, amidst
the everyday dust and dirt of his realist's observations, in his stories.

The Fiction of a Doctor
*James E. B. Breslin**

The change from *A Voyage to Pagany* to *The Knife of the Times* (1932) is
dramatic: we go from a novel which treats a grand theme in a confessional mode to a series of stories that treat mundane people with re-

*From *William Carlos Williams: An American Artist* by James E. B. Breslin (Chicago:
University of Chicago Press, 1985), 138–41. Reprinted by permission.

portorial objectivity. Williams's devotion to experience over ideas made him resist attempts to politicize art during the 'thirties; but the Depression clearly turned his sympathetic attention to the lower class inhabitants of his native locality. Moreover, the shift from the novel to the short story was natural enough for a writer who had made the episode the basic unit of his longer fiction. The story suited his new subjects— "the briefness of their chronicles, its brokenness and heterogenity [sic]—isolation, color. A novel was 'unthinkable'" (*SE*, p. 300)—and the shorter form was structurally liberating too: "One chief advantage as against a novel—which is its nearest cousin—is that you do not have to bear in mind the complex structural paraphernalia of a novel in writing a short story and so may dwell on the manner, the writing. On the process itself. A single stroke, uncomplicated but complete. Not like a chapter or a pharagraph." (*SE*, pp. 304–5). The style is no longer dense, reflexive, as in the poetry and fiction of the 1920's; instead, we get a spare, swift-moving colloquial language that has been purged of all stylistic pyrotechnics. This simplicity of manner opens Williams's fiction to the lives of the people in his locality, without the distortions any elegancies of form might impose. In fact, so casual in tone, so open to the contingent, are these stories that they strike many readers as mildly interesting vignettes of small-town life, but no more. Some of the stories in *The Knife of the Times* are slight; others depend too much on a superficial kind of shock for their effect. But before making any final estimate, we need to look at them from within the concerns of Williams's new project for fiction—to deal objectively with real characters moving in a modern locality.

One of the most memorable is the title story. Ethel and Maura, "intimates as children," separate after marriage but maintain a correspondence. Gradually, Ethel's letters become more intimate, expressing at first disappointment with her marriage and children, then openly avowing passion for Maura. At last, after twenty years, the two meet in New York City and there, in a pay toilet, Ethel presses herself on her friend, who submits. "What shall I do? thought Maura afterward on her way home, on the train alone. Ethel had begged her to visit her, to go to her, to spend a week at least with her, to sleep with her. Why not?" All this happens in three and a half pages. It is useful here, as in many of these stories, to consider what Williams has avoided doing. He has not written the story from Ethel's point of view, dwelling on the pathos of her frustrated yearning. He has not expanded a moment of moral crisis with an anguished Maura forced to choose between duty and passion; her reactions afterward on the train are deliberately played down and devoid of any moral considerations. Nor has Williams filled in any personal or social context that might make Maura's passivity more intelligible. Events are narrated objectively, yet from the "inside" in the sense that assessment of them from any external point of view is undercut. There is no cleverly executed plot, no deep probing of character, no moral critique of the issues; and these exclusions are typical of the entire collection. The reader will justly ask, what's left? The answer is the revelation of a lower, more mysterious, more profound motive—the repository of instinctive power which, Kora-like, is buried by the pressures of everyday reality. What draws Williams to Maura is her simple acceptance of passion: "Why not?" Acceptance of these instinctual drives is the beginning of all Williams's work; but whereas the irrational entered *The Great American Novel* because the author dared to follow the associational leaps of his own consciousness, it enters his fiction now as a motive operating in other people. By sticking to the surfaces of events and people, Williams yet arrives at a deeper psychology.

The psychology here is really the physio-psychology of the doctor, and while an attitude of natural acceptance generates all of Williams's work, it is in his fiction that the relation between that point of view and his medical training become most apparent. What Williams says of Old Doc Rivers is also true of himself: "things had an absolute value for him" (*FD*, p. 103). A doctor looks at things not with an eye to their social or moral value, but simply as natural facts; his perspective is clinical—neutral. In *The Knife of the Times*, emotions are conceived physiologically: "frightened, under stress, the heart beats faster, the blood is driven to the extremities of the nerves, floods the centers of action and a man feels in a flame" (*FD*, p. 102). Characters are often defined in terms of physical presence, as is one of the subjects in "The Colored Girls of Passenack—Old and New":

> Once I went to call on a patient in a nearby suburb. As the door opened to my ring a magnificent bronze figure stood before me. She said not a word but stood there till I told her who I was, then she let me in, turned her back and walked into the kitchen. But the force of her—something, her mental alertness coupled with her erectness, muscular power, youth, seriousness—her actuality— made me want to start a new race on the spot. I had never seen anything like it. (*FD*, p. 56)

The girl says nothing, does nothing significant; she is a mysterious figure through whom a profound physical force operates. In an early crude form, the passage illustrates one of the remarkable effects Williams achieves in his fiction: his ability through external description to create the sense of deep contact with a character. Of course, this passage also shows that the doctor's point of view has a value system of its own, which determines both the kinds of people Williams treats in his fiction and the way he treats them. . . .

Bells Break Tower: William Carlos Williams's Stories
*Warren Tallman**

If Pound, Eliot and Joyce are the most spectacular of the writing primitives, William Carlos Williams, the one who stayed home in New Jersey, has increasingly become the most influential on this side of the water. Among a number of reasons for his growing importance none is perhaps more germane than his constitutional inability to *make up* his mind. Joyce, Eliot and Pound all had incisive ambitions and intelligences, the latter two ranking as foremost literary pedagogues handing down enough directives, precepts and opinions to make Jonson, Johnson, Pope and Arnold seem reticent. Williams was as pre-occupied as the others with providing keys and clues to the new writing world. But there is a difference. The weather that fills any given day seems forgetful of that which had filled previous days, and Williams' head works in this weather-wise way. Each effort he makes to name his writing reads like a new attempt from which the memory of previous attempts had vanished. This is transience, an inability to dip his thoughts into the same stream twice. It makes for immediacy, an intensified pre-occupation with the matter at hand. One name for it is localism, not simply a matter of keeping his eye on the neighbors—though that is involved—but more nearly a matter of keeping attention concentrated close at home in the writing place.

The effects show clearly in the stories he wrote intermittently

*From *Boundary* 1 (1972):61–64. ©1972 by *Boundary 2*. Reprinted by permission.

throughout his career, many of them collected in the New Directions volume, *The Farmers' Daughters*. For many readers these stories must seem a little like boomerangs. You enter in and travel along only to discover that you haven't gone anywhere at all. For instance, "Four Bottles of Beer," one of a cluster based on his experience as a physician, in this case a house call. "He's asleep," it begins and the conversation between the sick child's mother and the doctor moves by turn from the child's illness as the doctor examines him; to the doctor's curiosity about what the woman's Polish-speaking mother is saying; to the woman's curiosity about the doctor's negro maid; to exchanging names and racial backgrounds of his family, then hers; to her dislike of negroes and negro cooking; to some noodles on the stove, half cooked because, "I wanted to scrub the floor before you came"; to the child's kinky hair; to earlier accusations by her father that her slapping the child had caused its illness; to complaints about her father; to a new, one hundred and sixty nine dollar 1930 radio and the music when she turns it on; to her wedding picture on the mantle; to the glass of home brew she now serves the doctor; to the four bottles of beer which at her mother's suggestion she gives him; to her husband's job deep-sea fishing at a nearby bay the name of which she can't pronounce— "Chipsabay . . . Sheepshead Bay you mean"; to her "I'll call you on the phone tomorrow," and "Look out you don't drop 'em," and "Goodby"—and that's all folks.

If I destroy the story with this perfunctory countdown it is in order to note a number of things Williams isn't trying to do. "Four Bottles of Beer" is utterly without that kind of referential reaching in which events and persons are labored in a search for deeper significance in farther rooms. The woman is crashingly ordinary, her circumstances likewise, her conversation more so. So be it. Her anxiety is evident in almost everything she says and does but Williams refuses to seek out deeper, subtler implications than those she in herself provides. The doctor is not led by that little child's diarrhea to contemplation of some greater life. The awful music on the expensive radio is awful music on an expensive radio. The beer tastes good but it goes down as beer rather than as baptism, regeneration, or, in homely guise, the body of our lord. In brief, here, as in all of the other stories, the incidents are kept local, a series of particulars that form into an unsummed sum. The reader, carried into the midst, is left there with the beer, sick child, awful music, anxious woman and foxy grandpa.

Which carries close to a beautiful difference between this casual yet careful story and those by writers still in the old world. Williams is as careful in his attention to the movement of speech as Pound is to the sounds of voices. It is in the nature of words as we call upon them that they move along somewhat as our feet do, step by step, word by word. Use of rhythm, which is so close to the heart of life that it may be life itself, figures prominently in both processes. From early infancy we begin to master the art of walking, and as we master it capacity increases. What begins as crawling goes on to toddling and tottering about which leads to walking, then hop skip jump and eventually, fanciest footwork of all, the dance. In between times we shuffle and shamble about, drag heels, stand still, start up again—a thousand permutations of the feet.

But notoriously, as we grow up we begin to neglect the art. The power that plucks at our feet—the beat beat beat—is subordinated. No more journeys as in childhood over the hill and a great way off. Instead our feet are forced to lug us along to the car the corner the bus, school, church, work, and home again home again and not jig a jig jig. And what has this to do with "Four Bottles Of Beer"? Plenty. For what is true of our feet is also true of words, which are the footsteps of the writer's voice. The most obvious sign of writing ability is the capacity to make words move in close response to the mood of the moment, a dance of thought that corresponds to the necessities and possibilities of the given occasion. Ablest writers are those who can keep moving while stumbling and fumbling around on the floor in the dark as well as step out on sure feet in response to invitations from any kind of dance. And much of the beauty, mystery and power of writing dwells in these movements of the words as they carry across from wherever the writer is to wherever the reader happens to be, also able to enter into the dance.

But art forgets as it grows up, and the wordsteps become subordinated to that which the writer seeks to master. A long history of this taming of the words eventuated in the deadening of the art of poetry that Pound found so oppressive circa 1900. Which is why he felt out of key not only with his own time but with poems like *Paradise Lost* in which the obedient scholars lines up row after row all spelling out a justification of God's ways. But it isn't only regulated pentameter pacing that signals subordination of the words and it isn't only form-dominated, pre-twentieth century England that practices it. No one gives more seeming freedom to the movement of words than William Faulkner in whose novels they often rush around like a huge confused pack of hounds. Yet however widely Faulkner lets them range, all are snuffling and baying after symbols and archetypes which collect into their overseer's myth of the south, justifying the ways of Old Massa to black people. In both Milton's ordered and Faulkner's scattered use, the moving, reaching, carrying power of words becomes a means to a further end: the building of the myth, the justification of God—truth, that is, in a tower.

All of which isn't to deny essential beauty and dignity to Milton and Faulkner but to point up the way in which Williams turns the proposition around by seeking to make all that he is capable of perceiving a means of arriving at a dance of words. The conversation in "Four Bottles of Beer" reads as a succession of advances and retreats as the doctor and the housewife struggle for the lead. In a deeper sense they are struggling for accord despite the fact that their life styles don't mesh. Her anxious pretensions and antagonisms push him away at the same time that her wistful if mismanaged attempts to please and impress him draw him close. The music isn't much, the dress she wears isn't as pretty as the one in the "monkey picture" on the mantle, and the beer isn't champagne. But at least she is present in each turn of the conversation, a figure in the dance rather than a proposition about life. Much of the story of Williams' career as artist is the story of his attempts to make ordinary speech so move—turn, turn again, return—as to draw people who counted into presence on the dance or threshing floor of words. Seen one way it is a dancing of the housewife and the doctor, clumsily, on one another's toes. Seen another it is a dancing of Williams' thought as he remembers or imagines the occasion. But whether one look at housewife, doctor, or artist all will be found caught up in the larger dancing of the words, which bend to them, moving as they move. And when the words become the sought place their greater magnitude opens out to the artist's lesser magnitude, drawing him on. . . .

The Man Who Loved Women:
The Medical Fictions of
William Carlos Williams

*Marjorie Perloff**

In one of William Carlos Williams' autobiographical sketches about the world of the big city hospital, a story called "World's End," the doctor-narrator recalls a particularly difficult little girl about six years old who was brought to the hospital kicking and screaming so violently that she could not be placed in a ward. The doctor decides to see what he can do: he takes the child to his office where she promptly bites him in the thigh, knocks off his glasses, and carries on like a wild little animal. Finally, not knowing what else to do, the doctor opens his desk drawer, takes out some crackers, and starts to chew on one. Here is the sequence that follows:

> The child quit her tantrums, came over to me and held out her hand. I gave her a cracker which she ate. Then she stood and looked at me. I reached over and lifted her unresisting into my lap. After eating two more crackers she cuddled down there and in two minutes was asleep. I hugged her to myself with the greatest feeling of contentment—happiness—imaginable. I kissed her hot little head and decided nobody was going to disturb her. I sat there and let her sleep.
> The amazing thing was that after another half hour—two hours in all—when I carried her still sleeping to the door, unlocked it and let the others in—she wakened and would let no one else touch her. She clung to me, perfectly docile. To the rest she was the same hell cat as before. But when I spoke severely to her in the end she went with one of the nurses as I commanded.[1]

This little incident provides us with a paradigm for all the medical stories collected in the volume called *Life Along the Passaic River* (1938). Consider the following points: (1) the patient, whether a child as in this case, or a teen-ager as in "The Girl with a Pimply Face," or an adult as in "A Night in June," is always female. In only one instance,

---

*From the *Georgia Review* 34, no. 4 (Winter 1980): 840–53. © 1980 by Marjorie Perloff. Reprinted by permission of the author. All rights reserved.

Marjorie Perloff

"A Face of Stone," is the baby a boy, and then Williams, who, by his own account, wrote these stories "at white heat" and "seldom revised at all,"[2] makes a remarkable slip:

> The man turned to his wife. Gimme the baby he said. . . . Give him to me. . . .
>   I hold her, the woman said keeping the child firmly in her arms.
> (*FD*, p. 168)

(2) The doctor-narrator, Williams' projected image of himself, is regularly presented as a no-nonsense, matter-of-fact type; if, in "World's End," he takes great pains for the little girl, he is also remarkably unflappable—a man who knows what needs to be done and does it. On the other hand, (3) although the doctor keeps his distance in the proper professional way and is designated throughout the *Passaic* stories as a married man whose emotional life lies elsewhere, his references to the treatment of the female patient are regularly couched in sexual language: in this case, he lifts the little girl "unresisting" into his lap where she "cuddled down," and he recalls that "I hugged her to myself" and "I kissed her hot little head." (4) In keeping with this subliminal erotic response of doctor to patient, the success of the "treatment" induces a sense of elation or victory that seems quite in excess of the actual event: "I hugged her to myself with the greatest feeling of contentment—happiness—imaginable." At the same time, (5) the patient is wary of all other doctors, which is to say of men who would or could have similar power over her. When the little girl wakens, she "would let no one else touch her. She clung to me perfectly docile. To the rest she was the same hell cat as before." Only his "severe" words can make her finally go with one of the nurses "as I commanded."

Critical commentary on these medical fictions has tended to rationalize their sexual component more or less as follows. Williams, both in his life and in his art, so the reasoning goes, was unusually sensitive and responsive to the human condition—especially to the condition of the ordinary poor people, many of them immigrants, who came to him as patients in his native Rutherford, New Jersey. His stance towards these people who become the characters of his short stories is, in James Breslin's words, at once "tough *and* sympathetic."[3] Williams does not sentimentalize their plight, yet he can see—in even the homeliest woman in her ninth month of pregnancy or in the "girl with a pimply

183

face"—a glimpse of what he calls "the hard straight thing in itself," the "Beautiful Thing" he was to celebrate in *Paterson*.[4] Williams' un-illusioned toughness and direct treatment of the thing gives the short stories their air of remarkable "authenticity." Or, as J. Hillis Miller has suggested:

> Williams' fiction is based on the power to put oneself within the life of another person and make him comprehensible by an objective report of his speech, movements, and facial expressions. There is none of the problem of knowing others which has long been a the-matic resource in fiction—all that play of perspectives and points of view, product of the assumption that each man is locked in the prison of his consciousness. . . . Williams' characters, like those of Virginia Woolf, penetrate one another completely and are known by a narrator who has transcended point of view so that he stands every-where in his story at once. His fiction, like that of the French "new novelists," is evidence of a Copernican revolution in the art of the novel. . . . Williams' people are not fixed personalities persisting through time, but are flowing centers of strength, polarizing them-selves differently according to each situation.[5]

But how *does* the poet enter the lives of those around him? "The reaction which gives Williams possession," Miller observes, "is strongly sexual." But since, in the Williams universe, one knows human bodies in the same way that one penetrates the life of flowers or fish, the sexual, Miller would argue, is more or less equated with the larger vitalistic, erotic pulse of the universe, the spirit celebrated from *Kora in Hell* to *Paterson* and beyond. In this context, Williams' ecstatic par-ticipation in the birth process of his patients (as, for example, in "A Night in June"), is read as emblematic of the poet's sense of creation, perpetual beginning. Birth is the opening of the field; the poet's mis-sion is "to make a start out of particulars."

No doubt Williams wanted his fiction to be read in this way. In his remarkably evasive *Autobiography*, Williams plays the role of genial in-nocent, the good fellow who has never quite figured out what, in his own words, makes women "tick." "I was an innocent sort of child," the first chapter begins, "and have remained so to this day. Only yes-terday, reading Chapman's *The Iliad of Homer*, did I realize for the first time that the derivation of the adjective venereal is from Venus! And I a physician practicing medicine for the past forty years! I was

Marjorie Perloff

stunned!"[6] But this "gee-whiz!" tone gives way, at moments, to its opposite: a cocky reminder that this poet-physician has been around. Consider the following passage in the Foreword:

> I do not intend to tell the particulars of the women I have been to bed with, or anything about them. Don't look for it. . . . I am extremely sexual in my desires: I carry them everywhere and at all times. I think that from that arises the drive which empowers us all. Given that drive, a man does with it what his mind directs. In the manner in which he directs that power lies his secret. We always try to hide the secret of our lives from the general stare. What I believe to be the hidden core of my life will not easily be deciphered, even when I tell, as here, the outer circumstances. (*Auto.*, unpaginated)

This is, as Herbert Leibowitz notes in a fascinating new essay on the *Autobiography*, "at once a warning and a challenge to the reader," as if to say, "keep your distance. Don't expect an easy intimacy with me."[7] In a later chapter of the autobiography called "Of Medicine and Poetry," Williams dangles the same key to his "secret life"—the "secret life I wanted to tell openly—if only I could"—in front of our eyes when he remarks:

> . . . my "medicine" was the thing which gained me entrance to these secret gardens of the self. It lay there, another world, in the self. I was permitted by my medical badge to follow the poor, defeated body into those gulfs and grottos. And the astonishing thing is that at such times and such places—foul as they may be . . . just there, the thing, in all its greatest beauty may for a moment be freed to fly for a moment guiltily around the room. In illness, in the permission I as a physician have had to be present at deaths and birth . . . just there—for a split second . . . it has fluttered before me for a moment, a phrase which I quickly write down on anything at hand, any piece of paper I can grab. (*Auto.*, pp. 288–89)

This astonishing passage is not just another account of the coming of the privileged moments that yield poetic vision. For the key word here is surely *guiltily*: "the permission I as a physician have had to be present," the poet's "medical badge," are what give him access to the "secret gardens of the self," but such access is perceived as somehow *guilty*. The medical metaphor, in other words, allows the narrator to

185

present his true feelings about women in the guise of safety and respectability. It would seem, then, that this narrator has not so much
"transcended point of view," as Miller suggests, as he has carefully
displaced it. In hugging the little girl who has finally stopped screaming and kicking, the doctor is, after all, behaving not abnormally or
inappropriately; his gestures are, in his own words, "not easily deci-
phered," and so the "hidden core" of his life is not violated. Indeed,
it is the poet's peculiar oscillation between "normalcy" (another routine house call with its trivial incident and predictable dialogue) and
the pressure of desire, a desire neither acted upon nor fully understood,
that gives the short stories of the thirties their particular poignancy.

"The Girl with a Pimply Face," for example, begins on a matter-of-
fact note:

> One of the local druggists sent in the call: 50 Summer St., second
> floor, the door to the left. It's a baby they've just brought from the
> hospital. Pretty bad condition I should imagine. Do you want to
> make it? I think they've had somebody else but don't like him, he
> added as an afterthought. (p. 117)

Challenged by his "afterthought" which presents him with an unknown rival, the physician-as-knight sets out on a quest to rescue, ultimately three damsels in distress: baby girl, mother, and surrogate
patient in the person of the baby' sister—"a lank haired girl of about
fifteen standing chewing gum and eyeing me curiously from beside the
kitchen table." The narrator's immediate response to this girl is "Boy,
she was tough and no kidding but I fell for her immediately." And after
some desultory talk about the baby's diarrhea, he notes: "This young
kid in charge of the house did something to me that I liked. She was
just a child but nobody was putting anything over on her if she knew
it."

Although, or perhaps perversely *because* her legs are covered with
scabby sores, her feet with big brown spots, and her face with terrible
acne, the unnamed girl attracts the doctor and he mentally undresses
her: "But after all she wasn't such a child. She had breasts you knew
would be like small stones to the hand, good muscular arms and fine
hard legs. . . . She was heavily tanned too, wherever her skin showed."
(p. 119). The physician's sensible advice as to what soap the girl should
use for her face, and his gentle reprimand that she should be in school

must be seen in the context of these fleeting thoughts about her breasts and legs; she is not just any patient but an ignorant, helpless girl to whom he can minister in the role of masterful, efficient male. Imagine Williams' story as "The Boy with a Pimply Face," and the point will become clear.

When the baby's mother finally arrives and the doctor examines the real patient, he finds that the infant has a severe congenital heart defect. Calmly and professionally, he notes that "she was no good, never would be," but he prescribes formula, calms down the mother, and writes out a prescription for "lotio alba comp." for the teen-age girl's acne. "The two older women looked at me in astonishment—wondering, I suppose, how I knew the girl." To them, he evidently appears as a miracle worker. It is a response nicely balanced in the story by the tolerant skepticism of the doctor's wife:

> What's it all about, my wife asked me in the evening. She had heard about the case. Gee! I sure met a wonderful girl, I told her.
> What! another?
> Some tough baby. I'm crazy about her. Talk about straight stuff. . . . And I recounted to her the sort of case it was and what I had done. The mother's an odd one too. I don't quite make her out.
> Did they pay you?
> No. I don't suppose they have any cash.
> Going back?
> Sure. Have to.
> Well, I don't see why you have to do all this charity work. Now that's a case you should report to the Emergency Relief. You'll get at least two dollars a call from them. (p. 126)

There is a fine irony in this last speech, for the wife cannot understand—as the reader does by this time—that her husband is getting much more than "two dollars" for his "charity work." He too is in need of a kind of "emergency relief." Indeed, the doctor is, in his own words, so "keenly interested," that even a colleague's account of the case—his warning that the mother is an alcoholic, the father a liar who pretends to have no money, and that the "pimply faced little bitch," as he calls her, has "a dozen wise guys on her trail every night in the week" and deserves to be run out of town—cannot alter the narrator's feelings. And in an oblique way, his "sympathy game," as the other doctor calls it, is rewarded. Here is Williams' conclusion:

The last time I went I heard the, Come in! from the front of the house. The fifteen-year-old was in there at the window in a rocking chair with the tightly wrapped baby in her arms. She got up. Her legs were bare to the hips. A powerful little animal.

What are you doing? Going swimming? I asked.

Naw, that's my gym suit. What the kids wear for Physical Training in school.

How's the baby?

She's all right.

Do you mean it?

Sure, she eats fine now.

Tell your mother to bring it to the office some day so I can weigh it. The food'll need increasing in another week or two anyway.

I'll tell her.

How's your face?

Gettin' better.

My God, it *is*, I said. And it was much better. Going back to school now?

Yeah, I had tuh. (p. 130)

This is not the inconsequential ending it appears to be. For the implication is that, consciously or unconsciously, the girl goes back to school in response to the doctor's wish. The baby is getting better, the mother is placated, the girl's skin is clearing up. Thus the "powerful little animal" with the bare legs has responded to the doctor's power.

To read "The Girl with a Pimply Face" as a story about the beauty, vitality and strength latent in even the most "venal and oppressive environment"[8] is, I think, to sentimentalize it. Like "The Young Housewife," in which the poet compares the woman to "a fallen leaf" and then declares, with humorous asperity, "The noiseless wheels of my car / rush with a crackling sound over / dried leaves as I bow and pass smiling,"[9] this short story is a fantasy of sexual possession. But it is important to note that unlike the fictions of such postmodern writers as Coover or Sorrentino or Kozinski, Williams' story is firmly wedded to the mimetic convention. The narrator, that is to say, is not about to engage in kinky sex with the pimply-faced girl. Rather, the focus is on the disparity between the doctor's external manner—so composed and matter-of-fact—and his sexual urges.

Another interesting variation on the paradigm I have described is found in "A Night in June." Here the doctor's quest romance takes him across town to deliver the ninth baby of an Italian woman named

Marjorie Perloff

Angelina. He approaches the prospect of the delivery (he has brought all but one of Angelina's children into the world and remembers with grief her first baby which he lost) as one would contemplate a love affair. Fondly, he prepares his instruments and puts them in an old satchel; lovingly, he sets out into the "beautiful June night." All is peaceful and still: "The lighted clock in the tower over the factory said 3:20." At the house, there is much to do and the doctor once again becomes his efficient self, selecting artery clamps and scissors, preparing the hot water, ordering an enema, and so on. Labor has not yet begun and he sleeps briefly, awakening to "the peace of the room" that strikes him as "delicious." Later, he gives Angelina a dose of pituitrin; "She had stronger pains but without effect." Here is the poet's reaction:

> Maybe I'd better give you a still larger dose, I said. She made no demur. Well, let me see if I can help you first. I sat on the edge of the bed while the sister-in-law held the candle again glancing at the window where the daylight was growing. With my left hand steering the child's head, I used my ungloved right hand outside on her bare abdomen to press upon the fundus. The woman and I then got to work. Her two hands grabbed me at first a little timidly about the right wrist and forearm. Go ahead, I said. Pull hard. I welcomed the feel of her hands and the strong pull. It quieted me in the way the whole house had quieted me all night.
>
> This woman in her present condition would have seemed repulsive to me ten years ago—now, poor soul, I see her to be as clean as a cow that calves. The flesh of my arm lay against the flesh of her knee gratefully. It was I who was being comforted and soothed. (p. 142)

Here delivery becomes deliverance. The physical ritual of the birth process becomes, in Williams' account, a variation on the act of love—the welcome feel of the woman's hands, the pressing down, the strong pull, the relief and relaxation: "The flesh of my arm lay against the flesh of her knee gratefully." By such contact, the doctor is "comforted and soothed." And yet this erotic experience is "permitted by the poet's medical badge" and hence domesticated, made safe. Within minutes, he is worrying about putting drops into the new baby's eyes and getting rid of the afterbirth. Again, he asserts his down-to-earth, "sensible" role as doctor, prescribing boric-acid powder to dry up the

189

belly button. Even this new belly button, I might add, belongs to a baby girl.

The medical metaphor thus provides Williams with a plausible evasion of a persistent problem. For curiously, in the rare stories in which the challenge becomes real, as it does in "The Venus" (the story originally at the center of *A Voyage to Pagany* which Williams removed, presumably because the publisher found the manuscript too long),[10] the self-assurance of the narrator dissolves. Here is the reaction of Dev (the protagonist of *Pagany* who is a thinly disguised version of Williams himself) to the German girl he meets on an outing to Frascati:

> This day it was hot. Fraülein von J. seemed very simple, very direct, and to his Roman mood miraculously beautiful. In her unstylish long-sleeved German clothes, her rough stockings and heavy walking-shoes, Evans found her, nevertheless, ethereally graceful. But the clear features, the high forehead, the brilliant perfect lips, the well-shaped nose, and best of all the shining mistlike palegold hair unaffectedly drawn back—frightened him. For himself he did not know where to begin (p. 212)

On Roman soil, stripped of his medical props and defining role, the Williams hero is like a knight stripped of his armor and his magic talisman which will open the gates to the castle. Face to face with a beautiful woman who has no reason to be dependent on him, he is frightened. "Not knowing what else to do or to say, he too looked (as the tram went through some bare vineyards) straight back into her clear blue eyes with his evasive dark ones." Confronted by this Venus who keeps asking him what America is like, the poet-doctor retreats. For to be an American is, as Williams knew only too well, to fear eros even as one is obsessed with it. America, he tells the Fraülein, "is a world where no man dare learn anything that concerns him intimately—but sorrow—for should we learn pleasure, it is instantly and violently torn from us as by a pack of hungry wolves so starved for it are we." But when the German Venus then asks him why, given his attitude, he should want to return to America, Dev replies: "It is that I may the better hide everything that is secretly valuable in myself, or have it defiled. So safety in crowds."

Here again is the guilty secret to which Williams alludes again and again. The "pagan grove" of Frascati is too openly erotic; Dev's last words to the German girl are "come on . . . let's get out of this." And we recall that it is "medicine" that gives him entrance to the "secret gardens of the self."

Indeed, the failure of medicine is oddly equated with the failure of desire. The very short story "The Accident," written as early as 1921 but included in the Passaic volume, begins with the sentence, "Death is difficult for the senses to alight on" (p. 221). The surprising word here is "senses" where we would expect "mind" or "heart." The narrator now explains: "After twelve days struggling with a girl to keep life in her, losing, winning, it is not easy to give her up. One has studied her inch by inch, one has grown used to the life in her. It is natural." From this deathbed image, the story now cuts abruptly to the following morning, a morning of spring sunshine in which the poet is driving somewhere with his baby son. Having so recently witnessed the girl's death, his mood is one of unrelieved sexual tension:

> What are you stopping here for! To show him the four goats. Come on. No? Ah! She blushes and hides her face. Down the road come three boys in long pants. Good God, good God! How a man will waste himself. She is no more than a piece of cake to be eaten by anyone. Her hips beside me have set me into a fever. I was up half the night last night, my nerves have the insulation worn off them. (p. 221)

In the Laurentian sequence that follows, the doctor converts his sexual energy into some "harmless" play with the goats; he tries, for example, to back the smallest goat "around the tree till it can go no further," whereupon the goat "tries to crowd between me and the tree." The doctor wins this particular struggle and lets the baby touch the goat's "hairy cheek" and stroke its flanks. We read: "The nozzle is hairy, the nose narrow; the moist black skin at the tip, slit either side by curled nostrils, vibrates sensitively." Here it is, of course, the father rather than the child who finds relief. Accordingly, when (on their way back to the car) the baby stumbles and "falls forward on his hands," his face in the dirt, the doctor-father is struck with guilt. For why did he bring the child here in the first place? And although the baby's fall is in fact a pure "accident," the narrator's guilt is oddly confirmed by the response of the "six women" whose heads appear, suddenly and mysteriously, "in the windows of the Franco-American Chemical Co. across the way." "They watch the baby, wondering if he is hurt. They linger to look out. They open the windows" (p. 224). The eyes of these strange women seem to penetrate what Williams calls the "hidden core" of his life; it is as if they challenge his erotic fantasy. But then, in a sudden transformation that recalls Surrealist film, the women are transformed: "They laugh and wave their hands." And indeed life, seemingly cut off by the death of the little girl as well as by his own baby's accident, goes on:

> Over against them in an open field a man and a boy on their hands and knees are planting out slender green slips in the fresh dirt, row after row.
> We enter the car. The baby waves his hand. Good-bye! (p. 224)

To read a story like "The Accident" is rather like looking at a relief map of what appear to be flatlands, only to see little mountain-shapes well up from beneath the surface and create peculiar irregularities. But before we can take the measure of these new mountains, canyons, and watercourses, the map collapses from somewhere within and flattens out once again. So in "The Accident," the baby's waving of the hand and the word "Good-bye" break the spell; the narrator's desire is once again enclosed in its secret chamber and "normalcy" is restored.

But what happens when the map undergoes no such transformations, when the tension between desire and the need for safety disappears? In such later fictions as "The Farmers' Daughters" (1957), the medical paradigm I have been describing undergoes some curious changes. The patient or patients are, as always in Williams, female: in this case, Margaret and Helen—both lonely and self-destructive women who turn to the doctor (here presented in the third person) for help. But this doctor is not called upon to deliver babies; rather he gives vitamin shots, advises the persistent Margaret on how to improve her breasts, and counsels Helen on her alcoholism. More important, the doctor of this story is no longer the tough but sympathetic narrator of "The Use of Force" or "A Face of Stone"; he is, on the contrary, deeply involved in the lives of the two women, even though he is himself safely married.

Throughout the story, there are allusions to his lovemaking, whether or not it is fully acted out, with both women, and especially with Helen, the stronger of the two, who turns out to be the survivor. Interestingly, in this story where the doctor's sexual interest in his patient becomes quite overt, there is never the moment of satisfaction that

occurs in "A Night in June" or in "World's End"—the moment of bliss
when the doctor finds the proper "treatment" for the patient. It is as
if Williams needed to hide what he calls the "inner core" of his life, to
keep the "Beautiful Thing" buried in the recesses of his being. When,
as in "The Farmers' Daughters," the sexual encounter moves from the
realm of fantasy to reality, a curious apathy—a kind of *post coitum tris-
tia*—occurs, an apathy coupled with a new irritatingly patronizing tone
toward women. Consider this passage:

> The doctor had a climbing rose in his garden named Jacquot which
> his wife and he both very much admired. It was a peach-pink ram-
> bler, the petals fading to a delicate lavender after the first flowering.
> More than that, the rose throve in their garden against odds thought
> by the man who sold them the plant to be overwhelming. . . .
>
> In spite of that its vigor was phenomenal, you couldn't kill it. It
> covered the trellis with a profusion of blossoms that in early June
> were a wonder to see. In addition it was delicately scented so that
> their whole yard smelled of it when it was in bloom. He had never
> encountered it in any other garden.
>
> Once he spoke of it to Helen and invited her to come over and
> see it and whiff its odor during the flowering season.
>
> They gave her a layered shoot; she planted it and it took hold at
> once. (pp. 366-67)

So the doctor keeps the rosebush for his wife but gives a shoot to
Helen: he has his cake and eats it too. Both Margaret and Helen have
had lovers and husbands, but they constantly assure their doctor that
he is the only man they can really love and trust, their only friend and
confidant. He is the recipient of Helen's favorite photograph, of Margaret's post-Thanksgiving banquet ("a poetic occasion, a love feast").
It is he who yearns for Helen's "Dresden china blue eyes," just as she
yearns for her little Dresden china doll—he who tells Helen, "When
you talk about that doll you're beautiful." Again, when Margaret decides to leave town in search of new adventure, he chides her gently
but tells her: "in many ways you are the best of us, the most direct,
the most honest—yes, and in the end, the most virtuous." Hearing
these words, Margaret predictably "wrapped her arms around his neck,
curled up on his knees and sobbed quietly." Finally after Margaret's
terrible death (she is murdered by her most recent fly-by-night husband), Helen tells the doctor:

No one came to the funeral but her family and me. They didn't open the casket. There were no flowers beside the bunch of red roses I'd sent her, her favorite flower.—How are you, my sweet? Take good care of yourself 'cause I can't afford to lose you. When she died, I died too, you're the only one I have left. (p. 373)

In his discussion of "The Farmers' Daughters," Thomas Whitaker concludes that each of the three characters sums up one facet of their common predicament: "in Margaret, the most desperate and naked loneliness; in Helen, a more vigorous if precarious thriving despite that loneliness; and in the doctor—imperfectly manifest through his own need—that non-possessive love which might cure the alienation from which all suffer."[11] This is, I think, to sugercoat the pill. For the doctor's "love" is *not* as nonpossessive as all that: he is, after all, charmed and titillated by the attentions of Margaret and Helen, by their openly declared love, their kisses and embraces. As opposed to the two women who are, in their different ways, losers, the doctor (however unfulfilled some of his yearnings may be) retains his position and his equilibrium; he is left, finally, with bittersweet and tender memories—memories that form the substance of the fiction itself.

Whitaker rightly points out that the doctor in this story is not the real focus of attention, that he is "hardly more than a mode of relating. . . . The narrative structure causes us . . . not to look *at* him so much as to see with his eyes."[12] But it is precisely this narrative stance that makes "The Farmers' Daughters" problematic. For whereas the earlier fictions delineate the quandaries attendant upon a dimly understood sexual tension, "Farmers' Daughters" is, as it were, carefully censored so as to give the reader no choice but to accept the narrator's overt evaluation of himself and of his two "patients." Unlike the protagonist of the earlier story, "The Use of Force," who suddenly remarks: "I could have torn the child apart in my own fury and enjoyed it. It was a pleasure to attack her," (p. 134), this doctor is careful not to drop his guard. Indeed, he resembles the speaker of "Asphodel, that Greeny Flower," who believes he can justify his countless infidelities to his wife by telling her:

> Imagine you saw
> a field made up of women
> all silver-white
> What should you do
> but love them?[13]

It sounds so simple, so earthy and natural. But as the recently published manuscript called "Rome" (the first version of *Voyage to Pagany*)[14] reminds us—and as Williams' best work makes clear—the Man who Loved Women never had quite so easy a time of it. For the "beautiful thing" flies only for a moment "guiltily about the room." Or, as Williams put it in a cancelled preface to "The Girl with a Pimply Face":

> How shall I say it? I who have wished to embrace the world with love have succeeded only in binding to myself a wife and children. . . ? I who have wished, in a general way, to die for love have suffered only the small accidents of fatigue, bewilderment and loss?
>
> Who feels enough confidence to say anything? All I know is that no matter what we have dreamed or desired it slips away unless by a supreme effort we struggle to detain it.[15]

It is this "struggle to detain" what "we have dreamed or desired" that gives force to Williams' finest stories, such as "The Accident" or "A Face of Stone." And the younger Williams knew, as perhaps the mature poet no longer cared to admit, that such struggle was a bloody business. In the ecstasy of the "guilty" moment, the poet's "medical badge" could become a kind of "open sesame." But, as Dev tells the beautiful Fraülein in "The Venus": "To me it is a hard, barren life, where I am 'alone' and unmolested (work as I do in the thick of it) though in constant danger lest some slip send me to perdition." (p. 216).

Notes

1. *The Farmers' Daughters: The Collected Stories of William Carlos Williams* (New York: New Directions, 1961). All parenthetical page references not otherwise identified are to this text.

2. Williams, *I Wanted to Write a Poem: The Autobiography of the Works of a Poet*, ed. Edith Heal (Boston: Beacon Press, 1968), p. 63.

3. *William Carlos Williams: An American Artist* (New York: Oxford, 1970), p. 154. Breslin's chapter "The Fiction of a Doctor," from which this phrase comes, is the best extended commentary on Williams' fiction available.

4. See Breslin, p. 160; Thomas R. Whitaker, *William Carlos Williams* (New York: Twayne Publishers, Inc., 1968). p. 103; Robert Coles, *William Carlos Williams: The Knack of Survival in America* (New Brunswick, N. J.: Rutgers Univ. Press, 1975), pp. 28–33.

The Critics

5. *Poets of Reality: Six Twentieth-Century Writers* (1965; rpt. New York: Atheneum, 1969), p. 323.

6. *The Autobiography of William Carlos Williams* (1951; rpt. New York: New Directions, 1967), p. 3. Subsequently cited as *Auto*.

7. See Herbert Leibowitz, "You Can't Beat Innocence: *The Autobiography of William Carlos Williams,*" *American Poetry Review* 10, no. 2 (March/April 1981):35–47.

8. The phrase is Thomas Whitaker's; see *Williams*, p. 101.

9. *Selected Poems* (New York: New Directions, 1969), p. 77.

10. See Harry Levin, "Introduction" to Williams' *A Voyage to Pagany* (1928; rpt. New York: New Directions, 1970), pp. xvi–xvii.

11. *Williams*, p. 118.

12. See Whitaker, *Williams*, p. 118; J. Hillis Miller, *Poets of Reality*, p. 323.

13. *Pictures from Brueghel and Other Poems* (New York: New Directions, 1962), pp. 159–60.

14. See "William Carlos Williams' *Rome,*" ed. Steven Ross Loevy, *The Iowa Review*, 9 (Summer 1978), 1–65. This improvisational diary abounds in four-letter words and "dirty" references, expressing the poet's anger and frustration at finding no proper outlet for his sexual desire.

15. Cited by Whitaker in *Williams*, pp. 103–4.

Chronology

1883   William Carlos Williams born 17 September, Rutherford, New Jersey.

1897–1898   Attends school in Switzerland and Paris.

1899   Attends Horace Mann School, New York City.

1902   Enrolls in medical school, University of Pennsylvania.

1906   Receives M. D. degree.

1907   Starts internship and specialty in pediatrics at Nursery and Children's Hospital.

1909   Moves back to Rutherford; meets Florence Herman; travels to Leipzig.

1910   Travels to England; sees Pound and Yeats; tours France, Italy, and Spain; returns to Rutherford and private practice as pediatrician and physician.

1912   Marries "Flossie."

1913   Establishes home and practice at 9 Ridge Road.

1915   Helps Alfred Kreymborg with little magazine *Others*.

1919   Publishes short stories in *The Little Review*.

1920   Starts *Contact* with Robert McAlmon; *Kora in Hell: Improvisations*.

1923   *The Great American Novel*.

1924   Travels to France with Flossie; meets Joyce, Hemingway, Stein, expatriates.

1925   *In the American Grain*.

1928   *A Voyage to Pagany*; "The Venus."

1932   Starts *Contact* again, now with Nathanael West; *The Knife of the Times and Other Stories; A Novelette and Other Prose, 1921–1931*.

1934   *Collected Poems, 1921–1931*.

1937   *White Mule.*

1938   *Life Along the Passaic River.*

1940   *In the Money.*

1946   *Paterson, Book 1.*

1947   Makes first trip as an adult to American West.

1948   *Paterson, Book 2.*

1949   Named fellow of the Library of Congress; *Paterson, Book 3.*

1950   *Make Light of It: Collected Stories; The Collected Later Poems*; wins National Book Award; lectures on the short story at University of Washington, University of Oregon, and Reed College.

1951   *The Autobiography; Patterson, Book 4*; has first cerebral hemorrhage; retires from medical practice.

1952   *The Build Up.*

1954   *Selected Essays.*

1957   *Selected Letters.*

1958   *Paterson, Book 5.*

1959   *Yes, Mrs. Williams: A Personal Record of My Mother.*

1961   *The Farmers' Daughters: The Collected Stories; Many Loves and Other Plays: The Collected Plays.*

1963   Dies, 4 March; wins Pulitzer Prize posthumously.

Selected Bibliography

Primary Works

Uncollected Stories

"Jean Beicke," "The Use of Force," "The Dawn of Another Day," "The Girl with a Pimply Face," and "A Night in June." In *Blast: A Magazine of Proletarian Short Stories,* edited by Fred R. Miller and Sam Sorkin, with William Carlos Williams as advisory editor. September 1933–November 1934.

"The Accident." In *Contact: An American Quarterly Review,* 1920–23, edited by William Carlos Williams and Robert M. McAlmon. New York: Kraus Reprint Corp., 1967.

Miscellaneous stories in the Williams archives at the Lockwood and Beinecke libraries include:

"A Black Democrat," "A Boy in the Family," "The Delicacies," "A Difficult Man," "The Fable of the Skunk Mencken," "The Drill Sergeant," "Effie Deans," "A Folded Skyscraper," "The Five Dollar Guy," "Genesis," "Sister under the Skin," "Pennsylvania Comes Through," "The Unfinished Refrain," "The Dying Priest," "The Ten Dollar Bill," "Long Island Sound."

Collected Stories

The Doctor Stories. Compiled and with an introduction by Robert Coles. New York: New Directions, 1984. Includes "Mind and Body," "Old Doc Rivers," "The Girl with a Pimply Face," "The Use of Force," "A Night in June," "Jean Beicke," "A Face of Stone," "Danse Pseudomacabre," "The Paid Nurse," "Ancient Gentility," "Verbal Transcription: 6 A.M."

The Farmers' Daughters: The Collected Stories of William Carlos Williams. Introduction by Van Wyck Brooks. New York: New Directions, 1961. Includes "The Farmers' Daughters," in addition to the stories first collected in *Make Light of It* (which also collected the stories of *The Knife of the Times* and *Life Along the Passaic River* as well as a subgrouping entitled "Beer and Cold Cuts").

Selected Bibliography

The Knife of the Times and Other Stories. Ithaca, N. Y.: Dragon Press, 1932; Folcroft Penn.: Folcroft Library Edition, 1974. Includes "The Knife of the Times," "A Visit to the Fair," "Hands across the Sea," "The Sailor's Son," "An Old Time Raid," "The Buffalos," "Mind and Body," "The Colored Girls of Passenack—Old and New," "A Descendant of Kings," "Pink and Blue," and "Old Doc Rivers."

Life Along the Passaic River. Norfolk, Conn.: New Directions, 1938. Includes "Life Along the Passaic River," "The Girl with a Pimply Face," "The Use of Force," "A Night in June," "The Dawn of Another Day," "Jean Beicke," "A Face of Stone," "To Fall Asleep," "The Cold World," "Four Bottles of Beer," "At the Front," "The Right Thing," "Second Marriage," "A Difficult Man," "Danse Pseudomacabre," "The Venus," "Under the Greenwood Tree," "World's End."

Make Light of It: Collected Stories of William Carlos Williams. New York: Random House, 1950. Includes all of the stories in *The Knife of the Times* and *Life Along the Passaic River* in addition to the following stories under the grouping of "Beer and Cold Cuts": "The Burden of Loneliness," "Above the River," "No Place for a Woman," "The Paid Nurse," "Frankie and the Newspaperman," "Ancient Gentility," "The Final Embarrassment," "The Round the World Fliers," "The Redhead," "Verbal Transcription: 6 A.M.," "The Insane," "The Good Old Days," "A Good-Natured Sloth," "A Lucky Break," "The Pace That Kills," "Lena," "Country Rain," "Inquest," "Comedy Entombed," and "The Zoo."

Poetry

The Collected Poems of William Carlos Williams. Edited by A. Walton Litz and Christopher MacGowan. Vol. 1, 1909–39. New York: New Directions, 1986.

Collected Poems, 1921–1931. Preface by Wallace Stevens. New York: Objectivist Press, 1934.

Paterson. New York: New Directions, 1958.

Selected Poems. Edited with an introduction by Charles Tomlinson. New York: New Directions, 1985.

Plays

Many Loves and Other Plays: The Collected Plays of William Carlos Williams. Norfolk, Conn.: New Directions, 1961.

Prose Other Than Stories

"An Approach to a Poem." In *English Institute Essays 1947*, 50–75. New York: Columbia University Press, 1948.

Selected Bibliography

The Autobiography of William Carlos Williams. New York: New Directions, 1951.

The Build Up. New York: Random House, 1952.

A Beginning on the Short Story (Notes) (Outcast Chapbooks, xvii). Yonkers, N.Y.: Alicat Bookshop Press, 1950; Folcroft, Penn.: Folcroft Library Edition, 1974.

"The *Contact* Story," *Contact: The San Francisco Journal of New Writing, Art and Ideas* 1, no. 1 (1959):75–77.

The Embodiment of Knowledge. New York: New Directions, 1974.

"Free Verse." In *The Princeton Encyclopedia of Poetry and Poetics,* edited by Alex Preminger, 288–90. Princeton: Princeton University Press, 1974.

"Letter," *Hot Afternoons Have Been in Montana. Poems with a Letter by William Carlos Williams.* Siegel, Eli. New York: Definition Press, 1957.

Imaginations. Edited with an introduction by Webster Schott. New York: New Directions, 1970.

In the American Grain. New York: New Directions, 1956.

In the Money, White Mule—part 2. Norfolk, Conn.: New Directions, 1940.

Kora in Hell: Improvisations. Boston: Four Seas Press, 1920.

A Novelette and Other Prose (1921–1931). Toulouse, France: Imprimerie F. Cabasson, 1932.

"Objectivism." In *The Princeton Encyclopedia of Poetry and Poetics,* edited by Alex Preminger, 582. Princeton: Princeton University Press, 1974.

Selected Essays of William Carlos Williams. New York: Random House, 1954. Published in a New Directions paperback in 1969.

The Selected Letters of William Carlos Williams, edited by John C. Thrilwall. New York: New Directions, 1957.

A Voyage to Pagany, New York: New Directions, 1928. Introduction by Harry Levin, 1970.

The William Carlos Williams Reader. Edited wth an introduction by M. L. Rosenthal. New York: New Directions, 1966.

White Mule. Norfolk, Conn.: New Directions, 1937.

Yes, Mrs. Williams. New York: McDowell, Obolensky, 1959.

Secondary Works

Museum Exhibition

"William Carlos Williams and the American Scene 1920–1940," Whitney Museum of American Art, New York, 12 December, 1978– 4 February 1979.

Bibliographies

Baldwin, Neil. 1947, *The Manuscripts and Letters of William Carlos Williams in the Poetry Collection of the Lockwood Memorial Library.* State University of

Selected Bibliography

New York at Buffalo. A descriptive catalog/Neil Baldwin, Steven L. Meyers; foreword by Robert Creeley. Boston: G. K. Hall, 1978.

Engels, John. *Checklist of William Carlos Williams*. Columbus, Ohio: Charles E. Merrill, 1969.

Rhodehamel, John. "The William Carlos Williams Holdings in the Lilly Library." *William Carlos Williams Newsletter* 3, no. 1:24–25.

Sten, Christopher. "William Carlos Williams: El Hombre at 100." *American Studies International* 21, no. 5 (October 1983):53–60.

Tashjian, Dickran. "Some New Williams Citations." *William Carlos Williams Newsletters* 3, no. 2:22–23.

Vose, Clemet E. "Addendum to the Williams Bibliography." *William Carlos Williams Newsletter* 3, no. 2:22–23.

Wallace, Emily Mitchell. *A Bibliography of William Carlos Williams*. Middletown, Conn.: Wesleyan University Press, 1968.

Interviews

Howe, Susan and Charles Ruas. "New Directions: An Interview with James Laughlin." In *The Art of Literary Publishing: Editors on Their Craft*. Edited by Bill Henderson. Yonkers, N.Y.: The Pushcart Book Press, 1980, 13–48.

I Wanted to Write a Poem: The Autobiography of the Works of a Poet. Reported and edited by Edith Heal. New York: New Directions, 1958.

Koehler, Stanley. "William Carlos Williams." In *Writers at Work: The Paris Review Interviews*, Third Series, edited by George Plimpton. Introduction by Alfred Kazin. New York: Viking Press, 1967, (Penguin, 1977).

Wagner, Linda W. *Interviews with William Carlos Williams: Speaking Straight Ahead*. New York: New Directions, 1976.

Criticism

Angoff, Charles, ed. *William Carlos Williams*. Rutherford, N.J.: Fairleigh Dickinson University Press, 1974.

Bell, Barbara Currier. "Williams' 'The Use of Force' and First Principles in Medical Ethics." *Literature and Medicine* 3 (1984):143–51.

Bettinger, James R. "Each Word Takes Claim: William Carlos Williams' *White Mule* and *The Great American Novel*." *Review of Contemporary Fiction* 4, no. 1:1984, 145–57.

Breslin, James E. B. *William Carlos Williams: An American Artist*. Chicago: University of Chicago Press, 1985.

Brinnin, John Malcolm. *William Carlos Williams*. Minneapolis: University of Minnesota Press, 1963.

Brooks, Van Wyck. Introduction to *The Farmers' Daughters: The Collected Stories of William Carlos Williams*. New York: New Directions, 1961.

Coles, Robert. *William Carlos Williams: The Knack of Survival in America*. New Brunswick, NJ: Rutgers University Press, 1975.

————. Introduction to *William Carlos Williams: The Doctor Stories*. New York: New Directions, 1984.

Christensen, Paul. "William Carlos Williams in the Forties: Prelude to Post-modernism." In *Ezra Pound and William Carlos Williams: The University of Pennsylvania Conference Papers*, edited by Daniel Hoffman. Philadelphia: University of Pennsylvania Press, 1983, 143–63.

Creeley, Robert. "A Visit with Dr. Williams." *Sagetrieb* 3 no. 2 (Fall, 1984):27–35.

Davies, John C. "'Which is the American?' Themes, Techniques, and Meaning in William Carlos Williams' Three Novels, *White Mule* (1937), *In The Money* (1940), and *The Build Up* (1952)." *Journal of American Studies* 6, no. 2 (August 1972):189–200.

Derounian, Kathryn Zabelle. "William Carlos Williams." In *Critical Survey of Short Fiction*, edited by Frank Magill. Englewood Cliffs, NJ: Salem Press, 1981, 2441–46.

Doyle, Charles, ed. *William Carlos Williams: The Critical Heritage*. London: Routledge and Kegan Paul, 1980.

Elliot, Emory, ed. *Literary History of the United States*. New York: Columbia University Press, 1988.

Ellmann, Richard, and Charles Feidelson, Jr. *The Modern Tradition: Back-grounds of Modern Literature*. New York: Oxford University Press, 1965.

Ellmann, Richard, and Robert O'Clair, eds. "William Carlos Williams." In *The Norton Anthology of Modern Poetry*. New York: W. W. Norton, 1973, 284–87.

Engle, Paul. "William Carlos Williams, M.D." *Horizon* 1, no. 4 (March 1959):60–61.

Engels, John. *Guide to William Carlos Williams*. Merrill Guides. Columbus, Ohio: Charles E. Merrill, 1969.

Fedo, David A. *William Carlos Williams: A Poet in the American Theatre*, (Studies in Modern Literature, No. 7, A. Walton Litz, general series editor). Ann Arbor, Mich.: UMI Research Press, 1988.

Fox, Hugh. "The Genuine Avant-Garde: William Carlos Williams' Credo." *Southwest Review* 59 (Summer 1974): 285–99.

Fredman, Stephan. "American Poet's Prose and the Crisis of Verse." *American Poetry* 1, no. 1 (Fall 1983):49–63.

Gallagher, Fergal. "Further Freudian Implications in William Carlos Williams' 'The Use of Force,'" *CEA Critic* 34, no. 4:20–21.

Graham, Theodora R. "A New Williams Short Story: 'Long Island Sound.' " *William Carlos Williams Review* 7, no. 2 (Fall 1981):1–3.

————. "The Courage of His Diversity: Medicine, Writing and William Carlos Williams." *Literature and Medicine* 2 (1983):9–20.

Selected Bibliography

Guimond, James. *The Art of William Carlos Williams: A Discovery and Possession of America.* Urbana: University of Illinois Press, 1968.

Hatlen, Burton. "The Quest for the Concrete Particular, or Do Poets Have Something to Say to Sociolinguists?" *Rhetoric 78: Proceedings of Theory of Rhetoric: An Interdisciplinary Conference,* edited by Robert L. Brown, Jr., and Martin Steinmann, Jr., 143–78. Minneapolis: University of Minnesota Center for Advanced Studies in Language, Style, and Literary Theory, 1979.

Hoffman, Daniel. "Poetry: After Modernism." In *Harvard Guide to Contemporary American Writing,* edited by Daniel Hoffman. Cambridge, Mass.: Harvard University Press, 1979, 439–95.

Holder, Alan. "*In the American Grain:* William Carlos Williams on the American Past." *American Quarterly* 19, no. 3 (Fall 1967):499–515.

Holton, Milne. "To Hit Love Aslant, Poetry and William Carlos Williams." In David J. Burrows, Lewis M. Dabney, Milne Holton, Grosvenor E. Powell, *Private Dealings: Eight Modern American Writers,* 50–69. Stockholm: Almqvist and Wiksell, 1969.

Jay, Paul L. "American Modernism and the Uses of History: The Case of William Carlos Williams." *New Orleans Review* 9, no. 3 (Winter 1982):16–25.

Kutzinski, Vera M. *Against the American Grain: Myth and History in William Carlos Williams, Jay Wright, and Nicholas Guillen.* Baltimore: Johns Hopkins University Press, 1987.

Koch, Vivienne. *William Carlos Williams.* Norfolk, Conn.: New Directions, 1950.

Laughlin, James. "For the Record: On *New Directions* and Others." *American Poetry* 2, no. 3 (Spring 1984): 47–61.

———. "Letters from Pound and Williams." *Helix* 13–14, (1983):97–108.

———. "Gists and Piths: From the Letters of Pound and Williams." In *Ezra Pound and William Carlos Williams: The University of Pennsylvania Conference Papers,* edited by Daniel Hoffman. Philadelphia: University of Pennsylvania Press, 1983, 197–209.

Levertov, Denise. "The Ideas in the Things." In *Ezra Pound and William Carlos Williams: The University of Pennsylvania Conference Papers,* edited by Daniel Hoffman. Philadelphia: University of Pennsylvania Press, 1983, 131–42.

Litz, A. Walton, Nathaniel Burt, and Lawrence B. Holland, eds. "William Carlos Williams." In *The Literary History of New Jersey,* 83–122. Princeton, N.J.: D. Van Nostrand Co., 1964.

Litz, A. Walton and Christopher MacGowan. "Further Notes on the Text of the Collected Poems of William Carlos Williams, Vol. 1: 1909–1939." *William Carlos Williams Review* 13, no. 1 (Spring 1987):7–13.

Loewinsohn, Ron. Introduction to *The Embodiment of Knowledge,* edited by and with an introduction by Ron Loewinsohn. New York: New Directions, 1974.

———. "Towards the Canonization of William Carlos Williams." *Massachusetts Review* 13, no. 4 (Autumn 1972):661–75.

Mariani, Paul. *William Carlos Williams: A New World Naked.* New York: McGraw-Hill Book Co., 1981.

Marling, William. *William Carlos Williams and the Painters, 1909–1923.* Athens: Ohio University Press, 1982.

Messerli, Douglas. "A World Detached: The Early Criticism of William Carlos Williams." *Sagetrieb* 3, no. 2 (Fall 1984):89–98.

Minter, David L. *The Interpreted Design as a Structural Principle in American Literature.* New Haven, Conn.: Yale University Press, 1969.

Miklitsch, Robert. "The Critic as Poet, Poet as Critic: Randall Jarrell, Deconstruction, and 'Dirty Silence.'" *American Poetry* 1, no. 2 (Winter 1984):35–48.

Miller, J. Hillis. "William Carlos Williams." *Poets of Reality: Six Twentieth-Century Writers.* Cambridge, Mass.: Harvard University Press, 1965, 285–360.

———, ed. *William Carlos Williams: A Collection of Critical Essays.* Englewood Cliffs, N.J.: Prentice-Hall, 1966.

———. "Williams' *Spring and All* and the Progress of Poetry." *Daedalus* 99, no. 2 (Spring 1970):405–34.

Monteiro, George. "The Doctor's Black Bag: William Carlos Williams' Passaic River Stories." *Modern Language Studies* 13, no. 1 (Winter 1983):77–84.

Narasimhaiah, C. C. "William Carlos Williams." *Literary Criterion* 10, no. 2, (1972):55–67.

Noland, Richard W. "A Failure of Contact: William Carlos Williams on America." *Emory University Quarterly* 20, (1964):248–60.

Oliphant, Dave, and Thomas Zigal, eds. *William Carlos Williams and Others: Essays on William Carlos Williams and His Association with Ezra Pound, Hilda Doolittle, Marcel Duchamp, Marianne Moore, Emanual Romano, Wallace Stevens and Louis Zukofsky.* Austin: Harry Ransom Humanities Research Center, University of Texas, 1985.

Ostrous, Alan. *The Poetic World of William Carlos Williams.* With a preface by Harry T. Moore. Carbondale: Southern Illinois Press, 1966.

Paul, Sherman. *The Music of Survival: A Biography of a Poem by William Carlos Williams.* Urbana: University of Illinois Press, 1968.

———. "Open(ing) Criticism." *North Dakota Quarterly* 50, no. 1 (Winter 1982):9–18.

Pearce, Roy Harvey. "The Poet as Person." *Interpretations of an Earlier Literature,* edited by Charles Feidelson, Jr., and Paul Brodtkorb, Jr. New York: Oxford University Press, 1959, 369–86.

Peden, William. *The American Short Story: Continuity and Change, 1940–1975.* Boston: Houghton Mifflin, 1975.

————. "The American Short Story During the Twenties." *Studies in Short Fiction* 10, no. 4 (Fall 1973):367–71.

Perkins, David. "The Impact of William Carlos Williams." In *A History of Modern Poetry: Modernism and After.* Cambridge, Mass.: Harvard University Press, 1987, 246–75.

Perloff, Marjorie. "The Man Who Loved Women: The Medical Fictions of William Carlos Williams." *Georgia Review* 34, no. 4 (1980):840–853.

————. "William Carlos Williams." *Voices and Visions: The Poet in America,* edited by Helen Vendler. New York: Random House, 1987, 157–204.

Peschel, Richard E., and Enid Rhodes Peschel. "When a Doctor Hates a Patient: Case History, Literary Histories." *Michigan Quarterly Review* 23, no. 3 (Summer 1984):402–10.

Poirier, Suzanne. "The Physician and Authority: Portraits by Four Physician-Writers." *Literature and Medicine* 2 (1983):21–40.

Procopiow, Norma. "Tradition and Innovation in William Carlos Williams' *The Great American Novel.*" *Modernist Studies: Literature and Culture 1920–1940* 4. (1982):160–75.

Rahv, Philip. "Dr. Williams in His Short Stories." In *Literature and the Sixth Sense.* Boston: Houghton Mifflin, 1969, 316–19.

————. "Paleface and Redskin." In *Literature and the Sixth Sense.* Boston: Houghton Mifflin, 1969, 1–6.

Rapp, Carl. *William Carlos Williams and Romantic Idealism.* Hanover, N.H.: University Press of New England for Brown University Press, 1984.

Riddell, Joseph N. *The Inverted Bell: Modernism and the Counterpoetics of William Carlos Williams.* Baton Rouge: Louisiana State University Press, 1974.

Rodgers, Audrey T. *Virgin and Whore: The Image of Women in the Poetry of William Carlos Williams.* Jefferson, N.C.: McFarland and Co., 1987.

Rosenthal, M. L. Introduction to *The William Carlos Williams Reader.* New York: New Directions, 1966.

————. "Is There a Pound-Williams Tradition?" *The Southern Review* (April 1984):279–85.

Sayre, Henry M. *The Visual Text of William Carlos Williams.* Urbana: University of Illinois Press, 1983.

Searle, Leroy. "Blake, Eliot, and Williams: The Continuity of Imaginative Labor." In *William Blake and the Moderns,* edited by Robert J. Bertholf and Annette S. Levitt. Albany: State University of New York Press, 1982, 39–72.

Sienicka, Marta. "Poetry in the Prose of *In the American Grain* by William Carlos Williams." *Studies Anglican Posnaniensia: American International Review of English Studies* 1, nos. 1 and 2 (1968):109–16.

Simpson, Louis. *Three on The Tower: The Lives and Works of Ezra Pound, T. S. Eliot, and William Carlos Williams.* New York: William Morrow, 1975, 195–318.

Sims, Patterson. "Introduction to 20th Century American Art: Selections from the Permanent Collection, Whitney Museum of American Art." New York: Whitney Museum of American Art, 1978.

Slate, J. E. "William Carlos Williams and the Modern Short Story." *Southern Review* 4, no. 3 (July 1968):647–64.

————. "William Carlos Williams, Hart Crane, and the 'Virtue of History,'" *Texas Studies in Language and Literature* 6, no. 4:486–511.

Sorrentino, Gilbert. "Polish Mothers and 'The Knife of the Times.'" In *William Carlos Williams: Man and Poet*. edited by Carroll F. Terrell. Orono: National Poetry Foundation, University of Maine, 1983, 391–95.

————. "The Various Isolated: W. C. Williams' Prose." *New American Review* no. 15, (1972):192–207.

Steinman, Lisa M. "Style, Science, Technology, and William Carlos Williams." *Bucknell Review* 27, no. 2, (1983):132–58.

Stevens, Wallace. Preface, to *William Carlos Williams: Collected Poems, 1921–1931*. New York: The Objectivist Press, 1934, 1–4.

Strom, Martha Helen. "The Uneasy Friendship of William Carlos Williams and Wallace Stevens." *Journal of Modern Literature* 2, no. 2 (July 1984):291–98.

Tallman, Warren. "Bells Break Tower: William Carlos Williams' Stories." *Boundary* 1 (1972):58–70.

Tapscott, Stephen. *American Beauty: William Carlos Williams and the Modernist Whitman*. New York: Columbia University Press, 1984.

Tarn, Nathaniel. "Child as Father to the Man in the American Universe." *American Poetry* 1, no. 2 (Winter 1984):67–85.

Tashjian, Dickran. *William Carlos Williams and the American Scene, 1920–1940*. New York: Whitney Museum of American Art, 1978.

Terrell, Carol F., ed. *William Carlos Williams: Man and Poet*. Orono: National Poetry Foundation, University of Maine, 1983.

Thirlwall, John C. "William Carlos Williams and John C. Thirlwall: Record of a Ten-Year Relationship." *Yale University Library Gazette* 14 (July 1920):373–84.

Van Duyn, Mona. "'To Make Light of It' as Fictional Technique: William Carlos Williams' Stories." *Perspective* 6, no. 4 (Autumn–Winter 1953):230–38.

Vendler, Helen. "Art, Life and Dr. Williams." *New York Review of Books* 22, no. 18 (13 November 1975):17–20.

Wagner, Linda W. "A Bunch of Marigolds." *Kenyon Review* 29, no. 1 (January 1967):86–102.

————. *The Prose of William Carlos Williams*. Middletown, Conn.: Wesleyan University Press, 1970.

————. "William Carlos Williams: The Unity of His Art." In *Poetic Theory/*

Selected Bibliography

Poetic Practice, edited by Robert Scholes, 136–44. Iowa City: Midwest Modern Language Association Conference, 1968.

Wakoski, Diane. "William Carlos Williams: The Poet's Poet." *Sagetrieb* 3, no. 2 (Fall 1984):43–47.

Watson, James G. "The American Short Story 1930–1945." In *The American Short Story 1900–1945: A Critical History,* edited by Philip Stevick, 103–46. Boston: Twayne Publishers, 1984.

Weatherford, A. Kingsley. "William Carlos Williams: Prose, Form, and Measure." *English Literary History* 33, no. 1 (March 1966):118–31.

Weaver, Mike. *William Carlos Williams: The American Background.* New York: Cambridge University Press, 1971.

Weisenburger, Steven. "Williams, West, and the Art of Regression." *South Atlantic Review* 47, no. 4 (November 1982):1–16.

Whitaker, Thomas R. *William Carlos Williams.* New York: Twayne Publishers, 1968; rev. ed., Boston, 1989.

Whittemore, Reed. *William Carlos Williams: Poet from Jersey.* Boston: Houghton Mifflin, 1975.

Williams, William Eric. "The School Physician's Notebook: A Cameo of William Carlos Williams." *Literature and Medicine* 2 (1983):3–8.

"William Carlos Williams: A 'Field' Symposium." *Field: Contemporary Poetry and Poetics* (Oberlin College, Oberlin, Ohio), no. 29 (Fall 1983):5–57.

William Carlos Williams. *Papers by Kenneth Burke, Emily Mitchell Wallace, Norman Halmer Pearson, A.M. Sullivan.* Canbury, N.J.: Associated University Press, 1974.

Worth, Katharine J. "The Poets in the American Theatre." In *American Theatre,* edited by John R. Brown and Bernard Harris, 86-107. London: Edward Arnold, 1966.

Index

Index

Index

The Author

Robert F. Gish is professor of English language and literature at the University of Northern Iowa, where he teaches courses in American and British literature. He is the author of *Paul Horgan* (Twayne Publishers, 1983), *Frontier's End: The Life and Literature of Harvey Fergusson* (University of Nebraska Press, 1988), and *Hamlin Garland: The Far West* (Boise State University, 1976). His criticism on the exoticism of Kipling, Conrad, Maugham, Forster, and Greene can be found in *The English Short Story, 1880–1945* (Twayne Publishers, 1985). He is a contributing editor to *The Bloomsbury Review* and has written extensively on the literature and history of the American West in such journals as *Western American Literature, New Mexico Historical Review, Southwest Review,* and *Prairie Schooner.* His stories appear in *The Cross Timbers Review, The North Dakota Quarterly,* and *The New Mexico Humanities Review.*

The Editor

General editor Gordon Weaver earned his B.A. in English at the University of Wisconsin-Milwaukee in 1961; his M.A. in English at the University of Illinois, where he studied as a Woodrow Wilson Fellow in 1962; and his Ph.D. in English and creative writing at the University of Denver in 1970. He is the author of several novels, including *Count a Lonely Cadence, Give Him a Stone, Circling Byzantium,* and *The Eight Corners of the World*. Many of his numerous short stories are collected in *The Entombed Man of Thule, Such Waltzing Was Not Easy, Getting Serious, Morality Play,* and *A World Quite Round*. Recognition of his fiction includes the St. Lawrence Award for Fiction (1973), two National Endowment for the Arts fellowships, (1974, 1989), and the O. Henry First Prize (1979). He edited *The American Short Story, 1945–1980: A Critical History*. He is a professor of English at Oklahoma State University and serves as an adjunct member of the faculty of the Vermont College Master of Fine Arts in Writing Program. Married, and the father of three daughters, he lives in Stillwater, Oklahoma.